PENGUIN BOOKS

ZERO WASTE HOME

A French-born artist with a hugely popular blog on Zero Waste living, Bea Johnson has appeared on *The Today Show*, NBC and CBS news, and been featured in the *New York Times*, *San Francisco Chronicle*, *People* and *Lianhe Zaobao* (Singapore) and online publications, including *The Huffington Post* and *USA Today*.

BEA JOHNSON

Zero Waste Home

The Ultimate Guide to Simplifying Your Life

PENGUIN BOOKS

PENGUIN BOOKS

UK | USA | Canada | Ireland | Australia
India | New Zealand | South Africa

Penguin Books is part of the Penguin Random House group of companies
whose addresses can be found at global.penguinrandomhouse.com.

First published in the United States of America by Scribner,
a division of Simon & Schuster Ltd 2013
First published in Great Britain by Particular Books 2013
Published in Penguin Books 2016
008

Printed in Great Britain by Clays Ltd, St Ives plc

A CIP catalogue record for this book is available from the British Library

ISBN: 978-0-141-98176-5

www.greenpenguin.co.uk

MIX
Paper from
responsible sources
FSC® C018179

Penguin Random House is committed to a
sustainable future for our business, our readers
and our planet. This book is made from Forest
Stewardship Council® certified paper.

To Max and Léo

Contents

ZERO WASTE HOME

Introduction

Not so long ago, things were different: I owned a three-thousand-square-foot home, two cars, four tables, and twenty-six chairs. I filled a sixty-four-gallon can of trash weekly.

Today, the less I own, the richer I feel. And I don't have to take out the trash!

It all changed a few years ago. The big house did not burn down, nor did I become a Buddhist monk.

Here is my story.

I grew up in the Provence region of France, in a cookie-cutter home on a cul-de-sac: a far cry from my father's childhood on a small farm, or my mother's upbringing on a French military base in Germany. But my dad was dedicated to making the most of his suburban tract of land. In the warm months, he would spend all his free time working the garden, true to his farming roots, laboring over growing veggies and quenching the soil with his sweat. In the winter, his attention would move to the garage, where drawers full of screws, bolts, and parts lined the walls. Deconstructing, repairing, and reusing were his hobbies. He was (and still is) the kind of person who does not hesitate to stop on the side of the road after spotting a discarded vacuum cleaner, radio, television, or washing machine. If the item looks repairable to him, he throws it in the back of his car, brings it home, takes it apart, puts it back together, and somehow makes it work. He can even repair burned-out lightbulbs! My dad is talented, but his abilities are not unusual for the region. People in the French countryside possess a certain kind of craftiness that allows them to extend the life of their belongings. When I was a child, my dad took the drum out of an old washing machine and turned it into a snail trap, for example, and I remember using the washer's empty shell as a (rather tiny and hot) playhouse.

Through my young eyes, my home was a modern version of *Little House on the Prairie,* a TV series I watched religiously in reruns as a kid. Though we lived in the suburbs, and my two brothers and I were not as helpful as the Ingalls brood (my older brother even had a phobia of the dish sponge), my dad was the handy type and my mom the accomplished homemaker on a tight budget. She prepared three-course meals for lunch and dinner. Just like Laura Ingalls's mom, my mom's week was organized around church, cooking, baking, cleaning, ironing, sewing, knitting, and seasonal canning. On Thursdays, she scouted the farmer's market for deals on fabric and yarn. After school, I would help her mark sewing patterns and watch her turn cloth into elaborate garments. In my bedroom, I emulated her ways and created clothes for my two Barbie dolls out of old nylons and gauze (the latter came from my parents' visits to the blood bank.) At twelve, I sewed my first outfit, and at thirteen, knitted my first sweater.

Apart from the occasional fraternal fights, we had what seemed a happy family life. But what my brothers and I hadn't perceived were the deep rifts between my parents that would ultimately turn their marriage into a sad divorce battle. At eighteen, ready to take a break from psychological and financial hardship, I set off to California for a yearlong au pair contract. Little did I know then that during that year I would fall in love with the man of my dreams, the man I would later marry, Scott. He was not the surfer type whom young French girls fantasize about, but he was a compassionate person who provided me with much-needed emotional stability. We traveled the world together and lived abroad, but when I became pregnant, my yearnings to try the American soccer-mom lifestyle (as seen on TV) brought us back to the United States.

MY AMERICAN DREAM: PLEASANT HILL

Our sons, Max and, soon after, Léo, were born into the trappings of my American dream: a three-thousand-square-foot contemporary home, on a cul-de-sac, complete with high ceilings, family and living rooms, walk-in closets, a three-car garage, and a koi fishpond in Pleasant Hill, a remote suburb of San Francisco. We owned an SUV, a huge television, and a dog.

We stocked two large refrigerators and filled an industrial-size washing machine and dryer several times a week. That's not to say that clutter ever crammed our house or that I bought everything new. The thriftiness that I inherited from my parents led me to shop thrift stores for clothes, toys, and furnishings. Nevertheless, on the side of the house, an oversize garbage can collected leftover house paint and mountains of weekly refuse. And yet we felt good about our environmental footprint because we recycled.

Over the course of seven years, Scott climbed the corporate ladder, making a very comfortable living that covered semiannual international vacations, lavish parties, a rich diet of expensive meats, membership to a private pool, weekly shopping trips at Target, and shelves of things you use only once and then throw away. We had no financial worries, as life rolled by effortlessly and afforded my Barbie-like platinum-blond hair, artificial tan, injected lips, and Botoxed forehead. I'd even experimented with hair extensions, acrylic nails, and "European wraps" (rolls of Saran wrap tightly wound around my body while I rode a stationary bike). We were healthy and had great friends. We seemed to have it all.

Yet things were not quite right. I was thirty-two, and deep down I was terrified at the thought that my life had settled and set. Our life had become sedentary. In our bedroom community, with large avenues and strip malls, we spent too much time in the car and not enough on foot. Scott and I missed the active life and roaming the streets of the capitals we had lived in abroad. We missed walking to cafés and bakeries.

A MOVE TOWARD SIMPLICITY

We decided to relocate across the bay to Mill Valley, a village boasting an active European-style downtown; we sold our house, moved into a temporary apartment with just the necessities, and stored the rest, with the mindset that we would eventually find a home to accommodate my Moorish decorating style and a whole lot of matching furnishings.

What we found during this transitional period is that with less stuff, we had time to do things we enjoyed doing. Since we no longer spent every weekend mowing our lawn and caring for our huge house and its contents, we now spent our time together as a family, biking, hiking, picnicking, and discovering our new coastal region. It was liberating. Scott finally understood the truth behind his father's words: "I wish that I didn't spend so much time caring for my lawn." As I reflected on the numerous dining sets I had acquired to furnish the kitchen nook, the dining room, and the two backyard patios in our old home, I also recalled a remark made by my good friend Eric: "How many sitting areas does one home need?"

I came to realize that most of the things in storage were not missed, that we had spent innumerable hours and untold resources outfitting a house with the unnecessary. Shopping for the previous home had become a (worthless) pastime, a pretext to go out and be busy in our bedroom community. It became clear to me that much of what we now stored had served no real purpose, except to fill large rooms. We had placed too much importance on "stuff," and we recognized that moving toward simplicity would provide us with a fuller and more meaningful life.

It took a year and 250 open houses to finally find the right home: a 1,475-square-foot cottage built in 1921, with no lawn, a stone's throw away from the downtown that we were originally told had no listings in our price range. Home prices were twice as much per square foot in Mill Valley as in Pleasant Hill, and the sale of our previous home afforded us half the house. But it was our dream to live within walking distance of hiking trails, libraries, schools, and cafés, and we were ready to downsize.

When we first moved in, our garage and basement were packed with furniture from our old life, but we slowly sold off what would not fit into the new small house. What we did not truly use, need, and love had to go. This would become our motto for decluttering. Did we really use, need, and love the bike trailer, kayak, Rollerblades, snowboards, tae kwon do gear, boxing and sparring gloves, bike racks, Razor scooters, basketball hoop, bocce balls, tennis rackets, snorkels, camping gear, skateboards, baseball bat and mitt, soccer net, badminton set, golf clubs, and fishing poles? Scott had some initial trouble letting go. He loved sporting activities, and he had worked hard to acquire all that equipment. But, ultimately, he realized that it was better to make decisions about what he truly enjoyed and focus on fewer activities rather than let golf clubs gather dust. And so, within a couple of years, we parted with 80 percent of our belongings.

FROM SIMPLICITY TO TRASH REDUCTION

As we simplified, I found guidance in Elaine St. James's books on simplicity and revisited Laura Ingalls Wilder's *Little House* collection. These books inspired us to further evaluate our daily activities. We disconnected the television and canceled catalog and magazine subscriptions. Without TV and shopping taking up so much of our time, we now had time to educate ourselves on the environmental issues that had been on our periphery. We read books such as *Natural Capitalism, Cradle to Cradle,* and *In Defense of Food,* and through Netflix we watched documentaries such as *Earth* and *Home* that depicted homeless polar bears and confused fish. We learned about the far-reaching implications of unhealthy diets and irresponsible consumption. We started to understand for the first time not only how profoundly endangered our planet is but also how our careless everyday decisions were making matters worse for our world and the world we'd leave behind for our kids.

We were using the car extensively, packing lunches in disposable plastic bags, drinking bottled water, dispensing paper towels and tissues (liberally), and using countless toxic products to clean the house and care for our bodies. The numerous trash cans I had filled with grocery bags in Pleasant Hill and the frozen dinners I had nuked in plastic also came back to mind. I realized that as we enjoyed all the trappings of the American dream, what thoughtless citizens and consumers we had become. How did we get so disconnected from the impact of our actions? Or were we ever connected? What were we teaching our boys, Max and Léo? On the one hand, what we learned brought tears to our eyes and made us angry for having been in the dark so long. On the other hand, it gave us the strength and resolve to drastically change our consumption habits and lifestyle, for the sake of our kids' future.

Scott felt strongly about putting his theories into practice, and although the economy was in recession, he quit his job to start a sustainability consulting company. We took the kids out of the private school we could no longer afford, and I tackled the greening of our home.

With the newfound knowledge that recycling was not the answer to our environmental crisis and that plastics were devastating our oceans, we switched from disposable to reusable water bottles and shopping bags. All it took was remembering to bring them along when needed. Easy. I then started shopping at health food stores and realized that the selection of local and organic produce was worth the extra dollar and that wasteful packaging could be avoided altogether by shopping the bulk section. So I adopted laundry mesh bags for produce and sewed cloth bags out of an old sheet to transport bulk. I designed them in a way that would eliminate the need for disposable ties. As I accrued a collection of empty bottles and storage jars, I slowly reduced our consumption of packaged goods, and soon had a pantry stocked with bulk. You might even say that I became addicted to shopping in bulk, driving far distances within the Bay Area, searching for suppliers. I sewed a dozen kitchen towels from the same old sheet and with the purchase of microfiber cloths broke our paper towel habit. Scott started a compost pile in the backyard, and I enrolled in botany classes to learn about uses for the wild plants we spotted on our local hikes.

As I had come to obsess about our kitchen's trash, I had overlooked the bathroom but soon proceeded to try waste-free alternatives there, too. For six months, I washed my hair with baking soda and rinsed with apple cider vinegar but when Scott could no longer stand the "smell of vinaigrette" in bed, I resorted to refilling glass bottles with bulk shampoo and conditioner instead. The high I used to get shopping in Pleasant Hill was replaced by the high of learning new ways to green our home and save money to survive the belt-tightening due to Scott's new start-up.

Max and Léo were doing their parts, too, riding their bikes to school, competing for shorter showers, and turning off light fixtures. But one day, as I chaperoned Léo's class on a school field trip to the local health food store, which included a stop in the bulk food aisle, I watched him stumble on his teacher's question "Why is it green to buy in bulk?" At that moment, it dawned on me: we had not yet informed the kids of our waste-reducing efforts. Provided daily with a homemade cookie, they hadn't noticed the lack of processed ones. That night, I pointed out the whys and hows of our atypical pantry and talked to them about other changes that they had already unconsciously adopted. With the kids now aware, and the whole family actively on board, we could aim at "Zero Waste."

When searching for alternatives, I had run into the term in reference to industrial practices. I did not look up the definition and ignored what it entailed for industries, but somehow, the idea clicked for me. It gave me a quantitative way to think about my efforts. We did not know whether we could eliminate every piece of trash, but striving for zero would provide a target to get as close to it as possible, to scrutinize our waste stream and address even the smallest items. We had reached a turning point.

TESTING THE EXTREMES OF ZERO WASTE

I examined what was left in our trash and recycling cans as a directive for our next steps. In the waste bin, I found packaging of meat, fish, cheese, bread, butter, ice cream, and toilet paper. In the recycling, I found papers, tomato cans, empty wine bottles, mustard jars, and soy milk cartons. I set out to eliminate them all.

I started presenting mason jars at the store's meat counter, generating looks, questions, and remarks from onlookers and employees. Explaining to the person behind the counter "I don't have a trash can" became my standby tactic. The pillowcase I brought to the bakery to collect my weekly order of bread drew remarks at first but was quickly accepted as the usual routine. With a new farmer's market opening, I tried my hand at canning, turning fresh tomatoes into a winter stash of canned goods. I found a winery that would refill our bottles with table red, I learned how to make paper from the handouts my kids brought home from school, and I tackled every bit of junk mail landing in our mailbox. There weren't books at the library on waste reduction, so I opened myself to suggestions and googled my way to substitutes for the items for which I couldn't find package-free solutions. I learned how to knead bread, blend mustard, incubate yogurt, craft cheese, strain soy milk, churn butter, and melt lip balm.

One day a well-meaning guest showed up on my doorstep with a pre-packaged dessert. It was then that I realized we would never achieve our Zero Waste goal without the help of our friends and family. I understood that Zero Waste starts *outside* the home, mostly at the store when buying in bulk and opting for reusables over single-use items, but it also starts with asking friends not to bring waste into my home when they come for a visit, and rejecting unneeded freebies. We added "refuse" to the sustainability mantra "reduce, reuse, recycle, rot," and I started a blog to share the logistics of our lifestyle, with a mission to let our friends and family know that our efforts were real and our Zero Waste objectives serious. I prayed for no more unwanted cake boxes, party favors, or junk mail, and I started a consulting business to spread my ideas and help others simplify.

We soon winnowed our recyclables to the occasional mail, school handout, and empty wine bottle. I contemplated moving toward the goal of Zero Recycling, and as we left for our annual trip to France, I daydreamed that my family might take Zero Waste to the next level when we got back and cancel our curbside recycling service.

FINDING BALANCE

Seeing all the trash at the airport and on the flight quickly brought me back to reality. I'd been living in a bubble. The world was as wasteful as ever. Spending a couple of months at my mom's, however, in a "normal" home, gave me the break needed to relax and let go of judgments and frustrations. I was also able to take a step back for a broader look at my frantic attempt to go Zero Waste. I saw clearly that many of my practices had become socially restrictive and time-consuming, and thus unsustainable. Making butter was costly, considering the amount needed to bake cookies weekly, and making cheese was high maintenance and unnecessary, considering that I could buy it from the counter. I realized that I had taken Zero Waste too far. I had foraged moss to use in lieu of toilet paper, for God's sake!

After all, it seemed that we would be more likely to stick with Zero Waste if we took it easy on ourselves and found some balance. Zero Waste was a lifestyle choice, and if we were going to be in it for the long haul, we had to make it workable and convenient to the realities of our lives. Simplification was once again in order.

Upon my return home, I decided to concentrate on letting go of extremes without compromising the gains we'd made on waste reduction. I reevaluated my tendency to fetch faraway bulk by finding satisfaction in available local supply instead. I also stopped making ice cream and instead refilled a jar at the local Baskin-Robbins. We accepted wine from visitors and gave up the idea of Zero Recycling. I stopped making butter and settled for composting the store-bought wrappers. Butter was (and still is) the only food we would buy in packaging. Within a month, Zero Waste became easy, fun, simple, and stress free.

Scott, who all along had a nagging fear that my passion for farmer's markets, greener alternatives, and organic bulk, in order to reduce packaging waste, was an overall drain on our finances, took the time to analyze our household costs. He compared expenses between our old (2005) and new (2010) lifestyles, reviewing past bank statements and taking into account that our two boys were eating significantly more (being five years older). What he found was better than either of us had dared hope: we were saving almost 40 percent on annual household costs! In his analytical mind, that number along with the amount of time that he knew we were saving—from living a simple lifestyle and taking fewer trips to stores—eliminated his fear.

Today, we are at peace with Zero Waste. The four of us have adopted practices into our daily routines, and we can fully enjoy all the lifestyle has to offer, well beyond the obvious ecological "feel good" aspects. With the implementation of Zero Waste alternatives, we have noticed undeniable life improvements: notable health benefits, along with considerable financial and time savings. We learned that Zero Waste does not deprive; on the contrary, through Zero Waste, I have found a sense of meaning and purpose. My life has been transformed—it's based on experiences rather than stuff, based on embracing change rather than hiding in denial.

ABOUT THE BOOK

Our country's environment, economy, and health are in crisis. Natural resources are running out, the economy is volatile, our general health is declining, and our standard of living is at a record low. What can one person do in the face of these monumental problems? The overwhelming reality of these facts can feel paralyzing, but we must remember that individual action matters and that change is our hands.

Natural resources are running out, but we buy petroleum-based products. The economy is weak, but we indulge in foreign products. Our general health is declining, but we fuel our bodies with processed foods and bring toxic products into our homes. What we consume directly affects our environment, our economy, and our health, by supporting specific manufacturing practices and creating a demand to make more. In other words, shopping is voting and the decisions that we make every day have an impact. We have the choice to either hurt or heal our society.

Many of us do not need to be convinced to adopt a green lifestyle, yet we yearn to find simple ways to do more, beyond recycling. . . . We found that Zero Waste offers an immediate way to feel empowered by meeting the challenges that we face head-on.

Zero Waste Home will take you beyond the typical eco-friendly alternatives covered well in other publications. This book will encourage you to declutter and recycle less, not just for a better environment but also for a better you. It offers practical, tested solutions to live richer and healthier lives using the sustainable, waste-free resources available to us today, while following a simple system in order: refusing (what we do not need), reducing (what we do need), reusing (what we consume), recycling (what we cannot refuse, reduce, or reuse), and rotting (composting) the rest.

Over the last years, I've learned that everyone has a different take on our lifestyle. Some think that it is too extreme because we do not buy junk food, for example. Others say that it is not extreme enough because we buy toilet paper or eat meat once a week or occasionally fly. What matters to us is not what people think but how good we feel about what we do. It is not the preconceived restrictions but the infinite possibilities that we have discovered in Zero Waste that make it a subject worth elaborating. And I am excited at the prospect of sharing what we have learned to help others better their lives.

This is *not* a book about achieving absolute Zero Waste. Considering the manufacturing practices in place, it is evident that absolute Zero Waste is not possible today. Zero Waste is an idealistic goal, a carrot to get as close as possible. Not everyone who reads this book will be able to implement all that I mention or be able to go as far as reducing his/her yearly household waste output to the size of a quart jar, as my family has. Based on my blog readers' feedback, geographic and demographic disparities come into play in determining how close to Zero Waste one can get. But how much waste one generates is not important. What matters is understanding the effect of our purchasing power on the environment and acting accordingly. Everyone can adopt the changes that are possible in their life. And any small change toward sustainability will have a positive effect on our planet and society.

I understand that given my viewpoint, many will call into question my decision to publish a printed book. But should valuable information be made available only to those who read electronic ones? At this point in time, a printed book is the best way for me to reach a maximum of readers. I believe it is my moral obligation to spread the word about Zero Waste as much as possible, to make every attempt to change our patterns of over-consumption, and to encourage companies to account for the products and choices that impact our health and use our finite resources. I've thought long and hard about this decision. And my cost-benefit analysis has led me to believe that inspiring one person to reduce their daily trash output is well worth the environmental cost of one book. I think it would be hypocritical for me not to print it, considering that I am an ardent patron of the library myself, and I would encourage you to donate the book to your library or pass it along to a friend when you no longer need it.

This is not a scientific book. Statistics and hard data are not my expertise. Numerous authors have done a great job at analyzing the underlying evidence to demonstrate the dire need for our society to adopt Zero Waste. In *Garbology*, Edward Humes exposes the ugly truth behind our waste problem, and in *Slow Death by Rubber Duck*, Rick Smith and Bruce Lourie raise awareness about toxicity in common household items. This book is different. This is a practical guide based on my experience.

It's my goal and ambition to offer readers the tried-and-true ways that have helped me to get as close to Zero Waste in the home as possible. I share with you what's worked and what's failed miserably! Some may dabble and others may decide to take it to the extreme. Whatever the case, my hope is that you'll find some useful alternatives regardless of personal or geographical circumstances.

The home should be a sanctuary. We—mothers, fathers, and citizens— have the right, if not the duty, and certainly the power, to bring positive change to the world through our daily decisions and actions.

A brighter future starts at home! Welcome to *Zero Waste Home*.

The 5 *R*s and the Benefits of the Zero Waste Lifestyle

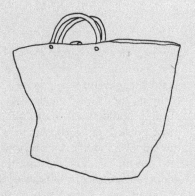

It's easy for you to be sitting there at home, in front of your television, consuming whatever you want, tossing everything in the trash, and leaving it out on the street for the garbage truck to take it away. But where does the garbage go?
—Magna, former recycling picker
at Rio de Janeiro's Jardim Gramacho landfill
in the documentary *Waste Land*

We drag the trash can to the curb at night, and by the time we get up the next morning, the cereal liners and dirty paper towels have disappeared, as if by magic. But when we say "we threw something away," what do we really mean? "Away" might take trash out of our sight, but that doesn't mean it should be out of our minds. After all, our discards don't just evaporate because the garbageman whisked them off. Our waste ends up in our landfills, spoiling our precious environment, leaching toxic compounds into our air and soil, wasting the resources used to create the discarded goods, and costing us billions of dollars each year in processing.

That's why Zero Waste is so crucial. So what is Zero Waste? Zero Waste is a philosophy based on a set of practices aimed at avoiding as much waste as possible. In the manufacturing world it inspires cradle-to-cradle design; in the home it engages the consumer to act responsibly. Many people have the misconception that all it involves is extensive recycling, when on the contrary, Zero Waste does not promote recycling. Rather, it takes into consideration the uncertainties and costs associated with recycling's processes. Recycling is regarded only as an alternative to handling (versus, ideally, eliminating) waste materials, and although included in the Zero Waste model, it is deemed a last resort before the landfill (as is composting).

What does Zero Waste entail for the home environment? Cutting waste in a household is quite simple if you follow these five easy steps: refuse what you do not need; reduce what you do need; reuse what you consume; recycle what you cannot refuse, reduce, or reuse; and rot (compost) the rest.

As illustrated in the graphic below, I have found that applying the 5 Rs *in order* naturally results in very little waste. The first and second Rs address the prevention of waste, the third R thoughtful consumption, the fourth and fifth Rs the processing of discards.

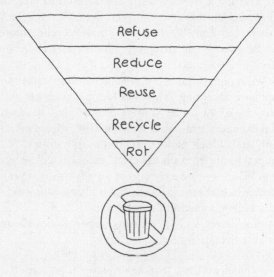

STEP 1: REFUSE {WHAT WE DO NOT NEED}

When my family embarked on the Zero Waste journey, it quickly became apparent that implementing Zero Waste in the home really starts with our behavior *outside* the home.

Curbing consumption is a major aspect of reducing waste (what we do not consume ultimately will not need to be discarded), but consumption does not occur solely through the obvious act of shopping. In our society, we start consuming the moment we step out the door and pick up a dry cleaning ad hanging on the knob or a plastic bag stuffed with a leaflet promoting landscaping services in the front yard. At work, business cards get handed out left and right and we leave the meeting with a handful. At a conference, we take one of the goody bags. We check the contents, and although we already have enough pens at home to last us a lifetime, we think: "Cool, a pen!" On our way home, we buy a bottle of wine; it gets double bagged with a receipt before we can say anything; and then we remove a flyer tucked under our windshield wiper. Once home, we check our mailbox and find it crammed with junk mail.

Zero Waste takes into consideration both direct and indirect forms of consumption. The first *R* (refuse) addresses the indirect type, the handouts and marketing materials that creep into our lives. We might be able to recycle most of them, but Zero Waste is not about recycling more; it's about acting on needless waste and stopping it from coming into our homes in the first place.

Every bit we accept, or take, creates a demand to make more. In other words, compulsive accepting (versus refusing) condones and reinforces wasteful practices. When we let waiters fill our glass with water that we won't be drinking and a straw that we won't use, we are saying: "Water is not important" and "Please make more disposable straws." When we take a "free" shampoo bottle from a hotel room, more oil will be rigged to make a replacement. When we passively accept an advertising flyer, a tree is cut down somewhere to make more flyers, and our time is unwisely spent dealing with and recycling something that is trivial.

In a consumer-driven society, refusing opportunities abound, and here are four areas worth considering:

1. **Single-use plastics (SUPs):** Disposable plastic bags, bottles, cups, lids, straws, and flatware. The intentional thirty-second use of a plastic product endorses toxic industrial processes; supports harmful chemicals leaching into our soil, food chain, and bodies; and subsidizes the manufacturing of materials that often do not or cannot get recycled and will never biodegrade. These products are the source of ocean pollution as found in the Great Pacific Garbage Patch and as seen daily around us, on roadsides, in our cities, and in parks and forests. This problem is monumentally overwhelming, but you can channel your frustration into action by simply refusing SUPs and by vowing never to use another again—the discipline of "vowing" can be extremely effective at achieving goals. SUPs can easily be avoided with a little planning and reusing (see "Step 3: Reuse").

2. **Freebies:** Hotel room toiletries, party favors, food samples, swag bags from conferences/awards/events/festivals (including sustainable events). I can hear you: "Oh, but they are free!" Are they? Freebies are primarily

constructed of plastics and made cheaply, which means that they break quickly (party favors often do not last any longer than SUPs). Any manufactured or plastic product comes with a heavy carbon footprint and associated environmental costs. Their accumulation in the home also leads to clutter, storage, and disposal costs. Refusing freebies requires strong willpower, but after a couple of practice runs, you'll quickly embrace the improvements you see in your life.

3. **Junk mail:** Countless people transfer junk mail from a mailbox straight into the recycling without a second thought. But this simple action has collective consequences that sustain the distribution of the 100 billion pieces of junk mail sent each year. Junk mail contributes to deforestation and uses precious energy resources to fabricate. For what? Essentially wasting our time and tax dollars. I have found that a no-tolerance policy (see "Junk Mail" on page 172) is the best way to fight it. Unfortunately, it is impossible to completely eliminate it with the mailing options currently offered by the United States Postal Service. As you will read in the pages ahead, I went to war against junk mail. And while I've mostly won, waging this battle has been the most frustrating part of my Zero Waste journey. I find it mind-boggling that I can block waste from entering my house but not my mailbox.

4. **Unsustainable practices:** These include bringing individually wrapped snacks to kids' sporting events because it's the "tradition," accepting receipts or business cards that we will never consult, buying excessive packaging and discarding it without urging the manufacturer to change. These examples show where our individual actions can have a tremendous effect in changing the way things are done, as they offer opportunities to speak up and get involved (see also "Active Discards" on page 256). Consumers can change wasteful processes if they let manufacturers and retailers know what they want. For example, the collective act of refusing receipts creates a need for offering alternatives, such as not printing and/or emailing them instead.

Of the 5 Rs that we will cover in this chapter, you might find that refusing is the most difficult to achieve socially, especially for households with children. Nobody wants to go against the grain or be rude when something is offered with no ill will. But a little practice and short justifications make it easy for us to decline the politest entreaties. All you have to say is, "I am sorry, but I don't have a trash can," "I am sorry, but I have gone paperless," "I am sorry, but I am trying to simplify my life," or "I am sorry, but we have too much at home already." People usually understand or respect a personal choice and will not insist. In some cases, we found that proactivity—such as taking our name off mailing lists before junk mail is sent out—works best.

Refusing is not aimed at making us feel inadequate in social situations; it is intended to cause us to reflect on our everyday decisions, the indirect consumption in which we partake, and the power that we hold as a collective community. While the individual act of refusing does not actually make the waste disappear, it creates a demand for alternatives. Refusing is a concept based on the power of collectivity: if we all refuse hotel freebies, then they will no longer be offered; if we all refuse receipts, then they will no longer need to be printed. And as a case in point, if you go into many retail stores (e.g., Apple) or hotel chains, you now have the option to receive an emailed receipt versus the printed statement. Give refusing a try. The occasions are infinite.

A couple of years ago, I was nominated for The Green Awards and the potential cash prize of twenty-five thousand dollars to spread the word about Zero Waste. The event was sponsored by Green Giant, which offered to fly me and a guest of my choice to the award ceremony in Los Angeles. I chose to bring my son Max and left with a plan to discreetly refuse (without offending my generous host) the probable swag bags and potential award. Refusing the former was easy, but the following night, when my name echoed on the microphone, I accepted the glass globe, blinded by elation and spotlights (no room for discreet refusal here). I posed for the press, award in hand, and for the rest of the evening, Max proudly held it under his arm, as he "always wanted a trophy." I reminded him that we did not come to win a physical object but to win the opportunities that the cash prize would afford instead. He insisted on taking the trophy home anyway. But a couple of months later, as the excitement of winning faded, so did his attachment to the award.

"Can I send it back to Green Giant to be reused for next year's participants?" I asked.

"Go for it," said my son.

And so I did. He has not regretted it one moment, nor have I. The pictures taken that night, the memories that we share, and the meaningful endeavors that the grant has since funded are reminders of a terrific evening. And I don't have to dust those things!

STEP 2: REDUCE {WHAT WE DO NEED AND CANNOT REFUSE}

It seems that if you have little in life, you have little to worry about. If you have much, it seems you have much to lose.
—Rick Ray in his documentary *10 Questions for the Dalai Lama*

Reducing is an immediate aid to our environmental crisis. It addresses the core issues of our waste problem and takes into consideration the imminent environmental consequences of population growth, associated consumption, and the finite planetary resources that cannot support the world's needs. Reducing also results in a simplified lifestyle that allows you to focus on quality versus quantity and experiences versus stuff. It encourages questioning the need and use of past, present, and future purchases. The things you own, you own because you need them.

Here are three practices we have implemented to actively reduce in our home:

1. **Evaluate past consumption:** Assess the true use and need for everything in the home and let go of the unnecessary through the process of paring down. Challenge yourself to consider letting go of things you always thought you had to have. For example through this process, we found out that we did not need a salad spinner. Question everything in your home, and you'll make many discoveries.
   - **Paring down forms better shopping habits:** The time and work invested in evaluating previous purchases lead us to think twice before bringing anything new into the home. Through the process, we learn to restrain resource-depleting accumulation and choose (repairable) quality over (disposable) quantity.
   - **Paring down supports sharing with others:** Donating or selling previous purchases supports the secondhand market and community (see "Step 3: Reuse"). It fosters collective generosity through sharing resources already consumed and increases used inventory (therefore making it easier to buy used).

- **Paring down makes Zero Waste manageable:** Simplifying makes it easy to plan and organize the logistics of Zero Waste. Less means less to worry about, clean, store, repair, or dispose of later.

2. **Curb current and future consumption in amount and in size:** Restraining shopping activity (new or used) clearly conserves valuable resources. It saves the resources needed to make new things and makes used items available to others. Areas to consider include: reducing packaging (Can I buy in bulk instead?); car usage (Can I bike more?); home size (Can I downsize?); personal effects (Do I need it?); technology (Can I do without?); and paper load (Do I need to print it?). Can I buy a lesser amount (maybe in a concentrated form)? Is the amount or size fitted to my needs? Question potential purchases, consider their life cycle, and choose products you can at best reuse or at least recycle (see "Step 4: Recycle," on selecting recyclable products, on page 24).

3. **Decrease activities that support or lead to consumption:** Media exposure (TV, magazines) and leisure shopping can offer a great deal of inspiration; however, the targeted marketing that funds the former and the clever merchandising that promotes the latter tend to aim at making us feel unfit, uncool, and inadequate. These feelings make it easy to succumb to temptations in order to satisfy perceived needs. Controlling our exposure can have a tremendous effect on not only our consumption but also our happiness. Find satisfaction with what you already have.

The practice of refusing is a pretty cut-and-dried matter. Simply say no. Reducing, in contrast, is a much more individual affair. You need to assess your comfort level given the realities of your family life, financial situation, and regional factors. For instance, eliminating car usage is not possible for most people living in rural or semirural areas, considering the unavailability of public transport. But reducing encourages us to consider maybe going down to one car and/or simply driving less. What it stresses, above all, is being aware of current consumption habits and finding ways to reduce unsustainable ones.

Reducing has been the most revelatory aspect and "potent secret ingredient" of my Zero Waste journey. Among the many benefits that voluntary simplicity has to offer, some unforeseen advantages have emerged.

When Scott quit his job to start a sustainable consulting practice in

OPTIONS FOR REDUCING

While thrift stores such as Goodwill or the Salvation Army can be a convenient way to initially let go, many other outlets exist and are often more appropriate for usable items. Here are some examples:

- Amazon.com
- Antiques shops
- Auction houses
- Churches
- Consignment shops (quality items)
- Craigslist.org (large items, moving boxes, free items)
- Crossroads Trading Co. (trendy clothes)
- Diggerslist.com (home improvement)
- Dress for Success (workplace attire)
- Ebay.com (small items of value)
- Flea markets
- Food banks (food)
- Freecycle.org (free items)
- Friends
- Garage and yard sales
- Habitat for Humanity (building materials, furniture, and/or appliances)
- Homeless and women's shelters
- Laundromats (magazines and laundry supplies)
- Library (books, CDs and DVDs)
- Local SPCA (towels and sheets)
- Nurseries and preschools (blankets, toys)
- Operation Christmas Child (new items in a shoe box)
- Optometrists (eyeglasses)
- Regifting
- Rummage sales for a cause
- Salvage yards (building materials)
- Schools (art supplies, magazines, dishes to eliminate class party disposables)
- Tool co-ops (tools)
- Waiting rooms (magazines)
- Your curb with a "Free" sign

the midst of the Great Recession, we were already well engaged in voluntary simplicity, but out of financial necessity, we were forced to reduce expenses further. We could no longer fund the family vacations and getaways that made life exciting, provided us mental respite from work, and offered a fresh view on our society. We consoled ourselves by embracing the evident benefits of the Zero Waste lifestyle. Downsizing had afforded a better neighborhood, and simplifying our lives made home maintenance easy. But at some point, we realized that these combined benefits allowed for one unexpected bonus: the occasional rental of our home. The first time required a bit of preparation before leaving, such as creating labels, writing a "Zero Waste Home Operating Guide" and reinstalling the trash/recycling cans for the renters. But our efforts were well rewarded: renting our home covered our flights and accommodations in France to visit my family and to immerse our kids in their second language. Making our house available has since afforded us weekend trips and even travel to warm destinations during the holidays. Now that's one perk we did not anticipate from this lifestyle!

STEP 3: REUSE {WHAT WE CONSUME AND CANNOT REFUSE OR REDUCE}

Use it up, wear it out, make it do, or do without.

—Ancient proverb

Many people confuse the terms *reuse* and *recycle*, but they differ greatly in terms of conservation. Recycling is best defined as reprocessing a product to give it a new form. Reusing, on the other hand, is utilizing the product in its original manufactured form several times to maximize its usage and increase its useful life, therefore saving the resources otherwise lost through the process of recycling.

Reuse has earned a bad reputation by association with the "hippie" lifestyle and hoarding. I used to confuse conservation with squirreling away resources, associating Zero Waste with containers cluttering kitchen countertops. But it does not need to be this way! Reusing can be simple and beautiful.

Since refusing and reducing eliminate the unnecessary, abiding by the hierarchy of the 5 Rs streamlines reusing. For example, plastic grocery bags can be repurposed (for packing as an alternative to bubble wrap or for transporting muddy shoes). But since they can also easily be refused, a Zero Waste home won't need to store or find uses for them. Much the same, reducing to the point where true personal needs are met controls the amount of reusables. How many reusable bags do I truly need? Through reducing, I evaluated my usage, and found that I need only three shopping totes.

Reusing is the tipping point of Zero Waste: it addresses both consumption and conservation efforts and offers an ultimate diversion from disposal. It can effectively (1) eliminate wasteful consumption, (2) alleviate resource depletion, and (3) extend the useful life of the goods purchased.

1. **Eliminate wasteful consumption:** Reusables can eliminate the need for packaging and wasteful single-use products through:
   - **Shopping with reusables:** Bringing the necessary reusables to the store reduces or eliminates the need for consumer packaging.
   - **Swapping disposables for reusables:** For every disposable item available, a reusable or refillable alternative exists. The practical chapters will focus on these further, but for starters, refer to the Basic Reusables Checklist on the next page.
2. **Alleviate resource depletion by:**
   - **Participating in collaborative consumption (sharing):** Many of the items we consume sit unused for hours or sometimes days at a time (lawn mowers, cars, houses, etc.). Through borrowing, loaning, trading, bartering, or renting peer to peer, we can maximize usage and even make a profit. Examples include but are not limited to such items as cars (RelayRides.com), homes (Airbnb.com), office space (desksnearme.com), and tools (sharesomesugar.com).
   - **Buying used:** Thrift stores, garage sales, consignment shops, antiques markets, Craigslist, eBay, and Amazon are great sources for buying used. Shopping should always start at these sites.
   - **Buying smart:** Look for products that are reusable/refillable/rechargeable, repairable, versatile, and durable. Leather shoes, for example, are durable and can be more easily repaired than plastic/synthetic ones.
3. **Extend the useful life of necessities through:**
   - **Repairing:** A trip to the hardware store or a simple call to the manufacturer will solve the problem in most cases.
   - **Rethinking:** Drinking glasses can double as penholders, and kitchen towels can be knotted to wrap and carry Zero Waste lunches.
   - **Returning:** Dry cleaning wire hangers can be returned to the store to be reused.

- **Rescuing:** Shipping boxes and single-side printed paper can be used again before getting recycled. Worn-out clothing can be used as rags before going to the landfill.

BASIC REUSABLES CHECKLIST

- ❏ Totes
- ❏ Widemouthed insulated cups
- ❏ Jars
- ❏ Bottles
- ❏ Cloth bags
- ❏ Rags
- ❏ Kitchen towels
- ❏ Cloth napkins
- ❏ Handkerchiefs
- ❏ Rechargeable batteries

STEP 4: RECYCLE {WHAT WE CANNOT REFUSE, REDUCE, OR REUSE}

Recycling is an aspirin, alleviating a rather large collective hangover . . . overconsumption.

—William McDonough, *Cradle to Cradle*

Often at parties when people find out that I run a Zero Waste household, they like to share with me that they too "recycle everything."

Of course, by now you know that a Zero Waste household is not all about recycling and that waste management starts outside the home by curbing consumption, which eliminates much recycling and greatly reduces associated concerns. These concerns include the fact that the broad system of recycling not only requires energy to process but also lacks regulations to guide and coordinate the efforts of manufacturers, municipalities, consumers, and recyclers. Recycling currently depends on too many variables to make it a dependable solution to our waste problems. For example, it relies on:

- manufacturers to **communicate** with recyclers, **design** products that are durable but also highly recyclable (mixed materials are costly to separate and often cheaper to send to the landfill than recycle; some things are recyclable in one city but not in another), and **label** their recyclability and recycled content accordingly (currently at their discretion)
- consumers to **be aware** of local recycling policies, to **recycle** responsibly, but also to **purchase** accordingly and **buy recycled** in order to create a market for recyclables
- municipalities to **provide** curbside recycling and collection locations for hard-to-recycle items and **share** residents' education with haulers (simple graphics and curbside feedback have proved to be efficient)
- haulers to **work with** municipalities in providing convenient and financially enticing service to residents (such as pay-as-you-throw rates), receiving adequate training from MRFs (see below) to **answer** customer questions (haulers are usually the only contact customers have with recycling services)
- materials recovery facilities (MRFs) to **sort** effectively and **offer** the greatest quality of sorted materials (i.e., with the lowest rate of contaminants), to **answer** customer questions, and to **contract** local recyclers (when sent abroad, recycling acquires a whole new set of variables)
- recyclers to **communicate** with manufacturers, to **make** their products visible and widely available, and to **encourage** upcycling and recycling versus downcycling (i.e., made into an unrecyclable lesser kind of product) markets

With every purchase, the entire life cycle of a product should be evaluated, including recyclability. Plastics are not only toxic to produce, consume (off-gassing and leaching) and recycle, but those that do get recycled (generally numbers 1 and 2) degrade in the process, are made into nonrecyclable products (downcycled), and are therefore destined to end up in the landfill.

An additional problem to take into consideration is the result of the emerging new green economy, which has manufacturers creating products made with mystery blends of materials (such as "biodegradable" or "compostable" plastics). These products create confusion among conscientious consumers and those in the recycling industry, and often end up tainting the recycling stream. If the purpose of recycling is to close our waste loops responsibly, then the processes need to be simplified to support this goal. In a Zero Waste world, recycling would be standardized across the globe, or even better, products would be designed for reuse and repair so that recycling would not even be necessary or at least would be greatly reduced.

We're not there yet.

The great news is that we consumers can greatly allay the concerns associated with recycling by applying the 5 Rs in order. By the time we have refused what we do not need, reduced what we do need, and reused what we consume, little needs to be recycled—also simplifying the guesswork around recycling (no need to find out whether a disposable cup is recyclable or not) and decreasing the trips to the hard-to-recycle collection sites.

When it's absolutely necessary, recycling is a better option than sending an item to the landfill. It does save energy, conserve natural resources, divert materials from landfills, and create a demand for recovered materials. Although it is a form of disposal, it provides a guide for making better purchases, based on the knowledge of what recycles best. When buying new, we should choose products that not only support reuse but also are made of materials that have a high postconsumer content, are compatible with our community's recycling program, and are likely to get recycled over and over (e.g., steel, aluminum, glass, or paper) versus downcycled (e.g., plastics).

I would love to be able to write here that we have achieved close to Zero Recycling in our home, but given the purchases that we made before embarking on the Zero Waste lifestyle and the current manufacturing practices in place, I have come to terms with the fact that it is not yet feasible (just as absolute Zero Waste is not yet feasible). We did give it a try but found it too restrictive (it forced us to refuse wine bottles offered by friends), too time-consuming (I had to make paper to recycle our kids' school papers), and not sustainable for the long term (for example, home maintenance cannot rely solely on the reuse of materials). But the experiment made me ask questions and learn a lot about the process. When we broke a couple of drinking glasses, I had to figure out how best to dispose of them: landfill or recycling? My searches on the Internet did not unanimously answer my questions and leaned toward sending them to the landfill, but I wanted to

HOME RECYCLING CHECKLIST

- ❑ Know by heart what your community can or cannot recycle at the curb. For example: incandescent lightbulbs, mirrors, crystal, Pyrex, ceramics and photo paper are not recyclable at my curb.
- ❑ Consider visiting your local MRF (materials recovery facility) or gain knowledge of plastics recyclability. Don't simply trust the chasing arrow. Some products with it are not recyclable, others without are recyclable.
- ❑ Allocate convenient recycling locations in the kitchen (under the counter is best) and home office. A Zero Waste bathroom or bedroom does not require any.
- ❑ Find collection sites for hard-to-recycle items (corks, worn-out shoes and clothes) and hazardous materials (batteries, paint, and motor oil). Earth911.com and its iRecycle app are a great resource.
- ❑ Allocate separate containers as per drop-off locations.

know for sure. It took visiting two different recycling centers, contacting twenty-one people, and shipping pieces of broken glassware to my glass recycler (tracking him down was not easy) to find out that my drinking glasses were recyclable after all (crystal ones are not, because they melt at a different temperature than most glass). I am not suggesting that you too put your glass in the bin (please first check with your local jurisdiction), but that you realize how complicated the system is, and reflect on the fact that for recycling to be successful, finding answers should be easy. Until then, recycle when necessary, but look to the other Rs first.

STEP 5: ROT {COMPOST THE REST}

My whole life has been spent waiting for an epiphany, a manifestation of God's presence, the kind of transcendent, magical experience that lets you see your place in the big picture. And that is what I had with my first compost heap.

—Bette Midler, quoted in the *Los Angeles Times*

Rotting describes the process of composting, which is simply the recycling of organic materials.

Composting is nature's way of recycling, allowing for organic discards to decompose over time and return their nutrients to the soil. At home, composting creates ideal conditions and speeds up the process for kitchen and yard waste to break down; therefore diverting waste from a landfill, where its natural decomposition would otherwise be inhibited and contribute to air and soil contamination. And considering that a third of household waste is organic, composting makes complete sense in terms of waste reduction.

I find composting satisfying. Composting is observable: you can put veggie scraps in a worm bin, witness the worms at work, watch them transform organic matter into nutrient-rich material, and use their tangible end product. The outcome of what we put in our compost is a certainty: rich soil, referred to as "black gold" by gardeners. On the other hand, the outcome of our plastic recycling is not. When we send away an empty bottle of contact lens solution, does it later become a deck? A bench? A toothbrush? Or landfill? Definitely landfill in the end. I used to picture compost as icky, smelly, messy, complicated, and scientific. I have found that none of these notions proved true.

As with recycling, I am not an expert on the subject—far from it. So many generations adopted it well before I'd even heard of it. But my family easily embraced it and in terms of Zero Waste, it has made a real difference. Rotting is a key component of this lifestyle, processing those items that cannot be refused, reduced, reused, or recycled. We've found it very useful in alleviating plastic consumption. We choose compostable wooden materials when metal or glass options are not available (such as toothbrushes).

Over time we've tried three different types of composting. We started with an open aerobic compost; we then added a worm composting bin; later, we adopted the city compost, letting go of our original open compost. But everyone's situation and composting success depends on different factors. And choosing a composting method can be overwhelming when faced with the multitude of options out there (especially for the novice). I created the "Compost Types Comparison Tool" on the following pages to ease your decision making.

There is a system out there waiting to meet your needs. Choosing a compost type is as much a personal choice as it is a functional one. Here is what to take into consideration:

- **Cost:** Some systems are free to set up, as they do not require a structure; some can be made from what you have on hand (leftover fencing, for example); while others entail investing in a secondary unit to enable the "curing" of the primary unit's output.

- **Location:** If you have a yard, you might want to adopt a compost system that will accept yard waste. If you live in an apartment, your choices will be narrowed mainly by the particularities of your location.

- **Aesthetics:** Some systems are simply ugly. Based on the space that you have available, you might want a system that blends with your decor, is compact, or is not visible. Sheet and trench composting, for example, are ideal in municipalities that do not allow exterior composting structures.

- **Food consumption:** Unless specified, most composting devices accept fruit and veggie scraps, tea leaves and coffee grounds, egg cartons, and crushed eggshells (more compostable items are described later in the book). But some can also process meat, dairy, and bones, which can be a real bonus in a nonvegan Zero Waste home.

- **End product:** Depending on where you live and what you grow (houseplants or edibles), you might have a use for compost or liquid fertilizer, or maybe not. Choose your system accordingly. Note that if your system delivers more end product than needed, you can donate it to gardening clubs or friends or post it for free on Craigslist.

- **Involvement:** In traditional composting, the correct ratio of brown (carbon) to green (nitrogen) materials is important. But if you want to keep the process carefree, some systems make this science optional (see "Compost Ratio—Margin of Error" in the "Compost Types Comparison Tool" table on the following pages).

- **Pests:** Pest control is obviously dependent on your diet (the furry pests generally go after the leftovers of a carnivore diet) and what you will be composting. Manufactured composters, for example, are usually engineered to not only speed up the composting process but also keep critters out of compost materials.

- **Pets:** If you have a pet, you might want to consider purchasing a pet waste composter or making your own (see the instructions on page 159). In any case, using the end product on edibles is not recommended.

- **Capacity:** Your system should accommodate your household's size and level of disposability. For example, paper towels, tissue paper, tea bags, coffee filters, cotton balls and bioplastics labeled "compostable" can be

COMPOST TYPES COMPARISON TOOL							
	Yard Waste	Pet Waste†	Pest Proof	Meat Dairy Bones	Speed	Cost	Urban
Cone	No	Yes	***	Yes	***	$$–$$$	No
Tumbler	Yes, small	No	***	No	**	$$	No
Bokashi	Yes, not practical	Yes, separate	***	Yes	***	$–$$$	Yes
Digester/Closed Holding Bin	Yes	Yes, separate	**	No	**	$–$$	No
Under Counter	No	Yes	***	Yes	***	$$$	Yes
Worm	Yes, non woody	Yes, separate	**	No	**	$–$$	Yes
Trench twelve feet deep	Yes	Yes, far from edibles	*	No	**	$	No
Curbside Pickup/Facility Drop-Offs	Yes	No	**	Yes	***	$$$	Yes
Sheet Composting	Yes	No	*	No	*	$	No
Heap/Open Holding Bin	Yes	Yes, manure	*	No	*–**	$–$$	No

†Special pet waste composters are also available, or you can make your own (see instructions on page 159)
* Low
** Medium
*** High
$ Inexpensive
$$ Moderate cost
$$$ Expensive

End Product	Aesthetics	Odorless	Curing Requires 2nd unit/ location	Comments	Compost Ratio— Margin of Error
None	**	**	Yes, for two weeks	Messy to empty (once every two years). Boost powder might be needed.	***
Compost	*	***	Yes	Bulky. Hard to turn.	**
Soil amendment/ liquid fertilizer	***	***	Yes	Needs Bokashi mix to work (make or buy). End product needs to be added to soil or compost.	***
Compost	**	**	Yes	Smelly and slow.	*
Compost	***	***	No	Requires electricity.	***
Compost/ liquid fertilizer	**	**	No	No garlic, onion, or twigs. Take inside when cold.	**
In-ground compost	***	***	Yes	Convenient when compost piles not allowed by municipalities.	***
Someone else's compost	***	**	No	Costly. Higher carbon footprint. Visit FindAComposter.com for drop-off locations.	***
Compost	*	*	Yes	Seasonal.	*
Compost	*	*–**	Yes	Dependent on turning.	**

composted (note that low temperatures in home composters will result in slow decomposition). However, applying the 5 Rs in order and the tips covered in the following chapters will provide alternatives to eliminate these products.

Note: Should you purchase a compostable or a recyclable item when buying new? To stay away from plastics, synthetics, or bioplastics, favor durability and recyclability in metal, glass, paper, and natural-fiber materials first; otherwise, choose a product made from compostable, renewable, and sustainably harvested resources, such as wood.

I have found rotting to be a revelation. The whole process has opened my eyes and helped me understand the simple workings of the natural world. I cannot get over the fact that I can grow an herb on my deck (with compost), feed its stalk to my worms, use their castings to grow more herbs, and use their "compost tea" to boost the growth of my houseplants, which in turn improve our home's air quality by absorbing pollutants such as formaldehyde and benzene. Their trimmings, along with the dust bunnies that I sweep, will also get composted and benefit the environment. Rotting represents the kind of big closed-loop waste cycle upon which our manufacturing model should have been based from the beginning.

BENEFITS OF THE ZERO WASTE LIFESTYLE

> *Zero Waste is the mother of environmental no-brainers.*
> —Jeffrey Hollender, CEO of Seventh Generation,
> as quoted in *The Story of Stuff*

Zero Waste offers evident and essential environmental advantages: it reduces pollution (decreasing hazardous solid and vaporous wastes) and encourages conservation (decreasing demand for natural resources). But the benefits of Zero Waste go way beyond ecological aspects. In the home, it undeniably improves one's standard of living. The uninformed might see Zero Waste as time-consuming and expensive (as I did). Yet these suppositions could not be farther from the truth!

Financial

The most quantifiable benefit of the lifestyle is financial. My husband, Scott, was not convinced about the Zero Waste lifestyle at first, but he jumped on the Zero Waste wagon once he accounted for money savings.

Here are ten ways Zero Waste makes financial sense:

1. Reduces consumption of products (focus on activities versus "stuff")
2. Reduces storage, maintenance, and repair costs
3. Eliminates the need to purchase disposables and offers amazing cumulative savings
4. Encourages buying bulk groceries, which are generally cheaper
5. Reduces (or at best eliminates) solid waste, therefore reducing disposal fees
6. Eliminates the purchase of trash liners ("wet discards" are compostable)
7. Favors buying quality, and therefore provides value for money spent
8. Supports a healthy lifestyle (see below), therefore reducing health care costs
9. Advocates selling unused items and renting seldom-used assets for a profit
10. Offers an option to sell recyclables directly to MRFs and compost material to gardeners

Health

The health benefits of the Zero Waste lifestyle are mainly associated with reducing our exposure to synthetics. The only downside (and this is actually a benefit) is that I am more sensitive to chemical smells and plastic tastes. But overall, my family is healthier and I feel confident feeding my kids foods that haven't been shrouded in health-harming plastics.

Here are ten ways in which Zero Waste improves the overall health of your family:

1. Discourages buying plastic packaging and products, thereby reducing risks associated with the growing concerns of plastic leaching into our food (such as BPA) and off-gassing into our homes (such as vinyl)

2. Supports reuse (i.e., buying used), which reduces off-gassing, since used products have already (mostly) released their gases
3. Promotes shopping in health food stores, which offer natural alternatives to common products, reducing exposure to such toxic chemicals as parabens, triclosan, and synthetic fragrances that are contained in toiletries and makeup
4. Encourages buying recyclable, reducing exposure to the harmful chemicals released when using nonrecyclable Teflon-coated cookware
5. Uses natural remedies and cleaning products, reducing exposure to unknown chemicals
6. Supports living with less, reducing dust collection and the accompanying allergies
7. Advocates outdoor activities, which help remedy vitamin D deficiencies, provide cleaner air (indoor air can be more polluted than outdoor air), and increase physical activity
8. Encourages buying whole foods, limiting the consumption of highly processed ones
9. Limits media/advertising exposure, reducing the cravings for unhealthy foods
10. Provides a leaner diet by reducing meat consumption

Time

Probably the most satisfying benefit of the lifestyle is that of time savings. And in an era when time is our society's most valuable commodity, who doesn't wish for more?

By refusing the accumulation of freebies, renouncing time-consuming habits (e.g., junk mail handling), and reducing home belongings, efficiency and time are reclaimed. Handling, storing, maintaining, cleaning, and organizing are simplified. Home management and Zero Waste are made easy. And reusing saves time otherwise spent shopping, transporting, or discarding disposables.

Anyone can benefit from a life freed from the burden of stuff and wasteful practices, and instead focused on experiences. Time also opens opportunities to get involved and participate in collective consumption, through which sharing, interacting, and reinforcing community bonds are possible. We discover like-minded people, no longer feel alone, and find hope that we never before saw in the future. But everyone's individual journey with Zero Waste will differ.

For me increased time has allowed for a richer life, doing the things I truly enjoy, spent with the people I truly care about. It has allowed me to find knowledge, wisdom, empowerment, confidence, passion, and a renewed life purpose. It has made room for greening my home, learning to forage, and experimenting with a multitude of crafts. It has engaged my artistic abilities to their full extent. It has permitted me to write a blog, write this book, and reconnect with nature. I have come to realize that stuff takes us away from our roots, from the outdoors. And with more time now spent outside, I no longer take the Earth for granted and I find my spiritual faith has been recharged.

Zero Waste has connected all the dots for me; it can do wonders for you, too.

In each of the following practical chapters, I will share with you some personal stories (I could not resist) and will let the 5 *R*s guide us to Zero Waste success, with these recurring elements: simplicity, reusability, and collection. *Simplicity* will cover the prevention of waste (refuse-reduce), *reusability* will address wasteful consumption (reuse), and *collection* will tackle the management of discards (recycle-rot).

Zero Waste is not all work. It can be fun, it can be beautiful. And you won't miss the smell of trash or the visual clutter of disposables, I promise.

Kitchen and Grocery Shopping

I had sworn off disposable packaging and was about to recycle our last empty jar of Dijon mustard when, out of curiosity, I took a peek at the ingredients on the label. Water, mustard seeds, vinegar, salt. How hard could it be to make at home? I had all but one ingredient on hand. Had anyone tried making it from scratch before? I ran to my computer, excited by the prospects, and within a few minutes I found a simple recipe.

How naive I had been to think that mustard was one of those things that you *only* buy from the store! Why did I not think of this earlier? Is it because I never watched my mother, an avid homemaker, whipping up the condiment? Is it because the concoction did not figure on my grandmother's pantry shelves? Is it because I did not recall Caroline Ingalls crafting the staple on *Little House on the Prairie*? (I did remember her churning butter . . . maybe I can, too, I thought.)

I collected some mustard seeds in the bulk section of my grocery store, and within a day I had a full jar of homemade mustard. I was hooked. I started thinking about the homemaking potential for the few packaged items left in my kitchen. I talked to my mom, mother-in-law, and friends, and I spent hours googling how-tos. I was willing to try anything.

One conversation with my girlfriend Karine led to kefir making. I added kefir grains (a live culture) to milk and got a fizzy yogurt drink overnight. How simple! The method was straightforward and my boys adopted this novelty with dispatch—and (I concede) a little added sugar. . . . But as their interest faded over time, I stepped beyond fermentation and into cheese making, a way to use the kefir we were producing and not drinking fast enough. I hung the homemade drink in a handkerchief above the sink and let the liquid condense into a soft cheese. It tasted just like the "real thing" and impressed family and friends. Their enthusiasm (and a bit of home-making pride) motivated me to further experiment with seasoning and texture: rolling in pepper, wrapping in bay leaves ("a total fail," as my boys called it), marinating in oil, pressing, drying, etc.

Kefir grains are tiny; they look like grains of white rice. But they are high-maintenance and depend on regular feeding. They soon loomed large in our family's life. We came to consider their welfare along with that of our dog, Zizou: Did you feed the kefir grains today? Do we take them camping this weekend? Do we carry them along when we fly to France this summer? A simple process had snowballed and complicated my life more than I cared to admit.

By the time I took a step back from the kefir madness, those little grains (and the mustard seeds before them) had forever changed my relationship with food, packaging, and even people.

What I appreciate most about making from scratch is learning how—and from what—common foods are made. Beyond satisfying my curiosity, making my own food also provides a sense of control and reassurance that comes along with handpicking the ingredients versus eating food made with a long list of things I can neither pronounce nor trust. While complicated ingredients disclosed on labels are common homemaking deterrents, I have found that most of what I used to buy in packaging can be made with only a few ingredients.

Manufactured goods offer convenience but at the expense of our connection with the making process. The less we make from scratch, the more reliant we become on manufacturing. We lose touch with how to do the basics that once afforded us freedom and survival. As we evaluate our environmental crisis and search for a connection to the things in our lives, we find ourselves going "back to basics" for solutions. Facilitated by Internet access and social media, homemaking provides grounds for collaborating and sharing knowledge. It reinforces ties across generational and cultural divides. I can even thank it for healing my relationship with my mother when physical distances separated us, and tightening bonds with my mother-in-law when cultural disparities had set us apart. I hope my kids, too, will benefit from it and so will their offspring (after all, savoir faire is the only heirloom I plan to leave behind—more on that later).

Okay, I'll be honest: my rebellious side also gets satisfaction from being able to make do without buying into corporations and their marketing engines. It gives me a sense of freedom, knowing that I do not depend on them, feeling as though I am outsmarting the system in place.

Now, you don't need to get carried away as I did. There's no reason to let kefir take over your life! After all, sustainability is really about adopting change that is feasible in the long run.

Today I no longer make cheese from kefir, nor do I tend to kefir grains. I composted them (with sadness) along with their high maintenance (with relief). I do not regret learning about a new process—I gained the ability to make cheese from yogurt if I have extra, something I now do frequently. I do not regret learning how to make butter, either, as I now understand and appreciate the amount of cream needed to make a pound. A pint of relatively expensive cream yields about a quarter cup of homemade butter. Given the amount of butter we use (my boys need their daily cookie), it became way too expensive to make from scratch.

My kitchen is a science lab. If I pull some beets out of the refrigerator, I might end up with a salad, a lip stain, or a watercolor dye. The options are infinite and limited only by my creativity. But I am careful about adopting change that I can maintain within my time and financial constraints. We found that the time required to make cheese and the expenses associated with making butter are not part of our long-term Zero Waste plan. We found that it's important to be diligent about finding sustainable balance between being easy and being green.

In this chapter, I will share how I have adopted Zero Waste in my kitchen. I'll show you how to set up a kitchen, how to shop, and how to plan meals. Zero Waste living inevitably involves some degree of home-making (to make the things that are not available in bulk), but you have to find the methods that are feasible for you in the long run. *Simplifying* is the key to making Zero Waste effortless. No need to become a homemake-aholic. The Zero Waste methods that work for you will soon become second nature in your kitchen. Ready, steady, go (slow).

KITCHEN SETUP

Turning a regular kitchen into a Zero Waste one is not as hard as you might think. It requires reorganization and a little research, but once a system is in place and the household is trained to use it, Zero Waste is a breeze.

Simplicity

Let's understand our simplifying goals before spinning into action.

The kitchen is a communal room, often referred to as the heart of the home. This is where we cook, eat, drink, collaborate, converse, and sometimes even read or do homework. With such high levels of activity, the kitchen is a key source of waste and clutter in our homes.

Look no farther than your kitchen cupboards, where accumulation is often overwhelming. Sandwich and ziplock bags, paper towels, disposable cups, and frozen dinners underscore a common cause for this surplus of stuff: we are searching for ways to save time.

In setting up a Zero Waste kitchen, efficiency is a crucial ingredient. It can bring peace and ease into meal preparation; it can bring joy to a task that we might otherwise consider a chore. In the kitchen, Zero Waste will not only prove to save precious time and free us from wasteful and unhealthy habits; it will save energy and money as well. But here is the catch: in order to reap the benefits, you need to make your kitchen a clutter-free zone. Depending on your current setup, decluttering may seem like a daunting task, but the editing process will make room for time to create more and clean less.

A Zero Waste kitchen makes cooking easier; it allots a place for everything (with extra breathing room around it); it addresses health concerns associated with known toxins; and it maximizes your investment on groceries. Our Zero Waste goal, as you can tell, addresses more than just solid waste.

Most kitchens are filled with gadgets that claim to make cooking and entertaining easier: sorbet makers, waffle irons, panini presses.... But are these really being used? If so, how often? What about the zester, the specialty cake pans, the cookie cutters, the dozen place mats, the fancy wine stoppers, the wine basket, the wine cooler, the champagne bucket, the second or third set of china, the wineglass stem charms, the shot glasses, and the tablecloth weights? Oh! And the candle that is too pretty to be lit? Think of the drawer filled with hot pads (aren't a couple enough?). Think of your junk drawer (what is in there that we can't live without?).

Manufacturers promise to turn us into Alice Waters, when in fact these items take up precious space, make it harder to find cooking essentials, create stress, clutter our lives, and waste time (not to mention valuable resources): they are an impediment to efficiency, they are an impediment to cooking. There is a good chance that most of the items mentioned here can be forgotten, simply donated, and replaced by something else (the cheese grater works just fine as a zester, for example). The fewer accessories you have, the less time it will take to prepare your food: one graded measuring cup is easier to ferret out from a drawer than multiple individual ones, and the less you will need to clean. The less will also eventually break and wind up, well . . . you know where. Alice Waters herself recognizes the importance of simplifying. She once said, "I think that the minimum amount of equipment in the kitchen is very desirable. When you get all those gadgets, you disengage with food, whereas if you use a mortar and pestle, or you're chopping instead of using a machine, you begin to feel empowered and you take responsibility for what you're making." Living with less does not deprive your life; it improves it.

Let's begin the decluttering process.

According to the Pareto principle, roughly 80 percent of the effects come from 20 percent of the causes. It'd be generous to say that 20 percent of household items get used 80 percent of the time. The remaining 80 percent of household items are not really that useful. In theory, simplifying a kitchen would be as straightforward as evaluating the 20 percent that we *do* use and letting go of the rest. But it's not always that easy. Our reasoning plays tricks on us and makes us hold on to things for a multitude of reasons. What if I wanted to host a Moroccan party? I need that tagine! A less aggressive way is to set aside a day (maybe two, depending on the speed of your decision making) to take *everything* out of your cupboards (including food) and put back only those items that survive the following questions:

- **Is it in working condition? Is it expired?** Keeping something that you had good intentions of repairing does not save it from the landfill, it only postpones its imminent demise. Repair it now, sell/donate it for parts, or discard it once and for all (compost expired food).
- **Do I use it regularly?** Have I used this item this past month? If you're not sure, stick a date on it and stash it away. If you do not reach for it within a month, donate it. But don't cheat yourself: using the fondue pot tonight just to prove me wrong does not count. Donate your fondue set and other kitchen items collecting dust.
- **Is it a duplicate?** Only one set of hands can reach into the oven at once. Pick your favorite pair of oven mitts. When dealing with duplicates, you might find it helpful to set a maximum number or devise space limitations for stuff, and combine foods.
- **Does it put my family's health in danger?** For example, Teflon (nonstick), aluminum, and plastics have proved to be health hazards. These should be discarded. This question proves particularly helpful in weeding out toxic items among duplicates (e.g., stirring spoons: recycle the plastic ones, keep the wooden or stainless ones). Eliminating these from

your everyday use will put your mind at ease and keep your family happy and healthy.

- **Do I keep it out of guilt?** If you are afraid of letting go a hostess gift, remember that your guests do not mean to burden you or instill guilt; they just want to offer a polite gesture. It's okay to let go of something that you never intended to purchase and don't really want. And when guests ask about the whereabouts of their gift, it is totally acceptable to express gratitude and then to let them know that you are simplifying your life. Be the king or queen of your castle.
- **Do I keep it because "everyone has one"? Is it too specialized? Does it truly save time, as promised?** We store and maybe even use many kitchen gadgets simply because of persuasive marketing. Evaluate the true need for egg slicers, grapefruit knives, a salad spinner, or a rolling pin. **Could another item achieve the same task?** A kitchen towel can act as a salad spinner, a bottle as a rolling pin. Often your fingers will do.
- **Is it worth my precious time cleaning?** Everything in your kitchen is to be considered, even the small items, even those hung on the walls or stored above your cabinets. Think of the decorative items that you have collected over the years: they serve no purpose yet they create visual clutter and require dusting. Are they worth it? The food processor is another high-maintenance item. By the time you have pulled it out of your cupboard and fiddled with and cleaned its bulky parts, you could easily have hand chopped twice as many onions. Is it worth keeping?
- **Could I use this space for something else?** If you view kitchen storage as real estate, then your junk drawer, for example, takes up some valuable space for just containing junk! If it is really "junk" that you are storing, then why keep it? If it is not, then the contents should go where they really belong, and the free space used to create breathing room between worthy items.
- **Is it reusable?** If not, can someone else make use of it? We'll look at reusability in just a bit.

Don't be afraid of letting go: focus on the benefits that you will gain from living with less.

Don't fear regretting things. Dreading the what-if is a normal part of this process. There will inevitably be one item that you'll regret giving away. But trust that this one item is a small sacrifice, a trivial price to pay in order to gain control of your kitchen.

Nothing should be overlooked. Get into the details of what you have. And if you end up keeping items "just to fill empty space" (yes, it happens!), then remove free-standing storage or shelves or consider moving to a smaller house with a smaller kitchen! Because to reach full efficiency, "fit" should marry "need." Anything beyond that union will ultimately be a waste of space, real estate, storage, maintenance, or heating.

Of course, paring down is a very subjective process, dependent on the size of your household and your cooking abilities and habits. But for illustrative purposes, I will list the kitchen items (I will cover the pantry later) we have chosen to keep in order to live a comfortable (rather than a wastefully lavish) life:

- **Dishes:** Twelve dinner plates, twelve small plates, twelve cups, and twelve bowls. We bought quality ware from a local ceramic studio. I have twelve because we can sit ten people at our table and I need a couple of extras for serving.
- **Glassware:** A shelf full of wineglasses, a shelf full of tumblers (about twenty-four each). These two shelves cover our party needs and eliminate resorting to disposables. We also use these glasses to serve cold soups and appetizers and to hold a variety of things, from loose salt to toothbrushes.
- **Flatware:** Setting for twelve
- **Cooking:** Three sizes of pans, three sizes of pots, one stockpot, three lids, a teakettle (all stainless)
- **Preparing and serving:** Three bowls and one platter
- **Baking:** Two pie dishes, one large casserole dish, one loaf pan, two baking sheets
- **Utensils:** Stainless ladle, spoon, spatula, tongs, and whisk, and one wooden spatula
- **Cutting:** One paring knife, one chef knife, one serrated knife, one pair of scissors, and one cutting board
- **Accessories:** Stainless colander, sieve, grater, steamer, funnel, one set of measuring spoons, a measuring cup, a scale, a bottle opener, a pepper grinder, two pot holders, two trivets
- **Small appliances:** An all-in-one blender and a toaster

What's missing?

Here are some examples of items that did not survive my list of questions above.

- **Food processor:** Hand chopping is not only faster (than cleaning a big apparatus) but also more sensuous. Connecting with the food as you cook makes the whole process pleasurable.
- **Microwave:** I did not like the amount of space that it took and we did not use it much other than to heat water. We kept our kettle instead.
- **Can opener:** Simply because we do not buy cans.
- **Salad spinner:** We use a colander or towel or mesh bag (see the grocery shopping kit on page 54) instead.
- **Rolling pin:** I find that my fingers can push the dough into a pie pan just fine, otherwise I use a bottle.
- **Cookie cutters:** There are plenty of items around the house that can do the job.
- **Zester:** I can use a plane grater or a knife instead.
- **Garlic press:** I use the side of a knife to smash the garlic out of its peel.
- **Basting brush:** I use a bundle of herbs, my hands, or a spoon instead.
- **Vegetable peeler:** Giving up my peeler has simplified my life by allowing me not to peel veggies that do not need peeling; it has reduced our compost output and provided us with increased vitamins stored in vegetable skins.
- **Loose cutting boards:** We use one that is integrated in the kitchen counter.
- **Cake pans:** I use my baking dishes instead.
- **Place mats and tablecloths:** I find that both get dirty too fast and are a waste of physical and electrical energy and detergent. Wiping a table is much easier than cleaning a place mat or tablecloth. Especially since having a place mat often requires cleaning the table, too!
- **Decorative items:** I don't want to spend any time cleaning or caring for something that has no use. Life is too short. I prefer to wrestle with my boys instead.
- **Rubber bands and bag clips:** Because we do not buy packaged foods, we do not need accessories or gadgets to seal them.
- **Formal dishware and a second set of flatware:** I could not justify the amount of space that these took or the extra care (hand washing) that they required.
- **Skewers:** We use rosemary branches instead, and they add great flavor to kebabs.
- And **disposables!**

Reusability

If your disposables somehow survived this decluttering process, let me tell you right now: you can reclaim the space that they take up, you don't need them. Keep your money where it belongs: in your pocket and out of the landfill! Throwaways can easily be replaced with reusable versions.

We all yearn to save time, at any cost (including the environment), so we buy into time-saving tricks that marketing campaigns promise. But who is disposability really benefiting in the end? Take a pack of disposable cups, for example: How does (1) ripping open its packaging, (2) carrying packaging and cups out to the curb with your recycling (or trash), (3) bringing that container back from the curb, (4) going to the store for more, and (5) transporting them from the store, on *multiple occasions,* save time compared to (1) grabbing reusable cups from the cupboard, (2) throwing them in the dishwasher, and (3) putting them away? It seems that we have been duped into thinking that multiple shopping and recycling trips required by disposability save more time than reusing a durable product. "Sweep them off a table, ours won't break!" the marketing teams behind disposables say. I think it's about time we reclaimed our adulthood: we're grown-ups, we can handle breakables.

Our family has replaced paper towels with microfiber cloths, and we never run out. We have eliminated the need for trash liners with composting. We have swapped plastic sandwich bags for kitchen towels, which I already had on hand. I have learned that I can easily live without wax paper or aluminum foil, and my husband appreciates the savings from no longer buying disposable plates, cups, or paper napkins. So many shopping trips have been eliminated!

If you stop buying single-use products for your kitchen, you will quickly realize that living without them is quite possible. Try it for a while. You'll find that some disposables can simply be eliminated; others, however, will require an up-front investment, one that will pay for itself in only a few months! Consume to save the environment? Yes, if your purchase replaces something that you would otherwise use only once. If you sold some items when you decluttered earlier, you now have money to invest in reusability. But please consider the recyclability of the materials you choose. Select metal, glass, or paper-based products, and avoid plastics.

Again, everyone's needs are different, but for illustrative purposes, here is a list of the disposables that my family has replaced with reusables:

- **Paper towels:** A pile of rags for wiping the counters and a pile of kitchen towels (made from an old sheet) for wiping hands. We use a knife to squeegee a wet piece of meat or fish.
- **Water bottles:** A stainless bottle for each member of our family; two regular (kids), two insulated (Scott and me). Bottled water is not only wasteful, it's also not as regulated as tap water, so you don't really know what you're drinking.
- **Cling wrap/sandwich and freezer bags:** A collection of canning jars. I have about a hundred in different sizes because I use them for canning, storing, freezing, and transporting food, and I store about ten empty ones in a cupboard for leftovers. I prefer French canning jars, not because I am French, but because the parts are integral and therefore easy to handle and wash (my favorite brand also uses an all-natural rubber gasket).
- **Paper napkins:** A pile of cloth napkins. I have about thirty, to accommodate our home's guest capacity. I chose medium size for versatility (they work for both cocktails and dinners) and patterned to hide the hard-to-clean grease stains. Each family member uses a monogrammed ring to identify and reuse his napkin between washes.
- **Tea bags:** A tea strainer. I chose a medium-size ball strainer based on the opening and capacity of our insulated stainless bottles.
- **Coffee filters:** A coffee press. Reusable coffee filters are also available for those using coffee machines.
- **Toothpicks:** Turkey lacers. About thirty, based on the maximum amount of guests that we can host at our house. You could also purchase reusable stainless-steel or titanium cocktail picks.

Reusability is not only about eliminating disposables, it's also about buying durable quality when replacements are needed. Buy secondhand professional gear, such as used chef's tools, when possible; alternatively, visit your local restaurant-supply store to locate products designed to withstand heavy use.

Collection

Appointing receptacles for the segregation of discards is another key element to a Zero Waste kitchen. It might help you, your family, and your visitors to post a list of what each container collects on each receptacle lid. Posting it on the fridge is an option, too, but it's less helpful. The sizes of the receptacles vary with your access to bulk foods, but ideally the smallest would hold landfill waste. Here is a description of the receptacles needed:

Compost

The first step to a Zero Waste kitchen is adopting a composting system that works for your needs, as those described on pages 30–31. Considering that a quarter of kitchen waste is compostable, you'll quickly notice a difference in your solid waste once you set up a system. Whatever type you implement, the most important part of composting is collecting compostable material. I have found that rotting is easiest when the receptacle (i.e., the container that collects compostable materials in your kitchen) is:

1. **Large enough:** A large container will reduce the number of trips to your composter, and pretty much any container will do. You can even turn your current kitchen trash bin into a compost receptacle. We empty ours once a week; meat and fish scraps are frozen until pickup day. Organic material smells bad only when mixed with nonbiodegradable items, as they are in a landfill, because the latter prohibit the former from decomposing properly. Since the preliminary stages of decomposition do not smell, you do not need to purchase a bin with a carbon filter—which needs to be replaced periodically. Your money can be better spent elsewhere.
2. **Aesthetically pleasing:** Many shy away from composting because they can't stand the idea of having a "dirty" container on their countertop. I don't blame them! But who said the container had to be displayed on your counter? We would never think of putting our soiled trash cans on our counters. Under counter is best. Out of sight but not out of mind.

3. **Within easy reach:** We keep ours in a slide-out container under the sink, which offers easy access when chopping veggies, for example. Simply rinse and cut the ends into the bin. Keeping your receptacle under the sink also makes it easy to empty your sink strainer as it collects wet and messy scraps and discard table scraps prior to loading the dishwasher.

Depending on your composting system, the list that you affix on your receptacle might include:

- Bamboo* or rosemary skewers
- Cellophane bags (make sure it's cellophane and not plastic!)*
- Coffee filters*
- Coffee grounds
- Egg cartons*
- Eggshells
- Expired food*
- Leftovers*
- Loose tea (tea bags, most of which are coated with polypropylene plastic, will not fully decompose)
- Matches
- Meat and fish bones*
- Nutshells
- Paper napkins*
- Paper plates*
- Paper towels*
- Shellfish (crustacean)
- Soiled paper and cardboard such as pizza boxes*
- Stale bread*
- Toothpicks*
- Vegetables/fruits
- Wax paper*, including butter wrappers

---

* Alternatives to discarding/composting these materials are covered throughout the book.

Recycling

Find out exactly what your community recycles (including what materials are considered hard to recycle) and allot containers accordingly. Hard-to-recycle materials are those items that are not included in your curbside pickup and need to be taken (or sent) to special locations. In our kitchen, for example, we have a can for mixed recycling; our community recycles glass, paper, aluminum and steel cans, and plastics numbered 1 through 7. We have a small container to collect cork corks, for taking to my grocery store, which upcycles them. We also have another for the sneaky plastic corks and the rare candy wrappers that make their way into our home. When it's full, I can ship the contents to TerraCycle to be upcycled (see "Resources" for more information). Considering the carbon footprint associated with shipping these resources, this is not a perfect solution, but it works until manufacturing and recycling processes improve.

Keep in mind that the amount that you currently recycle will change as you adopt Zero Waste: your recycling system needs to be flexible at least for the short term. For example, you might already have a container in place to collect plastic bags for reuse or recycling, but we'll eliminate the need for them in just a minute.

Landfill

Now that you are using your old trash can to collect compostable materials, you can use your old compost receptacle (usually the size of a small bucket) to collect landfill waste. No need for trash liners since the wet items that usually make them necessary are compostable.

The contents of this bin represent a call for action, starting with changing your grocery shopping habits.

GROCERY SHOPPING

Grocery and Errands Lists

Shopping lists are obvious time-savers. But I have found that they serve an even bigger purpose.

Through my business, I was surprised to find that three-quarters of the households that I consulted did not have an ongoing list, resulting in frequent grocery runs (sometimes daily) and impulse buys (sometimes buying what they forgot they already had).

We keep two shopping lists: one for groceries, one for errands. Both lists are conveniently located adjacent to our pantry and are made of strips of used paper (typically homework printed on a single side). I've clipped them together and attached a pencil. We fill the sheets from bottom up, so we can tear off the bottom and bring it to the store. Cell phones are good paperless alternatives but not as suitable for the participation of the whole family or on-a-whim jotting.

When one of us uses up a pantry item or notices butter running low, we make note of it on the *grocery list*. The whole family contributes to it. Léo once wrote, "10,000 bananas," out of frustration with our "local-only produce policy." I did not fully honor his request, but I did buy him a half dozen to reward his participation. I also use the list to jot down items needed for special occasions like extra cheese for a potluck. The grocery list is dedicated to items available at the grocery store that I visit on a weekly basis and that I have carefully chosen based on its bulk selection, location, and on-premise bakery.

When we want to get something from another store, we write it on the *errands list*. By the time I leave for my weekly shopping, I have typically found alternatives, or simply eliminated the need to buy many items on the list. I also use the errands list to jot down such things as donation drop-offs or "specialty bulk" items.

Overall, these lists have been great tools for saving time and money and reducing.

Bulk vs. Bulk

We have incredible power as consumers. We rely on grocery shopping for survival and restock a multitude of products weekly (sometimes daily), and our decisions can promote or demote manufacturers and grocers, based on the packaging or quality of food they provide. Where we spend the fruit of our hard labor should more than meet our basic need of filling a pantry shelf; it should also reflect our values. Because ultimately, giving someone your business implicitly articulates this message: "Your store satisfies *all* my needs and I want you to flourish." We can vote with our pocketbooks by avoiding wasteful packaging and privileging local and organic products. I have found that *bulk* shopping meets these considerations.

In the United States, most people associate bulk shopping with membership warehouse clubs: buying a shrink-wrapped bundle of three large containers of bay leaves, or purchasing a colossal tub of margarine. This "spend more to save more" business model provides the lowest price per unit possible for its customers and will prove economical in feeding a boarding school or a small army. It can also benefit the average-size family, but not always. Scott and I gave up our membership years ago, after buying that three-pound tub of margarine. Before we could reach the bottom, pieces of toast and traces of jam commingled with other unidentifiable bits. Did I cut your appetite? The sight of it eventually cut ours, and we ultimately sent the gross remains to the landfill. Remorseful for wasting money on something that we did not have the guts to finish, we never bought big-box bulk again, or margarine for that matter. Buying more than needed inevitably results in food boredom and racing against expiration dates, both of which ultimately lead to wasted food, space, money, resources, and precious time!

However, the kind of bulk mentioned in this book refers to that found in health food stores and co-ops, sold loose in bins, with no packaging. It's a kind of bulk shopping that allows consumers to refill containers and buy as much or as little as needed.

On the packaging front, both business models (membership warehouse clubs and health food stores) reduce packaging. But if we compare stocking up for staples at either location, the first involves storing very large amounts at home. My pantry would need to be the size of a dance hall if I were to shop at a big-box house for the selection of bulk that I keep in my kitchen today. On the other hand, you don't need a gargantuan pantry to house items purchased from bulk bins at a health food store. It should be said that health food stores don't eliminate packaging altogether (manufacturers use it to transport goods to the stores, and the items even sometimes come in the same fifty-pound bags found at membership warehouse clubs), but they allow the consumer to match purchases with true food needs and storage space. Because a regular-size household does not need one pound of stevia (I need half a teaspoon per month) or thirty pounds of pecans (I use one cup around the holidays) at once, the health food store represents our "dance hall"; it provides storage for the consumer.

People often assume that buying in bulk from a health food store is costly. In fact, we have been able to shave a third off our grocery bill by shopping this way. If you stay away from prepared foods, cut down your meat consumption, and are careful in picking affordable choices, just as you would when purchasing packaged goods from a supermarket, you'll see your grocery bill decrease significantly.

The health food store and co-ops provide a lot more local and organic choices, too. And because they generally do the groundwork in evaluating the ingredients and origin of the foods that they carry, it saves time spent decoding ingredient labels. Quality food does not come cheap, but in the long run is better for us and the environment and is an investment I am willing to make for the health of our family and the planet. The more we buy organic, the more likely we'll see prices drop, too. I am happy to vote: "Yes, more [bulk]" and "Yes, more [organic]" every time I shop. As I wish for less waste and more bulk bins in my kids' future, I feel good investing the fruit of my hard labor into that ideal every week.

We will be referring to bulk from now on as unpackaged goods of any type, including but not limited to groceries.

Locating Bulk Stores

Whether you end up adopting bulk grocery shopping will most likely depend on your access to it. Many tell me that they do not have bulk in their area. Until I tackled our waste, I had no idea that bulk bins existed in my town either! I have therefore created a bulk locating app, named Bulk, so you, too, can enjoy the benefits of shopping the package-free aisles. The app is free, points to bulk nearest you anywhere in the United States or

Canada, and provides a way to share locations that you discover or already use. Please take advantage of it!

Putting Together a Zero Waste Shopping Kit

To reduce packaging waste as much as possible while shopping in bulk, you will need:

- **Totes:** The array of shopping bags that have popped up on the market these past few years can be overwhelming. I've found it preferable to invest in a good sturdy bag than to purchase one for a buck. I use portable laundry hampers, made of a very sturdy canvas with metal handles.
- **Cloth bags (two sizes):** I made mine from an old sheet with their tare* on the front. You can also make them out of silk (light and quick drying) or buy them in the bulk section of your store. If they do not have a tare printed on them (they usually do not), have them weighed at the customer service counter of your store and permanently mark the tare on the front of your bags (many pens, permanent markers or leftover house paint will do). To eliminate the need for disposable wire ties, make or select a style that includes an integrated tie.
- **Mesh bags (optional):** You can use these for produce in lieu of cloth bags; the see-through quality of the mesh allows the cashier to read produce codes. Laundry wash bags or paint strainers work well but are synthetic. Natural fiber (usually hemp or cotton) options are available.
- **Glass jars (two sizes):** The same reusable mason jars mentioned above under "Reusability" (page 47) work great. I use one-liter (one quart) and five-hundred-milliliter (pint) sizes. Have them weighed at the customer service counter and make note or permanently mark the tare on them.
- **Bottles (optional):** Empty glass white vinegar bottles work well as they generally have a large screw top opening, but you can also reuse wine or lemonade (flip-top) bottles. Have them weighed at the customer service counter and make note or permanently mark the tare on them.

---

* The tare is the weight of your empty container, usually in pounds. The cashier can then deduct it from the total weight of the item purchased at checkout.

- **Washable crayon:** A washable crayon to note the item number directly on your bag or jar will eliminate the need for disposable labels commonly used in bulk stores.
- **Pillowcase:** Or a large bread bag made from an old sheet.
- **Your grocery list!**

Should you have difficulty putting together your shopping kit, please note that all items can be found on my website at ZeroWasteHome.com.

At the Store and at Home

Now that you have a shopping kit ready to use, here is what to do with it at the store and what to do once you get it home.

- Use the **cloth bags** to stock up on dry bulk, such as flour, sugar, beans, cereal, cookies, spices, etc. Use the washable crayon to note the bulk item number of your choice directly on your cloth bag before filling, and fill an estimated amount to match your storage container at home. (For spices, I prefer to bring and fill my empty spice jar to avoid overestimating.) These bags also work well for packing bread rolls from the bakery bins.

  At home: Transfer your dry goods into airtight containers. I use French canning jars of varying sizes for this purpose.
- Use the **mesh bags** (or cloth bags) to fill with produce.

  At home: Transfer produce to the high-humidity compartment of your refrigerator. If your produce drawer does not work efficiently (i.e., leafy greens wilt), add a damp towel or wet your cloth bag, or see "Resources," page 268. I put herbs in a glass of water. I transfer the larger items out of the bags, but use the mesh to store small items together (grapes, for example) and to quickly wash them (simply run the bag under water.)
- Use the **small-size jars** for "wet" bulk, such as honey, peanut butter, pickles, etc. and write the bulk item number on the jar with the washable crayon. Do not overlook the olive and salad bars; these are a great source of unpackaged foods.

  At home: Store directly in your pantry or refrigerator.
- Use the **pillowcase** to transport bread from the bakery. You can call ahead to place an order—though some stores allow on-the-spot order-

ing. Present your pillowcase at the time of pickup, and the bakery staff will slide bread into it. They hand you a price sticker or a barcode, which you can keep for future use. Once you have a system in place, you can set up an ongoing weekly order.

At home: Transfer the bread into another pillowcase (I cut our baguettes in half) to store in the freezer (it keeps for a week); thaw as needed.

- Use **bottles** to fill with liquids, such as olive oil, vinegar, maple syrup, etc. (bulk liquids are harder to find than counter products or grains). Sometimes the opening of the refilling pump is too large for bottles, in which case larger jars are more convenient. Don't forget to use the washable crayon to write the item number on the glass.

At home: Store directly in a cupboard on a lazy Susan for easy reach or in the refrigerator (maple syrup).

- Use the **large-size jars** for "counter" items, such as meat, fish, cheese, and deli. Simply ask the counter staff to fill your jar with your order. They will affix a price label onto your jar.

At home: Store directly in the refrigerator.

BYOC (bringing your own container) is uncommon and may raise eyebrows, but only if you show hesitation. I find it easier not to ask for permission to shop with reusables. For example, when facing new staff at the fish counter, I'll say, "Four calamari steaks, in here, please," as I hand out my jar, looking down at the calamari steaks, aloof. Staring at the staff for approval will only make them doubt you. I act as if jars were common practice (as if I had shopped this way my whole life), and when asked about the purpose of the jar, I simply reply, "I do not have a trash can." No one asks further questions. That said, I was recently turned down at a store where I have been refilling my jars for the past three years. The new staff member behind the counter firmly said, "It's against health and safety regulations." I urged her to check with her manager and she eventually filled my jar. But a comment like this would have deterred a first timer from ever trying again! Acceptance of BYOC does vary from one jurisdiction to another, and each application (counter, dispensers, dry goods, wet goods, etc.) depends on ever-changing federal, state, and local regulations. Different stores interpret rules differently, and some even choose to disregard them. When establishments or jurisdictions frown on the practice, it is usually for fear of getting sued; they do not want to be responsible for you getting sick because you did not properly clean your container. But don't take a store employee's word for it if you get turned down: ask for managers to produce the exact section and number of the law that forbids filling up your containers. I have found that they are rarely able to provide concrete evidence.

It takes guts to do the unconventional, but please do not give up; try another store, or even another day, if you get turned down!

Running all your errands on the same day, once a week, and with a list, will not only save you from impulse shopping, it will allow you to build a relationship with staff members, so you can feel comfortable shopping this way. Every Friday, I look forward to greeting Carl and his cheese team, sharing a few words with Kito as he hands over my order of warm bread, and absorbing Jay's eternal smile at the cash register. These guys and their patience are, after all, what makes this system possible, and I am ever grateful to them for accommodating our requests. Be friendly, be patient, be thankful.

Beyond the Grocery Store

What about those things that you cannot find in bulk at your local health food store or co-op grocery store? Or what if a health food store is not available in your area?

Bulk is not limited to health food stores: CSAs (community supported agriculture), farmer's markets, and specialty vendors can be a great source of package-free products, when their sustainable efforts are consistent. CSAs, for example, are a wonderful business model. They support the local community and promote the organic and seasonal industry. Unfortunately, the particular CSA we joined used plastic bags: ten bags times six hundred members per week resulted in six thousand plastic bags that my farm "released into nature" each week! I proposed solutions and urged the adoption of alternatives, but excuses were made as to why bagging was necessary for portioning. Other CSAs certainly provide package-free produce, but I have adopted my local farmer's market. It offers more seasonal variety in comparison and gives me a chance to chat with vendors and refuse plastic bags on the spot. Maybe one day the florist will consider selling his beautiful flowers sans plastic, too! Visit LocalHarvest.org to find a CSA or farmer's market near you.

Here are further package-free food options to consider beyond the store.

- Buy **eggs** from the farmer's market, a CSA, or a neighbor: both CSAs and farmer's market egg stands gladly take egg cartons back for reuse. But if you live in the countryside, you might be able to forgo the carton altogether by buying eggs directly from a neighbor. You can locate one through Eggzy.net.
- Buy **milk and yogurt** sold in a refundable glass jar. Depending on where you live, you can buy milk directly from a local dairy, from a delivery service, or sometimes from the refrigerated aisle of your grocery store. For the latter, a deposit fee is charged at the time of purchase and refunded upon returning the bottle to the store.
- Bring a jar or cloth bag to a **specialty store** for a refill, such as ice cream or candy. You may get turned down, but business in a jar is still business! And many retailers are open to it. The Maille store in Paris offers refills of its mustard, for example.
- Refill clean, empty **wine** bottles during a winery "bottling event." I like to reuse flip-top bottles for this purpose, no corks wasted. Wine refilling is hard to find, and depending on where you live, the option might not be available to you. Our bulk locator app will find such wineries for you; alternatively, you can call around or simply google "bottle your own wine events." An added bonus: refilling can be very cost effective.
- Refill a **beer** jug (i.e., growler) at a local brewery. Some breweries offer empty growlers and provide refills at the bar. Call around to locate participating establishments. If you get turned down, your inquiry may at least get them to consider it. Note: this method works only when you are ready to drink one gallon of beer at once; it will start to lose its carbonation overnight. Have some friends over!
- **Craft** what you cannot find in bulk form. For the sake of my sanity, I avoid making what is available in bulk. Instead of baking bread, I slide the buns sold loose in the bread aisle and the baguettes from the bakery into my pillowcase. To keep Zero Waste as simple and effortless as possible (sorry, kefir grains), I simplify, reprioritize my time, and make from scratch only the staples that are difficult to find unpackaged. Favor recipes that require only a few bulk ingredients and are easy to make.
- Consider **canning** the products that you are used to buying in cans. Home canning is a great alternative to store-bought cans, most of which

are loaded with MSG and can leach BPA. For simplifying reasons, I choose to can only tomatoes—because my family enjoys them out of season. I buy them at the end of the summer, from the farmer's market and at closing time, when I can bargain for large quantities at a low price. Visit my website ZeroWasteHome.com for a tutorial.

- Join or start a **buying club.** A buying club is generally an informal organization of people (typically seven or more families) who buy food together from a co-op distributor and share chores associated with collecting money and placing and dispatching food orders. Many wholesalers that supply stores and restaurants and specialize in natural and organic products provide goods to buying clubs as well. For households that do not have access to a health food store, buying clubs provide a great alternative for purchasing quality groceries in bulk and at a low price. CoopDirectory.org provides lists of distributors to get you started.

- **Grow your own.** Food that you grow at home will always be package and sticker free! For example, herbs are often sold in clamshells and/or in too-large quantities but can easily be grown in containers. Rosalind Creasy, author of several edible-gardening books, recommends that beginners boost their confidence by starting with high-yield vegetables: mesclun salad and stir-fry greens produce a lot in a short time; eggplants, chard, and kale deliver over a long period of time (large harvest-to-space ratio); indeterminate tomato varieties yield more fruit than determinate kinds. Pole beans, peas, and vining cucumbers grow vertical and for a long period; day-neutral strawberries fruit from early summer through fall; and radishes, lettuce, arugula, and green onions are in and out quickly.

- **Forage.** Clamshell packaging does not grow in the wild. Take a foraging class and tap in to your feral side. The activity has become a family favorite; sometimes Léo comes home with lips stained with blackberries, sometimes with a bucket of crayfish in his hand. Scott goes for fish and shellfish; I specialize in collecting greens. Foraging is a great way to supplement your weekly grocery shopping and save money!

A Typical Grocery Run

Some might think that we are obsessed with Zero Waste. Although it is an eminent part of our lifestyle, I do not consider it an obsession . . . anymore.

It might have started as such, but with the logistics now on autopilot, we can fully enjoy the financial, health, and time-savings benefits. Our success has hinged mainly on our shopping and organization skills. It did take practice to unravel our old habits, and it may take some time to find a system that works for you, but Zero Waste and the 5 Rs provide guidance for making the right decisions at the store. It might seem a lot to the untrained, but the way other people shop seems overwhelming to me now.

I'll share with you my Friday routine so you can get a sense of what it looks like:

My husband and I share the use of the family car. I have priority on Fridays to run errands and shop for groceries, because it coincides with the farmer's market.

I have three large totes (no need for more): two *grocery totes* and one *farmer's market tote*.

I keep the farmer's market tote (containing produce mesh bags) and one of the grocery totes (containing clean bulk bags, washable crayon, pillowcase, and a saved baguette bar code) in the trunk of my car.

In the house and next to my shopping lists, I keep the other grocery tote (*kitchen grocery tote*) handy to fill during the week with washed bulk bags, empty jars, empty containers to be returned for a deposit refund (milk and yogurt), empty egg cartons to return to the egg stand, and empty produce bags.

On Fridays, I take this tote down to the car with both shopping lists, making sure that I have a minimum of five one-liter jars to fill: (1) meat, (2) fish, (3) deli, (4) cheese, and (5) grated cheese. I transfer the egg cartons and produce bags to the farmer's market tote.

For optimum time and fuel efficiency, I number my errands list by stops, starting with the farthest errand and maximizing right turns (a tip from my husband, who worked with companies trying to maximize their fuel efficiency).

Then I work my route, crossing out the errands on my errands list as I go. My last three stops are usually the farmer's market, the grocery store, and the library.

At the farmer's market, I grab the farmer's market tote and go straight to my favorite veggie stand (veggies at the bottom of the tote), then my favorite fruit stand (usually softer than veggies). If I purchase berries in a small basket, I pour them into a mesh bag and hand the basket to the seller so he can reuse it. Finally, at the egg stand, I get my carton refilled. My purchase decisions at the produce stands are simply based on what looks good to me at that moment, and I make sure to buy enough to last us a week.

Then at the health food store:

- I load a cart with both grocery totes and make a first stop at the customer service stand to return yogurt and milk jars for a refund (I wrap the refund slip around my credit card, so I don't forget to use it during checkout).
- I then head to the bakery to order "Ten baguettes, no packaging." Ten baguettes are what I need per week for my family of four.
- I proceed to fill my jars at the salad bar (mostly for grated cheese at a low price), the olive bar (for condiments like capers, cornichons, and olives), and the deli, meat, and fish counters.
- I grab butter sold in wax paper, milk and yogurt sold in glass, while my jar gets filled at the cheese counter.
- I fill cloth bags and jars from the bulk aisle according to my list.
- I sometimes stop in the produce section for a specific item that I would not have found at the farmer's market (e.g., loose spinach), or the bakery bins for some croissants.
- My loop ends back at the bakery counter, where fresh out-of-the-oven baguettes await me and get placed in my pillowcase, giving me much-needed warmth (I get cold in grocery stores). The smell fills my senses with childhood memories as I make my way to the checkout stand.
- I unload jars first (because heavy items will need to go into the totes first), then bulk, and then bread. I pull out the baguette bar code and remember my deposit refund slip wrapped around my credit card as my totes get filled. The cashier deducts the tare weight of my reusable containers and the refund slip off my bill.
- I pay, refuse the store receipt, and head home, making a quick stop at the library.

As you can see, I have rolled my way through the fresh, healthier perimeter of the store, bypassing the overprocessed, overpackaged center aisles. The only disposable packaging that might result from a grocery run is butter, for the reasons mentioned earlier.

Once home, I unload the car, refrigerate cold items, fill storage jars with bulk, cut in half and freeze the baguettes in another pillowcase, store veggies in the produce keeper of the refrigerator, replenish the fruit bowl on the dining table, put dirty bulk bags on the washing machine, recycle my shopping lists, and put the totes back in place: two in the car, one in the home, ready for use the following week.

MEAL PLANNING

Much regular household trash is made up of convenience (fast food) packaging, making Zero Waste an unthinkable goal for many. But slow food is not that complicated. As with kitchen accessories, a little decluttering, organizing, and planning goes a long way.

Recipe Overhaul

Not so long ago, my cookbook was filled with recipes collected over the years, many of them calling for processed or canned goods. Not-so-healthy and/or wasteful recipes mingled among healthy, waste-free ones and not only crowded my recipe binder and made the healthy recipes hard to find but also made Zero Waste shopping difficult, complicated, and frustrating. Running around trying to find powdered sugar in bulk to accommodate my Bourbon Ball recipe did not make sense.

Then it dawned on me that if a Zero Waste kitchen called for Zero Waste shopping, then it followed that Zero Waste shopping called for Zero Waste cooking. Of course I had to "Zero Waste" my recipes!

I took my recipes through this much-needed decluttering and lifestyle-fitting exercise:

- **Select** recipes that contain only ingredients locally available in bulk.
- **Part with** those that require too many ingredients or too much time to make. Simple concoctions can taste just as good as elaborate ones.
- **Recycle** those that have not been tested. The weight of having failed to make them stressed me out. Letting them go freed my head and my to-do list.
- **Let go** of the dinner party recipes that cannot be prepared ahead of time. I have come to realize that when cooking with company, I lose focus, forget ingredients or my sense of time, and end up apologizing

for mishaps. I cook much faster and better alone. I manage dinnertime more accurately with reheating, and I am a better host to my guests if my attention is not lost worrying about recipe ingredients. Also, making the food in advance gives flavors time to blend beautifully.

- **Scan** the few remaining recipes including those bookmarked in a half-dozen books (you know, those books that you keep for the single recipe that you liked in them). I used CamScanner, a smartphone scanning app, to do this quickly.
- **Recycle** the loose sheets and **donate** the books so others can enjoy them.

Now that my recipes were scanned, I organized them into the following folders:

- Breakfast: pancakes, bread pudding
- Finger Foods/Appetizers: deviled eggs, pâté, stuffed mushrooms
- First Courses: individual goat cheese soufflés, leek flan
- Soups: cauliflower soup, garlic soup, gazpacho
- Grains: rice, quinoa, couscous
- Pasta
- Legumes: white-bean stew, lentil curry
- Potatoes
- Dough: pizza, tortilla
- Fish and Shellfish: sardine carpaccio, crusted salmon, trout meunière
- Chicken: the "eco" and affordable meat gets its own tab!
- Meat: lamb keftas, beef bourguignon, cherry duck
- Veggies: recipes not containing starch or meat
- Desserts: chocolate mousse, lemon soufflé
- Cookies/Sweet Snacks: biscotti, butter cookies, candied pecans
- Wild/Foraging: manzanita cider, thistle pesto
- Pantry: jam, mustard, vanilla extract
- Menus: a set of three to four well-coordinated recipes around a theme— Moroccan dinner or summer brunch
- Home/Body: hairspray, laundry detergent, glue, tooth powder

Digitizing recipes improves mobility. I have mine saved in cloud storage, which I can access from anywhere using my phone. But it also aids cross-referencing: one recipe can effortlessly be copied into multiple folders for easy referencing and menu planning. For example, cauliflower soup can be applied to these three folders: First Courses, Soups, and Veggies. Furthermore, since most recipes nowadays are sourced online, they can simply be saved into appropriate folders (instead of printing) and easily shared via email or the cloud itself.

Weekly Dinner Plan

I mainly refer to my recipes when planning for company; the rest of the week I rely more on matching flavors (or pairing foods). Great reference guides for this cooking method include *The Flavor Bible: The Essential Guide to Culinary Creativity, Based on the Wisdom of America's Most Imaginative Chefs* by Karen Page and Andrew Dornenburg. I also like to draw inspiration from restaurant menus or the prepared counter of the health food store. This approach feeds my creativity and fits my shopping style of buying seasonally or based on what looks good to me. Moreover, I can adapt it to a weekly plan that I've created based on our family's (1) access to bulk, (2) mostly vegetarian diet, and (3) schedule. My approach allows me leeway to use eggs, milk, and/or cheese as a source of protein for vegetarian nights and to adapt farmer's market finds to the dish of the day. This schedule below is neither a rigid guide nor one size fits all. A household can tailor it to its family needs, but having some type of schematic plan takes the guesswork out of weeknights and preemptively answers the kids' inevitable question: "What's for dinner?"

- Monday: Pasta
- Tuesday: Legume
- Wednesday: Dough (homemade quiche, pizza, or tortillas)
- Thursday: Bread (to go with our veggie "fridge-cleanup" soup or salad)
- Friday (shopping day): Potatoes and fish
- Saturday: Wild card, dinner with friends or dinner out
- Sunday: Grain and meat

Pantry Staples

Our pantry is organized to stock a limited and set amount of jars, which contain either a permanent staple or rotational staple. *Permanent staples* will vary from family to family. Ours include:

- Flour, sugar, salt, baking soda, cornstarch, baking powder, yeast, oatmeal, coffee, dry corn, powdered sugar
- Jam, butter, peanut butter, honey, mustard, canned tomatoes, pickles, olives, capers
- Olive oil, vegetable oil, apple cider vinegar, wine vinegar, tamari, vanilla extract
- A selection of spices and herbs

Rotational staples represent groups of foods that we used to buy in many different forms. In the past, our legume collection consisted of chickpeas, lentils, peas, red beans, fava beans, pinto beans, etc. Even though stocking many types of food appears to stimulate variety, the contrary is often the case. Similar to wardrobe items, pantry favorites get picked first while nonfavorites get pushed back and forgotten, take up space, and ultimately go bad (i.e., become rancid or bug infested). Today, instead of storing many versions of a staple, we have dedicated one specific jar and adopted a system of rotation. For example, our rotating jar of grain might be filled with rice one week, couscous another. Our rotating collection includes:

- Grain
- Pasta
- Legume
- Cereal
- Cookie
- Nut
- Sweet snack
- Savory snack
- Tea

This system has proved not only to maintain variety in our diet and free up storage space; it has also been efficient at keeping foods from going bad.

Reducing Food Waste

Beyond rotating staples, there are other ways of reducing food waste. We've talked about arming yourself with grocery lists before you hit the market, but by serving small portions, reheating leftovers, and utilizing freezing methods, you can further minimize the amount of unused/spoiled food that goes into the compost. You can for example freeze herbs in ice cube trays or separate leftovers into smaller lunch-size portions in glass jars and freeze them. I also use the meat and fish bones that I collect in my freezer to make stock before composting them.

Even the most dedicated Zero Waste kitchen is bound to generate some compostable waste. Here is my A-to-Z list for addressing those items that might fall through the cracks:

Add it: Leftover squash can make a great addition to savory pancakes. Or try using some of the water used for cooking pasta in your pasta sauce.

Bake it: My family is not enthusiastic about eating kale in general, but they love kale chips. Bake on a sheet with a drizzle of olive oil and salt for ten minutes at 350 degrees.

Collect it: I keep a jar in my freezer to collect bits of stale bread. When the jar is full, I make bread pudding. (See the recipe on page 75).

Dehydrate it: You can use a dehydrator, but sun and air-drying are most economical; I tie herbs in small bundles and let them air-dry indoors (the attic is ideal) to retain maximum color and flavor. Dried, ground celery leaves plus salt equals celery salt!

Edit it: My kids don't like raisins in their cereal; I remove them from their breakfasts and add them to a cookie recipe instead.

Ferment it: Leftover wine or fruit scraps are ideal for making vinegar at home. All you need to start your own wine vinegar is "a mother of vinegar," generally available through home-brewing stores.

Grate it: Grated apples can make a wonderful addition to salads, and grated stale bread (bread crumbs) is wonderful on veggies or casseroles.

Hang it: If yogurt passes its expiration date and is not moldy, I season it and hang it above the sink in a handkerchief to make a soft cheese (but you knew that already).

Ice it: Wilted lettuce can be revived in a bath of ice water.

Juice it: Don't compost those carrot tops; blend them with your green smoothie.

Knife it: When we have too much fruit, I cut it up and put it on a plate, and it magically gets eaten!

Ladle it: The day before my grocery run, I throw all leftover veggies in a pot with water and chicken bones and make soup. Artichoke leaves and pea shell discards also make wonderful bases to cream soups.

Marinade it: I learned from my mom to macerate extra grapes or dried fruit in brandy for a few months (sometimes years). It makes one potent dessert.

Neutralize it: If you are thinking of ditching your dish because it is too spicy, add lemon, dairy, alcohol, or sugar. Too sweet? Try salt, vinegar, or lemon. Too salty? A splash of white vinegar and pinch of sugar should tone it down. Too sour? Add baking soda.

Offer it to friends, school, food bank: If you overestimated your cooking or harvest, make someone happy with the extras. Everyone likes a surprise donation of Meyer lemons.

Preserve it: Ripe fruit can be turned into jam and extra veggies pickled.

Question it: Google will tell you what to do with your leftover.

Reinvent it: Use scraps of ham to flavor a pea soup, or bruised apples to make applesauce (you can also turn the sauce into fruit leather)!

See it: Proper storage is important to extend the life of your leftovers. The transparency of the canning jars that we use prevents foods from getting forgotten.

Thicken (or thin) it: Sometimes soups or sauces linger in the refrigerator because the texture is too runny or too thin. Using cornstarch to thicken or water to thin a soup will make all the difference.

Use it all: Not peeling is a great way to get the most out of your produce. But if you do peel the stem of broccoli (which usually gets discarded), you can add it to your recipe.

Vamp it up: I love throwing a cocktail party around leftovers. It's a fun way to clear out a fridge before a grocery run. Leftover pizza can be portioned into bite sizes, and small meat or grain mixtures can be scooped into endive leaves, mushrooms, spoons, or small glasses. Cake trimmings and leftovers can be layered with whipped cream and fresh fruit to make a trifle. In France they call this vamping up the art of "bluffing."

Wet it: Sprinkle water on a damp baguette and bake to revive it.

XYZ: eXamine Your Zipper; i.e., verify the integrity of your seals. Grains sealed improperly are subject to spoilage and bug infestation. A good seal extends shelf life: since we have been using (airtight) canning jars for storage, we have not spotted a single ant or beetle near our food.

ENTERTAINING

What should you consider when expecting company?

The most important aspect of entertaining in a waste-free manner is to *be proactive*. Take a preemptive approach to the eventuality of your guests bringing waste and clutter into your house. You worked hard to simplify your kitchen and embrace change: don't let your guests spoil your efforts. Let your friends know about your waste-busting determination. Mention the reusables that you have implemented, the worms that you have adopted. Draw attention to your decluttering efforts and proclaim the money savings that you discovered. Communicating the changes you've implemented will help you to avoid the frustration of having to deal with hostess gifts and throwaways. Give your friends the tools to understand and respect your choices.

Entertaining can be a great way to celebrate the Zero Waste lifestyle and put it to the test on a larger scale. It might even inspire others to adopt some of your practices.

Here are some ideas worth considering when putting Zero Waste into practice with visitors:

Food

- Bring extra jars to the grocery store to accommodate the extra servings that you will be preparing.
- Avoid using serving platters/dishes. Serving straight onto dinner plates simplifies, reduces dishwashing, and encourages plate presentation. It also allows you to control portions and therefore waste. Serve small and offer seconds.
- Favor finger foods for large parties. Finger foods—i.e., hors d'oeuvres—eliminate food waste otherwise collected by the use of plates, reduce dishwashing, and are a great way to use leftovers. Simply present these

treats with a pile of cloth napkins and a bundle of turkey lacers as a reusable alternative to toothpicks.

- Provide salad plates if your buffet requires the use of plates. These will encourage small portions and discourage food waste.
- Prepare large quantities of a small selection versus small quantities of a large selection. For a buffet it is more efficient to make twenty pieces for six different appetizers instead of six pieces for twenty different appetizers.

Drinks

- Add lemon wedges, cucumber slices, or rosemary to tap water in lieu of serving bottled sparkling water.
- Consider refillable growlers or kegs when serving beer to large groups.
- Purchase drinks based on the reusability of their container. I purchase vodka in a 750-milliliter flip-top bottle because I reuse the bottle for wine refills and the flip top eliminates the need for corks.
- Make your washable crayon available for guests to mark their drinking glasses. It will not only help them identify their glass and therefore reduce dishwashing but it also eliminates the need to store wineglass charms.

Decor and Ambience

- Using ceramic dishes, "real" flatware, and cloth napkins saves money and affords elegance at the same time.
- Find creative ways to decorate your table: Use napkin-folding tricks, houseplants, leaves/branches from the yard, candles, or simply seasonal fruit. Use a chocolate chip to draw on the table or scatter coral lentils, corn, or another colorful bulk grain to create designs. Children can use play dough (see the recipe, page 207 in the "Kids and School" chapter) to make flowers or shapes. A favorite in our home is drawing designs in one tablespoon of white flour sprinkled in the center of the table. Another favorite is scattering the fuzz from the head of an artichoke gone to seed. For buffets, I have set fern fronds in glasses of water and covered them with different-size jars so that these cloches staged my

serving plates (dinner and salad plates) at different levels, or I have filled jars with my choice of finger food and purposely spilled their contents on the table to display them.

- Make new votive candles from empty votive tins (and wick bases). You can fill them either with wax or olive oil. One-pound blocks of beeswax are available at health food stores (unpackaged) and lead-free wicks by the yard at craft stores. Simply stick a short wick into a base and fill the votive with melted beeswax. I find it easier to use the oil method as it simplifies refilling (see page 215 in the "Holidays and Gifts" chapter for more details). But I sometimes buy tapers (which are sold unpackaged) and melt their leftovers to fill votive tins. My candleholders are reversible and can hold either form.
- Download music to your iPod. Donate your CD player and CDs for others to enjoy, and connect iPod to your home sound system instead.

RECIPES

MUSTARD

INGREDIENTS

½ cup powdered mustard	1 beaten egg
6 oz white wine	1 tablespoon sugar
½ cup apple cider vinegar	1 tablespoon of flour

DIRECTIONS

1. Combine all ingredients in a mason jar.
2. Place the open jar in a medium saucepan with one inch of water over medium heat.
3. Whisk the mixture until thickened.
4. Let cool and refrigerate.

FLOUR TORTILLAS

INGREDIENTS

4 cups flour
1½ teaspoons salt
1 teaspoon baking powder

½ cup cold butter
1 cup warm water

DIRECTIONS

1. Combine dry ingredients in a large bowl.
2. Incorporate the butter into the mixture and mix with your finger-tips until it resembles coarse crumbs.
3. Add the water and combine until a soft dough forms.
4. Separate into 12 small balls.
5. Roll out each ball as thinly as possible and cook in a pan over medium heat for 20 seconds on each side.

VANILLA EXTRACT

INGREDIENTS

2 vanilla beans

½ cup brandy

DIRECTIONS

1. Slice the vanilla beans in half lengthwise.
2. Place in a small bottle.
3. Cover with brandy.
4. Seal and let sit for three days before using.

HOT SAUCE

INGREDIENTS

1 pound hot peppers (serrano or
    jalapeño, for example)
2 cups white vinegar

2 cups water
1 tablespoon salt

DIRECTIONS

1. Cut the peppers into large chunks.
2. Combine all ingredients in a medium pot.
3. Bring to a boil.
4. Simmer for 30 minutes.
5. Blend using an immersion blender.
6. Cool and transfer into a small bottle.

PIZZA DOUGH

INGREDIENTS

2 cups flour
2 teaspoons yeast
1 teaspoon sugar

½ teaspoon salt
2 tablespoons olive oil
¾ cup warm water

DIRECTIONS

1. Combine all ingredients in a large bowl.
2. Knead until well combined and gather into a ball.
3. Cover the bowl with a plate.
4. Let rise for 45 minutes in a warm place. (I turn my oven on to the lowest setting while I prepare the dough, turn it off, and use the warmth of the oven to rise the dough.) The dough should double in size.
5. Scrape the dough off the bowl with generously floured fingers and shape into a ball.
6. Spread the dough onto a greased baking sheet using your fingertips.
7. Top as desired and bake at 400 degrees for 25 minutes.

HORSERADISH

INGREDIENTS

1 cup grated horseradish root   ¼ teaspoon salt
¾ cup white vinegar

DIRECTIONS

1. Combine all ingredients in a small bowl.
2. Blend using an immersion blender.
3. Transfer into a small jar.
4. Use sparingly, this is potent!

SALT-PACKED ANCHOVIES

INGREDIENTS

1 pound anchovies   Coarse salt

DIRECTIONS

1. Remove the head and guts of anchovies (keep the bone in) and rinse.
2. Pack alternate layers of coarse salt and anchovies in a mason jar (start and end with a thick layer of salt).
3. Seal and refrigerate for three weeks before consuming (some of the salt will dissolve and turn into brine).

SOY MILK

I made soy milk during my homemake-aholic period and do not make it anymore, but I thought I would share it for those of you who are lactose intolerant.

INGREDIENTS

1 cup soybeans
6 cups water

Sugar, vanilla extract (optional)

DIRECTIONS

1. Soak the soybeans overnight in a medium bowl.
2. Drain.
3. Combine with 6 cups water and blend using an immersion blender.
4. Strain and squeeze in a handkerchief over a large pot.
5. Add sugar and vanilla to taste.
6. Bring to a boil and simmer for 10 minutes.
7. Let cool and refrigerate. (It will last for a week.)

PANCAKES

Many people buy pancake mixes, but making them from scratch is easy and much more delicious!

INGREDIENTS

1½ cups flour
3½ teaspoons baking powder
1 teaspoon salt
1 tablespoon sugar

1¼ cups milk
2 eggs
3 tablespoons melted butter or oil

DIRECTIONS

1. Combine all ingredients in a large bowl.
2. Pour ¼ cup batter into a lightly oiled pan and brown both sides.

BREAD PUDDING

INGREDIENTS

3 cups stale bread broken into
  chunks

4 eggs

2 cups milk

1 cup sugar

3 tablespoons melted butter

1 pinch of salt

1 pinch of cinnamon

DIRECTIONS

1. Spread out the pieces of stale bread in a greased baking dish.
2. Whisk together the remaining ingredients in a medium bowl.
3. Pour over the bread.
4. Bake at 350°F until a knife inserted in the center comes out clean (about 45 minutes).

More recipes are available on my website, ZeroWasteHome.com

5 *RS* CHECKLIST: 5 TIPS FOR THE KITCHEN

Refuse: Resist food packaging and disposable plastic bags.
Reduce: Pare down kitchen accessories and define pantry staples.
Reuse: Shop for groceries with reusables and rethink your leftovers.
Recycle: Appoint separate containers tailored to your recycling needs.
Rot: Compost food scraps.

ONE STEP FURTHER

Most of the ideas covered in this chapter addressed the visible and tangible aspects of waste, but the following tips on energy, water, and time savings will complete your sustainable efforts.

Energy

- Do not preheat your oven.
- Open your refrigerator only when necessary.
- Favor hand-operated to electrical tools and appliances.
- Invest in a pressure cooker.
- Match your pot to the right burner size.
- Keep your freezer and refrigerator stocked.
- Turn off your ice maker; use it only briefly to refill the ice container, or use ice cube trays instead.
- Test the seal of your refrigerator by closing the door on a dollar bill in various locations around the door. If the door doesn't hold the bill firmly in place, you probably have a leaky seal.

Water

- Use a sink strainer and compost the bits it collects. This saves water you'd use when running the disposal.
- Stop leaks. Read your meter before and after a two-hour period when no water is being used to find out if you have a leak.
- Install faucet aerators.
- Keep a water catchment container in your sink and utilize the water you collect when washing, steaming, or boiling vegetables to water your plants.
- Fill a sink or basin with water to rinse dishes throughout the day instead of running the faucet for every rinse.

Time

- Learn the professional tricks for slicing and chopping to maximize your time in the kitchen.
- Keep your chopping board at the sink where you rinse your produce.
- Prepare your meals at the sink; the sink acts as a catch-all.
- Store the bread knife with the bread.

- Dedicate water bottles for each member of the family to avoid the use of a glass.
- Place a wooden board behind your jars to keep them forward, if your shelves are deep, so they don't slide back and out of reach.
- Keep an aloe vera plant on the counter for quick burn relief: simply cut a small piece of a leaf and apply to the burn.
- Throw a bone into your soup instead of making stock separately.
- Toss salads using your bare hands.
- Outfit oil and vinegar bottles with pourers.

Bathroom, Toiletries, and Wellness

Before adopting Zero Waste, I was an ardent consumer of beauty and grooming products. But when I started to learn more about the chemicals they're loaded with, and the negative impact they have on health, I began to feel like a guinea pig. When I decided to eradicate waste and toxins from our lives, I became the tireless subject of my *own* research. At first, I needed all the energy I could summon to navigate a field of products, many of them harmful to health and to the environment. I found that the beads in common store-bought exfoliators carry tiny plastic particles that end up in our water, that the paper wrapper around many soaps is lined with plastic and is therefore not recyclable, that many organic brands care about ingredients but not the impact of packaging on the environment. And then I had to wade through all the green-washed claims. "If it is great for the environment, it will be great for your skin!" Don't believe everything you read. One product made my skin red as if I'd spent all day in the sun unprotected. Not a pretty sight. Another time, I bought into the natural claims of an international brand of solid conditioner sold by weight, only to find that the ingredients (fragrances) gave me a headache. I couldn't stand it and put the bar outside, which cured my headache immediately, but the next day I found the expensive product melted into our concrete patio. What a mess; what a waste of money: I should have double-checked the ingredients before buying.

Disappointments associated with packaging, ingredients, and effectiveness subsequently led me to experiment with making my own. That way I could avoid packaging by enlisting products available in bulk as well as control ingredients and cost.

My homemade trials did not come without failures. I went out to dinner wearing one of my mascara experiments only to find out that (a) my girlfriends do not warn me when I have a makeup malfunction and (b) my makeup had melted and given me raccoon eyes.

I got my hair cut for the sake of the environment, too, to reduce my electricity consumption used to dry it, to use less shampoo to clean it, and to take quicker showers to rinse it. Unfortunately, the haircut did nothing for my face. And regrettably, a magazine came to shoot our family shortly after. When my mom received a copy of the publication, her feedback to me was: "What's with the hair? It does nothing for you. . . ."

Fortunately hair grows back . . . even the hair that I ripped off trying eighteen different recipe combinations of homemade wax. I got blisters on my fingers trying to achieve the right consistency. Over the few years of research, I have tried four different brands of mascara and twenty-two different types of mascara recipe combinations, four deodorant alternatives, seven brands of shampoo bars, three tooth powder dispensers, and six different brands of tinted moisturizers. I have used mango, lemon, avocado, sugar, salt, eggs, coffee grounds, oatmeal, honey, yogurt, milk, different types of oils, baking soda, apple cider vinegar, charcoal, cornstarch, cocoa powder, aloe vera, onion, coconut oil, sage, cucumber, tea, grapefruit, glycerin, vitamin E, white clay, green clay, papaya, a burned matchstick, horseradish, moss, and stinging nettle on my skin.

My poor family! When I ran out of hair to wax, I tested my product on Max's legs (with his consent, of course!). To test color alternatives, I collected my boys' hair from the floor after a cut, tied it into twelve small bundles, and dipped them in different concoctions to dry on the kitchen counter at dinnertime. Not very appetizing. Scott tried seven brands of soap to use in lieu of shaving cream, including the soap I made using leftover plumbing lye and leftover bacon fat. Surprisingly, after you use it, it does not smell as if you had spent the day petting a pig; it smells just like Ivory soap. The lather was not great, though, and once I ran out of lye, I did not see the point in buying a plastic container of it if I could simply buy soap loose, already made!

Apart from having made a fool of myself in public and having inflicted discomfort on my family, I enjoyed coming up with my own substitutes. I feel as though I am "cheating the system."

That said, while anything is worth trying, not everything is worth adopting. I don't recommend stinging nettle as a lip plumper; I found that it provides uneven, painful results. Baking soda in lieu of shampoo is an option worth investigating if you have short hair; it made my long hair so frizzy and stringy that my friends immediately noticed when I switched back to regular shampoo. On the other hand, I found that a menstrual cup is to the bathroom what reusable cloths are to the kitchen. Once I realized the savings and the ease of implementing the alternative, I beat my head against the wall for not using it earlier. You might just make similar discoveries!

In this chapter I tell you about the products, the mixtures, and the recipes that have worked well for me. You might have to do a little experimenting to adopt the methods that best suit your lifestyle, but trust that I have done most of the guinea pig's groundwork, so you don't have to.

BATHROOM SETUP

The bathroom is probably the second-biggest source of recurring waste in the home, but here, too, it can easily be avoided with decluttering, implementing reusables, and deploying collection receptacles.

Simplicity

While the basic function of bathrooms is to serve our everyday health, hygiene, and grooming rituals, I have found most households tend to breed duplicate shampoo containers, expired prescriptions, and disposable remnants of all types. But the signs of personal obsessions and self-doubts that we also attempt to hide behind closed cabinet doors are hardly a secret: many bathrooms are filled with miracle creams claiming to take years off, with cosmetics promising to cover up our imperfections and bewitching perfumes claiming to attract the opposite sex. These products set us back hundreds of dollars each year, and they often end up gathering dust and then entering the garbage can. Who can blame us for hoarding such items? Everywhere, the media blinds us with touched-up photographs of flawless faces and toned bodies; every season, advertisers dream up must-have new eye-shadow palettes and high-tech skin care. All of this makes it hard to feel beautiful, and it shows in our bathroom cabinets. Our insecurities clutter our lives.

The first step to beauty (and therefore bathroom) simplicity is to try to limit our exposure to the media and store merchandising. It's true that unless we live in a remote area, it is nearly impossible to completely avoid, but reducing our exposure is certainly possible, and with practice, you can even acquire selective vision! It's important to keep in mind that beauty cannot be bought; you cannot find in a bottle what comes from within.

The National Association for Continence finds that the average American spends about an hour of his or her (very busy) day in the bathroom. Along with the recent rise of spa culture, it seems that in our stressful lives we aspire to find relaxation and make the most of the only room in the house that affords undisturbed time. The commercial success of disposable bathroom cleaning supplies (e.g., disposable toilet scrubbers) further underscores the appetite for a space that is easy to clean and encourages efficiency.

Simplification is the second step to a Zen-like bathroom, and it starts with emptying cabinets and drawers and evaluating what is truly necessary.

- **Is it in working condition? Is it expired?** Old cosmetics provide havens for bacterial growth and can become health hazards, just as combs with missing teeth can hurt your hair. Recycle the former through the Return to Origins Recycling Program (at any Origins location; see page 269) and the latter with your number 1 plastics. Expired medicines work to a certain point but can sometimes make your condition worse. Contact your pharmacy to inquire about proper disposal in your area, or look for the nearest National Prescription Drug Take-Back Day (organized by the U.S. Drug Enforcement Administration; see page 269).
- **Do I use it regularly?** You might have bought a large container of lotion at Costco fifteen years ago, but you have since adopted a different brand. That lotion is waiting to be used and probably never will be. Don't deny the facts: if you do not use it at least once a month or if it's dusty, let it go.
- **Is it a duplicate?** How many brushes or combs does one really need? What about hair ties? If you match ties to your hair color, you do not need a plethora of colors to match your outfits. If the only hairstyle you ever really do is a ponytail, then one tie should suffice; if you fancy pigtails, then two. Combine dried-out bars of soap: soften by soaking, and mold them together. Combine half-used bottles, samples, and hotel freebies into one shampoo dispenser. When editing duplicates, favor those that promote efficiency or dry faster (choose waffle weave towels over terry cloth ones, for example).
- **Does it put my family's health in danger?** Chemicals used in bathroom products can cause health problems. Make your health and that of your family a priority. Check the EWG (Environmental Working Group)'s Skin Deep Cosmetics Database to rate your products and declut-

ter accordingly. According to the David Suzuki Foundation's "Dirty Dozen," the chemicals to be most wary about are:

1. BHA and BHT
2. Coal tar dyes
3. DEA-related ingredients
4. Dibutyl phthalate
5. Formaldehyde-releasing preservatives
6. Parabens
7. Parfum (a.k.a. fragrance)
8. PEG compounds
9. Petrolatum
10. Siloxanes
11. Sodium laureth sulfate
12. Triclosan

- **Do I keep it out of guilt?** Perfume is a common gift, and many fragrances are toxic (and should likely have been eliminated based on the prior question). But consider whether or not you are holding on to a product out of guilt because the bottle is pretty or someone spent a lot of money for it. Reassure yourself knowing that recycling it is unavoidable; if you don't discard it, someone else after you certainly will.

- **Do I keep it because "everyone has one"?** Question your need for everything in the bathroom, including those items that you have always considered necessities. I used to buy mouthwash, Band-Aids, and Q-tips because everyone had these items. I thought I needed them, too, but I no longer do. Could something else achieve the same task? Your pinkie (called the "ear finger" in French) is a great alternative to Q-tips.

- **Is it worth my precious time dusting and cleaning?** Moisture and dust are not best friends. If you clean decorative items in your bathroom, you know how hard it is to clean stuck-on dust. Is the nautical theme worth it? Probably not. Send the ship to the kids' playroom.

- **Could I use this space for something else?** Hair rollers take a lot of room; if you let them go, you could use the space to store towels in the empty cabinet, instead of on a rack where they collect dust.

- **Is it reusable?** Disposables take up space, too, and we will eliminate them in this chapter, but for now, your stash could help someone in need. Men's shelters need disposable razors; women's shelters feminine hygiene products. The latter could also be dropped off in a public bathroom (some provide baskets full of feminine products) to aid someone in an emergency.

Did the process empty a shelf? Remove it and patch the holes if it was attached to the wall. Work on emptying external bathroom storage and making the best use of the space provided inside built-ins (under-counter space and medicine cabinets). Clearing out horizontal surfaces (counters, floors) and eliminating them when possible (shelving, over-the-toilet stand) not only make a bathroom peaceful and spacious but also simplify your cleaning routine!

Decluttering a kitchen usually engenders fear of what-ifs; I have found the bathroom generally involves giving up expensive products in which we invested high hopes. But your money is already spent: don't dwell on your financial loss; focus on the bright side—you are learning to identify your spending habits and make wiser future decisions. The price that you paid for the item that you are now recycling was worth every penny if you take away better consumption habits from the decluttering process. Look forward to saving money with reusable or package-free alternatives!

Again, decluttering is a very personal affair. But for illustrative purposes, here are some of the items that we have eliminated through this evaluation process:

- Bathrobes
- Bathroom decor
- Body sponges
- Candles
- Deodorizing spray
- Duplicate combs, brushes, tweezers, and scissors
- Expired medications
- Extra cosmetic bags
- Extra prescription glasses
- Extra towels (two per family member is enough: one for everyday use, the other for the occasional swim or overnight guest)
- Extra hair ties and accessories (one is enough for me)
- Eyebrow powder
- Highlighting cream
- Fake eyelashes and nails
- Freestanding storage

- "Party" makeup color palettes
- Hair-bleaching kits
- Hair-coloring kits
- Hair-specific shampoo bottles
- Hand sanitizer
- Hand cream
- Hand towels
- Hotel kits
- Loofah and pumice stone
- Body lotion
- Magazine holder
- Mouthwash (no one in our family really used it)
- Nail art
- Nail polishes
- Perfume
- Q-tips
- Rubbing alcohol
- Samples
- Teeth-whitening gel
- Toilet brushes
- Trash cans!
- Washcloths
- Waterproof mascara
- Wonder creams

No longer purchasing these items gives you an idea of the money we are now saving.

Reusability

Other than toilet paper, we no longer buy single-use products; we have adopted either reusable or package-free alternatives for them instead. Relying heavily on available bulk, our system includes using our grocery shopping kit for transport: cloth bags for dry goods and bottles for wet items. At home we store these items in jars and dispensers, much to the benefit of our bathroom's aesthetics.

Collection

Collection is unavoidable in the kitchen; however, in the bathroom, receptacles can become obsolete. Whether you need bathroom receptacles (compost, recycling, and landfill) will greatly depend on your access to bulk and your ability to switch to reusables. To simplify housekeeping, it's best to store containers under the counter.

Recycling

Many households limit their recycling efforts to the kitchen. For years we, too, sent toilet paper tubes and shampoo and conditioner bottles to the landfill, simply because we had not dedicated a recycling container to our bathroom and did not bother separating our discards. Today, we have reduced our bathroom recyclables to a couple of unavoidable pieces per year and do not need a receptacle for them, but during our transitional period, we found it handy to have one close to the shower stall.

Compost

Depending on the type of composter at your disposal, consider composting the following hygiene items:

- Bamboo or wooden toothbrushes*
- 100 percent cotton swabs (with cardboard sticks)*
- 100 percent cotton balls*
- 100 percent cotton facial pads*
- 100 percent cotton gauze*
- Facial tissue*
- Hair from a brush or electrical shaver
- Loofahs*
- Sea sponges*
- Nail clippings

* See the following pages for alternatives to discarding/composting these materials.

- Silk floss
- Tampons (including the cardboard applicator)*
- Toilet paper*
- Unfinished-wood combs
- Urine* (particularly useful in accelerating a compost pile)

Whether you need a compost receptacle in your bathroom will greatly depend on your dedication to Zero Waste alternatives. In the end, if all you compost is hair or nails, you might not need a dedicated container at all! I simply discard hair from my brush out the window, for birds to reuse as nesting material.

Landfill

As you now know, the fastest way to get to Zero Waste is to find alternatives to your disposables. Try this: remove your trash can (reassign it for your recyclables until you can eliminate it altogether) ... whatever waste you have to carry out to your landfill receptacle in the kitchen calls for a substitute.

GROOMING AND HYGIENE

Many of the products that our parents, grandparents, or great-grandparents used were reusable or minimally packaged, and some of the substitutes you'll find here may make you nostalgic for the olden days. I have had great fun and pleasure rediscovering them. I even enjoy their aesthetics so much that I could not envision going back to cabinets filled with plastic containers and disposable products. The items below have also thoughtfully been chosen based on efficiency. Keep in mind that the choices you make should integrate well into your daily routine.

For each disposable, many alternatives exist. But here are a few guidelines on making selections:

- Keep an open mind.
- Let your specific needs be your guide in defining what to adopt.

- Watch out for the Dirty Dozen in the products that you do purchase.
- Be patient. Some alternatives require a transitional period for your body to adjust.
- Have fun. Maintain a good sense of humor when you stumble upon alternatives that don't work for you.

Skin

Hand/Body/Face Soaps

- **Bar:** Solid soap is the best option in terms of waste if you can find it sold loose or in recyclable paper (to see if the packaging is entirely made of paper, tear a small piece and look for a plastic layer). A rich lather eliminates the need for many other products. You can use it for washing hands, face, and body, shaving and shampooing. When we run low, I simply mold the leftover sliver onto a new bar.
- **Bulk liquid:** If you absolutely must use liquid hand soap, castile is multipurpose and works great. Since it is however quite pricey, consider making your own (see page 147).

Lotion

- **Bulk lotion:** Lotions can be bought in bulk. All you need is a container to fill, but watch for synthetic ingredients.
- **Bulk oil:** A natural alternative to lotion, cooking oils are my preferred choice (no need to read ingredient labels). They also serve a dual purpose in the kitchen! Choose canola or soy for normal skin; olive, peanut, safflower, sesame, soy, or sunflower for dry skin; grape seed for oily skin.

Deodorant

- **Homemade:** Recipes for solid deodorants abound but require too many ingredients (baking soda, cornstarch, and melted coconut oil are the most popular), and I was not satisfied with the results. They left either white rings on the skin (not ideal when wearing sleeveless or tank tops) or oil stains on clothing.

- **Alum stone:** Also referred to as crystal deodorant, it is easy to use and does not involve homemaking. We simply wet the stone, apply it, and dry it after use. The stone can crack if dropped but lasts for years (in contrast to a jar of homemade deodorant) and works on healing razor nicks, too.

Please note that although these methods kill odor-causing bacteria, they do not prevent perspiration. Store-bought antiperspirants contain a type of aluminum, which has been linked to serious health problems. Poor planning will trigger public discomfort. I know from experience. Dress in clothes that won't show wetness when you know you'll face a stressful situation.

Sun Protection

I personally believe in moderate sunscreen use. I worry about skin cancer as much as I worry about vitamin D deficiency. My family uses clothing and hats as sun shields (the rays penetrates them in a small percentage) and uses sunscreen for prolonged exposures. I also use it on my face every day (see below) for reasons related to vanity.

- **Bulk sesame oil:** Used alone, it provides some amount of sun protection. Its exact SPF level has however not been proved, so it is ideal for light exposures.
- **Homemade:** Making your own sunscreen is as simple as mixing zinc oxide or titanium dioxide powder into the sesame oil or your bulk lotion, but I have yet to find these powders sold loose. For an SPF 20, combine 2 ounces of weighed powder to 8 ounces of weighed lotion.
- **Store-bought:** For long exposure to the sun's powerful rays and those reflected by water, sand, or snow, we have selected a manufactured organic brand. Look for glass or metal containers.

Hair

Making shampoo at home calls for too many packaged ingredients, which defeats our purpose! Making your own does not decrease your waste, so why bother?

- **No poo:** Consider joining the "no-poo" community, if you have short hair. Cleaning your hair without shampoo consists of rinsing it, sprinkling baking soda on your scalp (a spice shaker works well), massaging baking soda in, then rinsing with apple cider vinegar for shine, and rinsing again (and again) with water. Both ingredients are available in the bulk aisle.
- **Solid bars:** Shampoo and conditioning bars are great for travel and require little packaging. Unfortunately, many of them are either packaged in laminated paper or contain toxic ingredients (take a close look!). We purchase a regular bar of soap with a rich lather instead. We pick a bar sold unpackaged or wrapped in paper, and it serves all our soap needs.
- **Bulk:** You can also buy shampoo and conditioner in bulk at the health food store by refilling your own bottles and transferring them into pumps. These liquid dispensers not only eliminate half-empty shampoo bottles cluttering the shower; they also control the amount used and limit waste. This method obviously does not eliminate plastic, as it is still needed to transport the liquids from the manufacturer to the store, but it invests money in bulk shopping and future development (ideally containers would travel back and forth between the two). I buy conditioner this way.
- **Dry Shampoo:** To go longer between washes, I substitute cornstarch sold in bulk for dry shampoo. Stored in a spice shaker, you can sprinkle it on the oily roots of your hair, massage in, and brush. Enjoy the added volume!

To simplify, I highly recommend sticking to one shampooing and one conditioning option for the whole family.

Shaving

There are many alternatives to single-use razors and disposable cartridges. You might get a few nicks and bumps during the transitional/adaptation stage, but stick with it and you'll find things smooth out.

- **Straight-edge razor:** This tool requires regular sharpening, courage, and agility (especially on underarms). Since the blade never needs replacing, it is the number one Zero Waste alternative! Note that it is not allowed in carry-ons when flying.
- **Electric shaver:** It requires energy but it is allowed in carry-ons.
- **Double-edge razor:** Closest in feel to a disposable razor, my husband prefers it. By drying his razor between uses, he is able to extend the blade's wear to six months. A pack of ten blades (they come in a tiny cardboard box) therefore lasts five years. This type of razor is accepted in carry-ons without the blade (which must be checked in or bought at the destination).
- **Soap:** A rich bar makes a wonderful substitute for shaving cream. Scott usually uses the same brand that we use for shampooing. He rubs it directly onto his skin to lather.

Supplemental options for women:

- **Tweezers:** Although a time-consuming endeavor, tweezing is manual (does not require product or electrical use) and over time will stop the hair from coming back. It is particularly useful for small areas (eyebrows or mustache) in lieu of toxic bleaching products.
- **Laser hair removal:** An expensive alternative, but with prices dropping, it is becoming affordable. Some fine light hair, invisible to the laser, may remain, but time and money saved in the long run are well worth it. I found that it has simplified my life and routine tremendously.
- **Sugaring:** Waxing with sugar originated in ancient Egypt and is still used in Arab countries today. Also referred to as *halawa* (meaning "sweet"), it can be a dessert or a great alternative for those adept at waxing! It is tricky but well worth the effort.

DIRECTIONS

1. Combine ½ cup sugar (I use bulk evaporated cane sugar), 1 table-spoon water, and 1 tablespoon lemon juice in a small skillet.
2. Boil on high until the temperature reaches 255 degrees (I borrowed a friend's candy thermometer to time mine and it takes 3 minutes with my cooking equipment).
3. Immediately pour onto a wet, heatproof plate and let cool.
4. When cool to the touch, and before it completely hardens, gather the mixture into a ball.
5. Knead and stretch the ball (it will change from clear amber to an opaque ivory color and should be sticky).
6. With your thumb, spread the ball into a strip against the hair growth and remove quickly in the direction of hair growth. Repeat on other areas with the same ball.
7. Store the remaining wax in a mason jar for future use and reheat the jar in a water bath when needed.

Dental

Toothpaste

In theory, toothpaste is not necessary to effectively brush your teeth. The act of brushing alone is what really matters in avoiding cavities (many people around the world use sticks). Our family likes using a brushing agent for added freshness and has switched to a homemade tooth powder. Used in moderation, tooth powders provide a great alternative to the store-bought pastes. Again, other recipes exist but include too many hard-to-get ingredients to be sustainable. If you're used to paste, tooth powder can be difficult to adopt; you will probably have to focus on your positive impact on the environment and visualize the Great Pacific Garbage Patch every time you brush, but before you know it you'll be hooked. I recently tried a friend's regular toothpaste and no longer like the way it feels. (My teeth did not feel thoroughly cleaned.) Much the same, Max tried some "kids" toothpaste, disliked the taste, and asked me for some baking soda.

DIRECTIONS

In a spice shaker (choose one with a cap dial to control dispensing), combine 1 cup baking soda and 1 teaspoon white stevia powder (optional: used to cut the saltiness of the baking soda).

APPLICATION

Sprinkle sparingly on a wet toothbrush.

Added bonus: White teeth! And toothpaste sludge in and around the sink, no more!

Note: I have found that not all baking sodas are created equal; some brands are coarser than others. You might want to test a few bulk suppliers to find the finest brand. Also, this tooth powder does not include fluoride, but many of us already have fluoride in our water.

Toothbrushes

- **Twigs:** California natives used wooden twigs from the red osier dogwood (*Cornus sericea*) to brush their teeth, a tradition that is still very common around the globe. Many different types of wood, notably those of the neem (India) or peelu (Middle East) trees are used, but olive, walnut, and sweet gum are more common on our continent. Called chewing sticks, they are fashioned by peeling the end of a piece, chewing it to loosen the inner fiber into "bristles," and gently rubbing teeth and gums. Studies have shown that they can even be more efficient than toothbrushes. They do not involve toothpaste and when grown at home, do not require packaging or transport. After use, the end can be cut for another time. When they are too short to reuse, they can be composted. Having trouble motivating our kids to use a simple toothbrush, I do not consider them a viable option for our family. But I believe they are the only true Zero Waste option at this time, one that I would definitely use while camping.
- **Store-bought:** Unfortunately, as far as store-bought toothbrushes are concerned, the ideal option is not yet on the market. Some are made

of recycled plastic and are recyclable but then turned into unrecyclable decking or benches; others feature a disposable bristle head on recycled plastic handles. All-natural alternatives made with wooden handles and boar-hair bristles exist but are sold in plastic packaging. With an array of not-so-ideal options, we have settled for a compostable bamboo toothbrush sold in cardboard, but made in China, until better alternatives show up on our local market.

Floss

- **Swishing:** As simple as it seems, swishing water within twenty minutes of eating can make a big difference in avoiding cavities, says my dentist.
- **Gum stimulator:** This tool is reusable and effective in keeping gums healthy, but flossing is still the preferred choice for removing plaque.
- **Silk:** The closest, strongest, and most efficient alternative to store-bought floss that I have found is silk thread. To eliminate the packaging associated with the purchase of thread, you can simply unravel a piece of organic silk fabric. Twisting a couple of threads together works best. The threads can then be composted. According to the American Dental Association, "It's not what type of floss you use, but how and when you use it."

Eyes

- **Laser:** Nearsighted folks can get their eyes lasered; farsighted folks can only resort to making better purchasing decisions in selecting eyewear or contact lenses.
- **Glasses:** They are reusable; contact lenses are not. Favor the former.
- **Contact lenses:** Homemade contact lens solutions are not safe, and contact lenses will never be sold in bulk, but the packaging of the lenses and that of the cleaning solution is recyclable, depending on your city's recycling policies. By using them only on occasion, you can extend their lifetime.

Tissue

- **Handkerchiefs:** Sadly a thing of the past, handkerchiefs are ideal for the occasional sniff.
- **Fabric scraps:** For bigger jobs, you can cut six-by-six-inch squares from an old T-shirt and stuff them into a jar for easy dispensing.

To clean either form, wash in hot water; to sanitize, simply steam iron.

Toilet Paper

This is one crappy subject I never expected to ever write about . . . but here are my two cents: adopting toilet paper alternatives should reflect individual circumstances, societal customs, and visiting guests.

- **Your hand:** Many countries do not use toilet paper. A hand and access to a bucket of water does the job and is the most waste-free alternative out there. In our western society, guests would not appreciate this option.
- **Cloth:** Some households provide a bucketful of clean reusable wipes, another for dirty ones (which are then laundered for reuse). This system is viable for light jobs (urine) but not hefty ones.
- **Washlet:** This high-tech solution can be outfitted to toilet seats. It requires a water connection for rinsing and electrical wiring for drying. Solar electricity makes this option feasible when the installation expense is no issue. I had a lot of hope for this technology, but my trial proved disappointing. I found that it did not eliminate the need for toilet paper altogether.
- **TP:** 100 percent recycled, unbleached TP, individually wrapped in paper (to bypass the common plastic wrapper on multiples) is not 100 percent waste-free, but it is the best option for our household today. . . . Hotel- and restaurant-supply stores sell singles and large quantities of individually wrapped toilet paper in a box at a lower price than the health food store.

Feminine Products

- **Reusable cup:** Forget about tampons and disposable menstrual cups; switch to a reusable menstrual cup. If allergies to latex are not an issue, consider one made with natural rubber; otherwise, synthetic options also exist. These require an up-front investment and take a couple of months of getting used to, but once you get the hang of it, you won't go back to disposables.
- **Reusable pads and liners:** These can simply be washed and steam-ironed (to sterilize them). You can buy them in a health food store or through my online store, but I made mine from an old cotton flannel shirt, and so can you, provided that you know how to sew. For instructions on how to sew pads, see "Resources," page 270. For liners, simply enlarge the template below to cut a few pieces from cotton flannel (I cut three per liner), layer them, and zigzag them together. Add snaps at each bullseye.

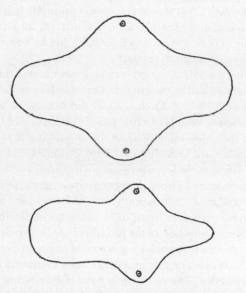

Who knew when I went to fashion school that the pattern that I would one day publish would be that of a menstrual liner . . . life is full of surprises.

COSMETICS

In my previous life, had I heard about Zero Waste, I would have pictured a community of practitioners with dreadlocks, weathered skin, and unadorned faces. What I found though is that through the application of the 5 Rs, you don't have to reject cosmetics.

Close review of the ingredients contained in my beauty routine (which proved to contain all of the "Dirty Dozen") led me to stock my makeup bag (the result of years of research for the drugstore products that worked on my oily skin) at the local organic store. Choosing healthy alternatives for my toxic products would have been easier had I disregarded the packaging they came in. What should have been a satisfying greening experience turned into real frustration. For example, one product gave me zits on my eyebrows. I did not even know that could happen! In another case, I found out that the packaging of the organic brand of mascara that I had assumed recyclable was not. How disappointing. I should have looked into the recyclability of the packaging before buying.

Defining cosmetics that would (1) contain nontoxic ingredients, (2) use minimal packaging, and (3) work for my skin type, all at the same time, was challenging. There was so much to think about before spending, so much uncertainty, so much to research.

It seemed that I would never get it right. I was making the same mistake in the bathroom as I had in the kitchen. Driving all over the San Francisco Bay Area in search of bulk Oreo cookies did not make any more sense than buying different brands of brow pencils in pursuit of the improbable "one." I found the solution, once again, in simplifying my routine. Once I identified my essentials, I slowly used up my products and adopted pantry replacements. Using main ingredients in their purest form would cut out the toxic middleman and afford an inexpensive organic selection of (bulk) substitutes. It took me a while to unravel my old ways but I have found that my present alternatives offer much more satisfaction, flexibility, and comfort knowing the composition of the products I use. The only manufactured cosmetic I now purchase in packaging is a glass bottle of organic SPF tinted moisturizer, which conveniently and organically combines daytime coverage and sun protection. The rest I either have eliminated or now make.

Lots of homemade scrubs use a combination of perishable (eggs) and sometimes exotic produce (papaya, avocado); they even sometimes require more packaging than the store-bought kind! For simplification, I personally like to stick to those alternatives that work just as well with one or two (bulk) pantry ingredients.

Finding replacements is not easy, but maybe some of my recipes and secrets can help:

BLUSH

DIRECTIONS

In a small jar, mix cocoa or carob (brown), cinnamon (orange), and beet root (pink) powders to achieve the color of your choice. These can also be used alone.

APPLICATION

Immediately after the application of your moisturizer, lightly tap a round brush onto the powder and apply to the face where color is needed. The moisturizer will fix the powder.

KOHL EYELINER (IF YOU ARE TOO CHICKEN FOR PERMANENT MAKEUP)

Used by the ancient Egyptians, this method provides a black powder, ideal for creating a smoky eye or lining lashes.

DIRECTIONS

1. In a metal sieve, placed over a mortar, burn ten almonds, one at a time (it takes a few minutes to get one completely lit).
2. Sift the ashes into the mortar below and grind them as finely as possible with a pestle.
3. Add a tiny drop of oil, and grind again. The mixture should remain powdery (if not, you've added too much oil).
4. Transfer the black powder into a small jar or a kohl container (see "Resources").

For a **smoky eye:** Dip the applicator (integrated within a kohl container) or a toothpick presoaked in olive oil into the powder, shake the excess off, place along the waterline, close your eye and pull the applicator out. Smudge with your finger.

For a **defined line:** Wet a small, chiseled brush in hairspray recipe (page 103) and mix with some kohl powder before applying. For larger quantities of "cake eyeliner," mix kohl and hairspray solution into a paste and transfer to a small tin container. Let the paste dry and solidify. To use, simply wipe a wet chiseled brush over the dry mix before applying.

EYEBROW LINER

DIRECTIONS

Mix cocoa powder and kohl (recipe above) to match your eyebrow color, or use either color alone.

APPLICATION

Simply wet a small, chiseled brush in water or the hairspray recipe (page 103) for a stronger hold and mix with some powder before applying.

EYE SHADOW

COLORS

Pastel green: French clay

Army green: Sage powder

Gold: Turmeric powder

Brown: Cocoa powder

Black: Kohl recipe on page 99

APPLICATION

Use fingertips or a small brush to add color to moisturized lids. Your moisturizer will fix the powder.

MASCARA

DIRECTIONS

1. In a small glass jar, combine 1 teaspoon beeswax, 1½ teaspoons coconut butter, and ¼ teaspoon kohl (recipe on page 99).
2. Place the jar in a small saucepan with 1 inch of water and stir on medium heat until the mixture is melted.
3. Remove from heat and stir ½ teaspoon honey into the mixture.
4. Let cool to solidify.
5. Stir vigorously to make a paste and transfer to a jar or a small tin.

APPLICATION

Roll a clean mascara wand into the paste, scrape off excess and wiggle onto the lashes. This is not your typical mascara; repeat applications are needed to achieve desired thickness.

Note: Since this is a product applied to the eye, please use hygiene common sense and keep your wand clean. Also please note that this is a nondrying, water-resistant and conditioning formula.

FACE POWDER

Face powders are used to hide imperfections, control oil in the T zone, and set your overall makeup. Cornstarch is a great substitute to the store-bought powders.

DIRECTIONS

Transfer cornstarch to a small jar. Use alone or add green clay if you want to correct skin redness. Or add bronzer (recipe on page 133) to match your skin color.

APPLICATION

Dip a large brush in the powder combination of your choice, shake off excess on the back of your hand and lightly dust the face where needed.

LIP/CHEEK STAIN

1. Slice beets and simmer in water until cooked.
2. (Eat the beets).
3. Reduce the leftover juice.
4. Remove from heat and let cool.
5. Pour into a glass roll-on tube, leaving room to top with a splash of vodka.

APPLICATION

Simply roll on the lips. Reapply to achieve a deeper shade.

MULTIPURPOSE BALM

DIRECTIONS
1. In a small glass jar, combine 1 tablespoon beeswax and 4 tablespoons oil (any oil will do, but I prefer sunflower oil for its high levels of vitamin E).
2. Place the jar in a small saucepan with 1 inch of water and stir on medium heat until the mixture is melted.
3. Pour in small tin and let cool.

APPLICATION

Use on lips and nails for shine, on crow's feet and hair tips as a moisturizer, and on cheekbones or brow bones as a highlighter.
Note: Stored in a separate container, you can also use this as a leather protector and wood polish!

DIRECTIONS

1. Cover 2 sliced lemons (you can use the discards of squeezed ones) with 2 cups of water in a pot.
2. Boil on high for 20 minutes to reduce.
3. Strain and pour into a spray bottle.
4. Add 2 tablespoons vodka to preserve.

APPLICATION

Simply spray, then style and let dry.

Hair Color

Henna, a ground leaf, can be purchased in bulk and is the fastest way to naturally color hair a reddish hue or black, when mixed with indigo. (See "Resources," page 270.) But if you do not have access to it or are after a less dramatic change, your pantry offers many coloring alternatives. The process is slow and requires daily application until color is achieved, but the subtle effects are well worth it.

Note: Results vary depending on hair color and type.

- **To darken:** Boil a handful of walnut hulls in 2 cups of water until reduced by half. Strain, apply to hair for 30 minutes, and rinse. Repeat daily until desired color is achieved and then weekly for maintenance.
- **To lighten:** Massage lemon juice into hair before spending time in the sun. Wear a visor to protect your skin from the sun. Repeat until desired color is achieved. I also add a strong chamomile tea to my conditioner.
- **To turn gray strands into blond:** Apply a tea of turmeric to hair for 15 minutes, checking the color change every 5 minutes, then rinse.

For daily maintenance and easy touch-ups, keep a paintbrush in the solution of your choice.

MY ROUTINE

Once tied to expensive products, I now make do with the rich soap mentioned earlier to wash my body from head to toe. I use the conditioner brands available in bulk and wash my hair every other day. On off days, I wear a ponytail or hat and occasionally use cornstarch as dry shampoo. I have simplified my cosmetics down to the essentials, and now solely rely on homemaking and using straight bulk items for all my beauty products, except for my SPF tinted moisturizer.

In the morning, my routine consists of using my drying towel to gently exfoliate my face after a shower. After I get dressed, I apply the SPF tinted moisturizer, and then use a large round brush to swipe cocoa powder across my cheeks and hairline. I apply the homemade eyeliner with an antique kohl powder applicator and blend it with my fingers for a smoked look. I apply the homemade mascara to my lashes, and I am good to go. On my way out, I reach for the homemade balm stored in my purse to add shine to lips, nails, cuticles, and I deposit the excess from the tips of my fingers through the ends of my hair to smooth them out.

At night I simply wash off my makeup using the bar of soap and apply grape seed oil to lightly moisturize my face (I concentrate on the crow's-feet and lips).

For special events, I intensify my day makeup (I apply two coats of tinted moisturizer and make my eyes darker or tint my lips with the beet lip stain) and I define my brows with a wet brush dipped in cacao. Sometimes I use cornstarch to add volume to my hair and add a curl to it. The day before a big event, I like to treat myself to a home manicure or facial.

Facial

Long gone are the days when my bathroom drawers were filled with facial products. When I am in the mood for a facial, I simply head to the kitchen: everything I need is stored in my pantry (no reason to store duplicates in a separate location), and the size of the kitchen sink keeps my ablutions contained.

1. **Cleanse:** Wash with homemade liquid soap (which I dispense at the kitchen sink, see page 147)
2. **Steam:** Sprinkle thyme in a bowl and fill with boiling water. Lean over the bowl and cover the head with a towel for five minutes.
3. **Exfoliate:** Over the kitchen sink, scrub a small handful of baking soda in a circular motion to exfoliate, rinse, and pat dry.
4. **Mask:** Mix a small amount of bulk clay (use French or bentonite for oily skin; kaolin for normal and dry skin) with apple cider vinegar to make a paste. Apply to the face, and rinse with lukewarm water when dry. **Note:** A dab of the mask can also double as an overnight spot treatment.
5. **Tone (optional):** Apply apple cider vinegar with a cotton round (consult Wellness, on the next page).

Mani-Pedi

Long gone are the days when I spent hours carefully applying polka dots and fluorescent pinks; in middle school, teachers would publicly comment on my daily change of nail color. After more than twenty years of continuous use, I tried the naked look with reservations but have not looked back. I have since noticed the ridges on my nails miraculously disappearing.

Tools needed:
- Clippers
- Cuticle cutter
- Stainless-steel file with a cuticle pusher on one end
- Multipurpose balm

Before a shower:
- Cut nails to desired length.
- File to desired length.

After a shower (cuticles will be softened):
- Use a towel to push cuticles back.
- Use the end of the stainless-steel file to lightly scrape the nail bed clean and swipe it under your nails.
- Use a cuticle cutter to cut stray pieces of skin (not the cuticles) around

nails. While this can also be done with nail clippers, cuticle cutters provide a cleaner, closer cut.

- Apply the multipurpose balm to nail tips and cuticles and rub your hands together to disperse the excess up the fingers.

A couple of times a year, I get my nails professionally buffed, but I schedule my manicure at the time of the salon opening to reduce exposure to the harmful chemicals they use during the day: usually, by the next morning, the strong odors have dissipated. I have noticed that such substances, which did not bother me in the past, now make me nauseous. A downside to reducing my exposure to harmful chemicals and greening my life, I guess.

WELLNESS

People who visit our house feel like they've hit the jackpot when they see our "pharmacy" container: "Aha! Do I spot packaging over here?" they ask, teasing. They might have discovered the three products that we preemptively store (pain reliever, cold tablets, and poison oak ointment), but what goes unnoticed is the intentional reduction work behind it.

Our process for addressing the wellness alternatives involved much trial and error. One day, excited about finding a dispenser of medicinal herbal tinctures (sold by the ounce at the local health food store), we filled small jars with decongestant and flu relief. Our enthusiasm subsided at the cash register and took a further beating on the first trial. Besides costing an arm and a leg, they did not seem to even work; at least not as efficiently or as quickly as the packaged stuff that we were accustomed to using. Maybe we should have given the elixirs more time, but with my son's symptoms intensifying, I did not have the heart to subject him to tests. An over-the-counter tablet provided him instant relief that night. After all, if Zero Waste could make allowances for toilet paper and makeup use, it could definitely make room for the inevitable medicinal need. No matter how dedicated I am to the lifestyle, I do not envision ever refusing medical advancements or jeopardizing our survival for the sake of our Zero Waste goals. I am not one to refuse necessary medication because of its packaging, but we can:

1. Eliminate the need for much medication by healthy living (prevention).
2. Eliminate the amount that we buy by resorting to home remedies when possible (home remedies).
3. Evaluate packaging use and our true need for what we keep on hand (over-the-counter).
4. Keep a tight inventory of prescribed medications (prescription).

Prevention

Clearly, I am a mom, not a doctor. It is not my place to make health claims or make medical recommendations, but I can tell you that we have noticed a net improvement in our family's health since embarking on this lifestyle: we simply do not get as many colds, rashes, or allergies as we used to. The positive impact of the new lifestyle on our health did not reveal itself immediately, but rather gradually. We saw fewer and fewer medical issues year after year. For example, Scott's chronic sinus infections have disappeared. And this year, for the first time, none of our family members caught a cold, and our doctor's visits were limited to routine checkups. I knock on wood as I write this.

Sadly, many people seek out Zero Waste's specific health benefits only after getting ill. They consider illness as a wake-up call to improve health, which leads them to research and adopt healthier alternatives. Some people have told me that they were not interested in changing their eating habits because they were too old to do so; some even dared tell me that they were going to die anyway, implying that they fully knew about the adverse effects of products found in the middle aisles of the grocery store but were giving up the fight. However, when sickness knocked on their partner's door, they looked for ways to eliminate toxins, live healthier, and adopt many of the alternatives mentioned in this book.

The activities involved in this Zero Waste lifestyle, such as shopping the fresh perimeter of the store, reducing our exposure to toxic chemicals, eliminating packaging that could leach into our food, spending more time outside, etc., improve our overall health. Don't wait to be sick to adopt change! Do what you can now to preventively maintain your health.

Home Remedies

No matter how healthy, our lives are colored by bruises, cuts, sniffs, and stubs. When our bodies cooperate, we take them for granted, but when we stub that toe, boy do we feel alive! In an instant, nothing else matters. Luckily, the cure is often no farther than a Zero Waste pantry (or the wild). We researched and tested a few natural alternatives. Here are our favorites in alphabetical order. (All but white vinegar, which is alternatively sold in a glass bottle, are available in bulk, of course!)

Allergies: Consume local honey daily.

Bruises: Apply half an onion on the area for fifteen minutes.

Coughs and sore throats: Gargle salt water and suck on a lozenge (recipe is on page 109).

Digestion: Chew on fennel seeds or drink an anise tea.

Eczema: Take an oatmeal bath and apply olive oil.

Foot odors: Spray apple cider vinegar on your feet and sprinkle baking soda in your shoes.

Gout: Drink coffee or eat cherries.

Headache: Drink an espresso, rub mint on the temples, or roll a fresh California bay leaf into your nostril. (I agree, it's not a great look, but it works for me!)

Insect bites: Apply white vinegar to the bites.

Jellyfish stings: Apply white vinegar to the stings.

Kidney stones: Mix ¼ cup olive oil with ¼ cup lemon juice and drink at once, followed by a large glass of water.

Lacerations: Use honey to heal small cuts.

Menstrual cramps: Drink chamomile or yarrow tea and apply a warm pad on the belly (i.e., a bottle filled with hot water, sealed tight, and placed in a sock).

Nausea: Consume ginger candied or in the form of a tea.

Oral thrush: Gargle a saltwater solution.

Prostate problems: Drink a tea of corn silk and eat tomatoes.

Quick heartburn relief: Drink 1 teaspoon baking soda in a glass of water (use only on occasion) or consume ½ teaspoon mustard.

Runny nose: Use a sea salt solution in a Neti pot.

Sunburn: Apply a generous amount of apple cider vinegar or olive oil.

Toothache: Gargle a chamomile tea or apply ice to the area.

Urinary tract infection: Eat cranberries.

Vaginal yeast infection: Eat yogurt.

Warts: Fix a piece of orange or lemon skin soaked in white vinegar to the affected area and repeat until gone.

XYZ: Etc. . . . google it!

LOZENGE RECIPE

I accidently created this recipe when perfecting my sugar wax!

DIRECTIONS

1. In a skillet, combine ½ cup honey, 1 tablespoon lemon juice, and 1 tablespoon of a strong herbal tea. You can use thyme, sage, peppermint, eucalyptus, or ginger (I use foraged yerba santa, a local plant with great expectorant properties).
2. Boil on high 3 to 4 minutes or until the mixture turns an amber color.
3. Turn off the heat and let cool until it can be handled.
4. Roll into small balls with your fingertips.
5. When completely cool, roll in powdered sugar.
6. Store in an airtight container filled with powdered sugar.

Note: Please do not give these to children under the age of three.

Over-the-Counter

Sometimes even with our best efforts, we end up at the drugstore. But do not despair; you can prove your conservation skills here, too.

- Choose tablets in a glass or, at default, a plastic jar (usually a recyclable number 2), instead of the tablets individually wrapped in aluminum/plastic and then a box.
- Refrain from buying jumbo-size medication jars. Although cheaper by the count, they'll expire before you can finish them. Be realistic.
- Choose a medicated cream in a metal tube instead of plastic.

Band-Aids

Running out of Band-Aids a couple of years ago made me happy: we were no longer going to be subject to marketing companies and their cartoon characters. Before buying more, I wanted to test our true need for them. I decided to wait until we needed one to go to the drugstore. I am still waiting. We have found that by not having them, we simply have lost our need for them. We wash small scrapes and cuts with soap and let them air-dry instead. We keep surgical paper tape on hand for deeper cuts but have been using the same roll for the past decade. While it seemed that we were applying Band-Aids on a regular basis, we now wonder: "How often do you really need a Band-Aid?" My son Léo used to reach for them freely thinking that they were a cure-all, that an "owie" would immediately feel better covered with SpongeBob. . . . He now agrees that a smoothie works just as well.

Cotton Rounds

Sometimes cleaning a wound requires a cleansing pad. While 100 percent cotton gauze is compostable, we have replaced it with reusable pads. Made with cotton flannel for absorbency, they can simply be washed and steam-ironed to sterilize. They are available online, but if you are inclined to sew them, you need to cut 2¼ inch circles in three layers of cotton flannel and zigzag your way around the pile to make one pad.

Prescription

Shit happens. And occasionally it leads to the doctor's office and then the pharmacy. And although our worries often surpass those of ecological conservation in those situations, here are a couple of things you can do to follow the 5 Rs:

- Discuss your need for prescriptions with your doctor; discuss alternative medicine options.
- At the pharmacy, refuse the bag and the instructions for the medications that you already know.

- Consider donating empty prescription bottles (it is illegal for most pharmacies to refill them) to the Humane Society, some of which accept them for reuse.

5 RS CHECKLIST: 5 TIPS FOR THE BATHROOM

Refuse: Don't let hotel shampoo bottles clutter your space and synthetic ingredients harm your health.
Reduce: Incorporate multipurpose products into your daily routine.
Reuse: Adopt the reusable hygiene alternatives mentioned above.
Recycle: Make your own cosmetics using bulk ingredients to eliminate recycling.
Rot: Compost hair, nails, and the lemon peel used for the hairspray.

ONE STEP FURTHER

Most of the ideas we covered in this chapter addressed the visible and tangible aspects of waste, but the following tips on energy, water, and time savings will complete (and further reward) your sustainable efforts.

Energy

- Insulate your hot water pipes.
- Set your water heater thermostat to 120 degrees Fahrenheit.
- Use a timer to keep your showers under two minutes.

Water

- Check for leaks: drop some beet juice in your toilet tank. If the color appears in the bowl without flushing, you have a leak and need to fix it.
- Put a brick in your toilet tank; it will reduce the amount of water used per flush. You won't notice a difference (until you see your water bill), and you'll forget it is in there.

- Consider installing composting (check your city codes) or low-flow (check for rebates) toilets if you remodel.
- Apply the flushing mantra: "If it's yellow, let it mellow. If it's brown, flush it down." Or better yet, use a waterless toilet or occasionally pee in your compost or citrus plants instead (urine provides them with a great soil amendment).
- Do not flush any product other than toilet paper down the toilet, even if it claims to be flushable.
- Install faucet adapters, which release water only when needed by applying pressure to a handle. Consider installing solar automatic faucets if you remodel.
- Swap for a low-flow model, if it takes less than twenty seconds for your showerhead to fill a gallon bucket.
- Collect water in a bucket while your shower heats; water your plants with it. Better yet, check your city and state codes and install a gray water system to use sink, baths, and showers for landscape irrigation.
- Take navy showers: turn the water on to quickly wet hair and body, off when washing and shampooing, then back on to take a quick rinse, and off as soon as you're done.

Time

- Install a mirror inside your medicine cabinet's door if it does not have one, so you don't have to close it every time you need a mirror.
- Use clear glass water tumblers to organize task items together (e.g., place all the manicure tools in one glass). You can then take the glass to your desired spot when needed (in front of the fireplace in the winter; out to the deck in the summer).
- Install a couple of clothes hooks to keep your toilet lid clear of clothes when taking a shower.
- In the medicine cabinet, dedicate one shelf per person, and one for common items such as tooth powder.
- Line up hygiene and cosmetics products in order of use on your shelf (e.g., moisturizer, then blush, then eyeliner).
- Maintain clear surfaces!

Bedroom and Wardrobe

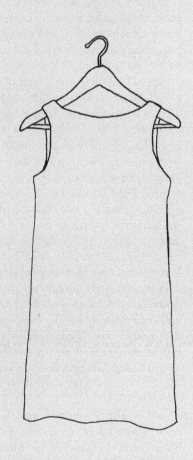

A number of years ago, Scott came home to find our apartment had been burglarized and my jewelry collection reduced to my wedding set. Lacking proof of broken entry and therefore presuming the burglars used keys to penetrate, our insurer refused to compensate us for our loss. What a waste of money invested in years of paid insurance premiums. I should have accepted the robbery as a sign of "natural selection." Instead I worked on rebuilding my collection. After a trip to India, I started wearing anklets and after a belly-dancing class, a chain around my waist. I quickly acquired more than I had lost. And when I discovered that my adopted country had a guideline (set by the diamond industry to stimulate sales, mind you) that a groom should spend two months' salary on an engagement ring, I gauged the wealth of new female acquaintances based on the size of their setting. I am ashamed to say I even convinced Scott to upgrade mine for another twice the size. What had become of my modest upbringing? By pursuing my American dream, I had come to associate "bling" with success and hierarchy. Blinded by greed, I gave too much importance to something that could vanish into thin air. On trips to underprivileged countries, I worried about exhibiting the ring. On resort grounds, I hesitated to leave it in the room. At the beach, I feared the ocean would rob it; at home, the housekeepers. Last year, when I grabbed a flat of tomatoes from the coarse and hardworking hands of the vendor whose fair prices I had bargained, it caught his eye: "Nice ring," he said. At that moment, I realized that it no longer suited me. With the rest of my collection, it had become a burden of upkeep and an article of the very kind of consumerism that I was fighting. I have since auctioned it off which brought me an inexplicable sense of relief.

As a girl, I admired and envied my grandmother's jewelry collection. When I look at it now, I see that it has caused her much worry. She's been the victim of numerous break-ins and repeated street-snatching incidents, and she's now spent more on insurance and safe-keeping than the jewelry is actually worth. Today, she stores the few surviving items in a safe-deposit box; wearing her favorite necklace requires a trip to the bank. I've changed my mind about wanting to inherit her collection.

It's true, after all, that a smile is the best accessory.

Of course, there is more to adopting the simple life than refusing a jewelry inheritance. Assessing my jewelry fixation was just one part of the process of simplifying my wardrobe and furnishings.

BEDROOM

Considering that we spend about a third of our lives sleeping, paying particular attention to creating a healthy and restful environment in the bedroom is of utmost importance.

While the eco-market pushes the consumption of organic mattresses and sheets in order to "green" a bedroom, I believe that the most important step you can take is to reduce clutter. It is effective, easy, and free! Since furnishings, rugs, and fussy window treatments harbor allergens and can release harmful chemicals into the air, a minimalist bedroom will no doubt yield considerable health benefits.

No need to consume to green your bedroom; simply reduce!

If we evaluate common bedroom activities: sleeping, reading, getting dressed, and sometimes "shagging," then we can let go of the furnishings and accessories that do not directly facilitate these tasks. Here are some ideas worth considering when simplifying this important space without compromising comfort.

- Computers, TVs, and workout equipment are best kept in living areas. This is especially true for the kids' rooms.
- Bulky nightstands tend to collect jewelry, prescriptions, unloved books, old magazines, used tissues (at best handkerchiefs), etc. Smaller surfaces discourage pileups. Consider using a stool, windowsill, or bed pockets instead.
- Dressers use up precious room and take time to dust: make the most of your closet space and eliminate the need for them.
- Chairs or valet stands inevitably invite clutter and collect dirty clothes meant for the hamper. Removing them enforces on-the-spot decision making: dirty and smelly go straight into the laundry bin; otherwise back into the closet or on a valet hook.

- Valances serve no other purpose than collecting allergy-causing dust. Consider taking them down; the fabric can be salvaged and repurposed into something more useful.
- Purely decorative pillows hinder efficiency: they need to be moved for sleep, put back after bed making, occasionally cleaned, and sometimes dry-cleaned or repaired. A couple of pillows for back support when reading usually suffice.
- Duplicate linen sets can monopolize a full cupboard (linen closet). They are also unnecessary if those in use are placed back onto beds post-laundering. One set of linens per bed (at most two if you line-dry or rent your house) in one neutral color throughout the house eliminates laundry separation and supports interchangeability.

All a bedroom really requires is curtains for privacy and insulation; a bed outfitted with a fitted sheet, a comforter and/or flat sheet, and a pillow for sleeping; a second pillow and light for reading; a closet (or an armoire); a plant to rid the air of indoor pollutants; maybe a couple of handkerchiefs tucked under the mattress to tidy up postintercourse.

Simplifying the bedroom provides not only better air quality but also makes it a breeze to clean and straighten up every morning.

The most common clutter problem and potentially the most wasteful element of the bedroom, however, is undoubtedly the wardrobe.

WARDROBE

The fashion industry is the prime example of an activity dedicated to using up resources, not to create satisfactions, but to create dissatisfactions with what people possess—in effect to create obsolescence in otherwise perfectly satisfactory goods.

—Ezra Mishan, English economist,
as quoted in *Less Is More*, by Goldian VandenBroeck

Boy, it seems as though fashion would be the antithesis of Zero Waste, and sustainable apparel an oxymoron in a society consumed by ever-changing trends. I agree that fashion (even if organic), when associated with "fast fashion" or trends (i.e., ephemeral and disposable wardrobes dictated by glossy magazines, Hollywood celebrity sightings, and marketing campaigns), is wasteful. But it does not need to be. As a matter of fact, I believe that fashion actually completes my Zero Waste lifestyle quite perfectly.

I love fashion. In my twenties, I studied at the London College of Fashion, where I learned how to turn a thought into a garment: how to draw the figure, design outfits, make patterns, sew, and have my creations fitted onto runway models for the graduation show. But I also learned that fashion in schools and couture shows is not about abolishing trends and creating new ones. It's about expressing one's creativity, putting outfits together, creating new combinations, and conveying a mood. In the confines of my closet, I see it as the art of getting dressed, of making the most of my inventory.

Trends and *style* might influence each other, but they are not the same thing. I agree with Yves Saint Laurent: "Fashions fade, style is eternal." Fashions defined as *trends* are indeed ephemeral, expensive, and environmentally destructive; on the other hand, fashion defined as *style* is accessible to anyone and is limited only to one's creativity and confidence.

After all, staying on top of trends does not necessarily mean that you have a fashion sense; neither does a large wardrobe.

Simplicity

Women and men alike often have reservations about paring down their wardrobes for fear of losing options or outfit combinations. Ironically, the same individuals often simultaneously complain of having a *closet full of nothing to wear*. I have come to learn that decluttering unexpectedly makes options clear and easy.

Large wardrobes fog our minds (decision making gets lost in a sea of possibilities) and when combined with our general lack of time, we end up picking the same garments week after week. Favorites (which are most likely comfortable and fit body shape and sense of style) move forward while dislikes get pushed back to less-visited racks and hard-to-reach shelves—therefore taking up valuable space, collecting dust, and hoarding precious resources. In a capsule wardrobe, each piece is carefully selected, equally worn, and as democratically displayed/visible as any other piece. In other words, the small wardrobe promotes *a closet full of things to wear*.

In theory, editing a large selection down would consist of evaluating favorites (those front, top-of-the-pile items) and letting go of the rest. But pretexts often hinder boldness. To downsize, take it all out, and for each item, ponder:

- **Is it in working condition? Is it outdated?** A few of those items that have holes, rips, and stains beyond repair/repurpose (refer to my alphabetical guide below for ideas) can be used as rags; the rest can be recycled (see "Recycling" section below). If you cannot flaunt past trends, donate or sell them; you'll make a vintage enthusiast happy.
- **Do I use it regularly?** Maybe you hold on to that bridesmaid dress for the what-if occasion. Donating it will clear space in your closet and make everyday wear more visible and accessible. Also, let your skinny clothes go: if you lose the weight, you'll want to treat yourself to a fresh wardrobe.
- **Is it a duplicate?** Seasonal accessories such as duplicate scarves and bathing suits take up space all year round: pick a favorite and let go of the rest. Same goes with underwear and socks: evaluate the amount needed between washes and let go of the extras (many thrift shops gladly accept them because many people gladly buy them).
- **Does it put my family's health in danger?** Formaldehyde, polybrominated diphenyl ethers (PBDE), perfluorochemicals, and phthalates respectively found in wrinkle-resistant (no-iron), fire/flame-retardant, Gore-Tex (also labeled Scotchgard or Teflon), and vinyl clothing are detrimental to our health. Nylon, polyester, and acrylic can also cause dermatological allergies. Consider letting go of these materials to reduce your exposure to them; contact the manufacturer for disposal suggestions.
- **Do I keep it out of guilt?** Jewelry is commonly gifted or passed down as an heirloom. Despite good intentions, these pieces often do not meet our personal aesthetics. It's okay to pass them on to those who will make use of them: a family member, consignment shop, or charity auction.
- **Do I keep it because society tells me that I need one ("everyone has one")? Could something else achieve the same task?** Consider everything in your closet. Powerful ad campaigns show sneakers as a must-have, but if your regular exercise routine involves yoga, leisure biking, and walking, you might just as well use a nonathletic comfortable pair of shoes instead.

- **Is it worth my precious time dusting and cleaning?** Neither decorative items nor storage containers have their place in a small wardrobe. Hat and shoe boxes not only hide their contents but also collect dust, take up room, and impair efficiency. Think out of the box: consider storing items on an open shelf instead. You will more likely use them and you will eliminate unnecessary cleaning. Let dust be your decluttering guide.
- **Could I use this space for something else?** If the previous questions did not convince you to donate or sell your wedding dress, consider relocating it to the attic and reclaim the space for conveniently storing your travel carry-on in your closet.
- **Is it reusable?** Such items as disposable underwear (yes, they do exist and are marketed to travelers!) or glue-on earrings (I wore them as a kid) clearly do not have their place in a Zero Waste closet. But when paring down, reusability is evaluated in terms of versatility and quality. Favor those items that can be paired with more than three pieces, reject those with little prospects. More on that in a moment.

Keep in mind that streamlining (any room) is an ongoing process, that it involves keeping an eye on use. If you notice a piece moving to the bottom of the pile or the back of the closet, make use of it or relinquish it. Otherwise, *nothing to wear* will lurk back into your life.

To prevent a wardrobe from growing again, I find it helpful to:

1. Set and stick to predetermined shopping days throughout the year: For example, I choose to shop mid-April for spring/summer and mid-October for fall/winter. It discourages leisure shopping (and therefore avoids compulsive buys) and encourages extending the useful life of the contents of your wardrobe.
2. Keep a tight inventory: Before a seasonal shopping trip, you can highlight the items on your list that you wore out (holes, tears, or stubborn stains) or simply grew tired of wearing, and need to replace. It supports the rule "One in, one out," by sticking to a predefined number.

Reusability

A Zero Waste wardrobe should not only be minimal, it should support reusability through: (1) buying secondhand, (2) buying versatile pieces, and (3) repurposing.

Buying Secondhand

The greenest product is inarguably the one that you already own. I believe in reusing before buying into green claims, in shopping our closets (ours and that of other family members), thrift stores, vintage shops, consignment boutiques, or flea markets before buying a new garment that is organic, vegan, recycled, recyclable, compostable, or biodegradable. Craigslist, Freecycle, and garage sales can also provide tag-free preowned apparel. Although it comes with the environmental impact of transportation, eBay can also meet very specific clothing needs; simply make sure to check the "preowned" box in your search. In my opinion, eco-friendly products will be a good alternative only when we have exhausted and worn out those already manufactured.

According to the Bureau of International Recycling (BIR), over 70 percent of the world's population use secondhand clothes—isn't it time our society did, too?

Many shoppers cringe at the idea of buying secondhand for many reasons, but misconceptions need to be abolished.

1. **Hygiene:** "It's dirty, someone else wore it." We tend to believe that new clothing is cleaner than its used counterparts, when in fact new clothing that has been tried or possibly returned can be dirtier (worn and never washed) than a laundered preowned garment. Furthermore, buying new clothing does not ensure that it will be bug free. Large retail chains have had well-publicized problems with infestations. Newly bought clothes (new or used) should be washed before wearing, regardless of their origin.
2. **Organization:** "I can't find anything in that mess." Just like retail stores, secondhand venues can set themselves apart through merchandising. Although secondhand markets provide cheap clothes, they are often

run by volunteers, ignoring the rules and powers of marketing or simply lacking presentation skills. If you do not enjoy rummaging through the messy piles of a garage sale, then pick an organized shop (Goodwill arranges its garments by color, for example) or, better yet, a consignment shop as they tend to run smaller, well-organized boutiques. EBay also makes it easy to narrow a search down to specifics. For example, you can hunt down a preowned "fitted denim women's shirt with pearl buttons in extra-small size."

3. **Smell:** "Thrift stores stink." Most people associate the smell of new plastics (i.e., synthetic off-gassing) and department store perfumes (i.e., toxic phthalates) with the high of shopping. On the other hand, resale shops sell items that have lost most of these toxic volatile compounds and therefore provide a somewhat healthier shopping experience than their retail counterparts.

4. **Standards:** "I find it demeaning to buy secondhand when I can afford to buy new." Again, it is not what you wear that defines who you are but who you are that defines what you wear. Also, the secondhand market can cater to financial standards of all kinds. The high end resells designer brands and vintage looks. In fact, the latter is now associated with cool, rare, and quality pieces.

Let's embrace the hunt for the unusual clothing and the carbon footprint redemption of buying used! But first, here are the rules to follow when shopping secondhand for a Zero Waste wardrobe:

- **Dress lightly.** Leggings paired with a fitted tank top, for example, make it easy to try things on in the aisles.
- **Bring your shopping tote.** Too often we think about the reusable bag for bringing home groceries but not clothes or shoes. Reduced shopping trips inevitably decrease incidences, but "where there is a will, there is a way." If you forget your tote, you can simply wrap small purchases into larger ones (accessories in a T-shirt, for example).
- **Bring your inventory list** (possibly accessible from your phone). Don't let the minimal price tags of secondhand shopping undermine your decluttering efforts; stick to finding and buying only those items highlighted on your list.
- **Favor durability.** While *new* purchases come with the uncertainty of how they will stand up to regular wear, *used* ones, on the other hand,

offer pretested apparel. The large majority of the resale merchandise has undergone an undefined amount of use (wearing, washing, drying) that the shopper can exploit to buy smart. If a garment was poorly designed to shrink, twist, or pill, then by the time it hangs on a thrift store rack, it will most likely show the defect. Furthermore, its condition gives a clue of how it will stand the test of time (pills on a sweater predict future pilling). Aim for quality materials, including leather shoes and belts, and metal accessories, which not only last longer but are more easily repaired than synthetic ones.

- **Favor natural fibers.** I have found it easy to eliminate plastics in the kitchen, but much harder to stay away from synthetics in the bedroom or wardrobe. Lycra is now commonly added to jeans, acrylic to socks and sweaters, and polyester to sheets. Yet pure cotton, linen, silk, hemp, bamboo, wool, and jute possess "breathing" properties, eliminate the risk of allergies caused by synthetic fibers, do not require static guards in the dryer, and are biodegradable (in theory, even compostable). If you must buy synthetic, seek the Patagonia brand (see "Recycling," page 128).
- **Expand your search.** Don't overlook costume, lingerie, party wear, or menswear racks, which can offer unusual pieces and silhouettes for everyday wear.
- **Inspect thoroughly.** The higher-end shops (such as consignment, designer resale, or vintage) pay particular attention to the condition of their merchandise. Thrift stores, on the other hand, are not as thorough. Test buttons and elastic bands and examine the seams. Be on the lookout for stains or holes. If your expertise can remedy a defect (i.e., postpone the garment's trip to the landfill), ask for a discount.
- **Be ruthless on fit.** Not only have sizing standards changed over the years and varied across the brands, but an item might also have been washed and shrunk. Don't trust the size label. This is where you choose a garment for its fit, not its size tag or brand. Don't waste your time and money. Try it on.
- **Launder before wearing.** Welcome it into your wardrobe and make it yours!

Living sustainably requires discipline. It involves learning how to resist fast fashion; it requires protecting oneself from the marketing campaigns found in fashion magazines, on billboards, and at bus stops and intended "not to create satisfactions, but to create dissatisfactions with what people possess." A used wardrobe undeniably takes persistence, willpower, and some getting used to. A fervent mall-goer won't commit to the secondhand market overnight. But gradual change holds significance. A great way to ease into adjustment is to first adopt a hybrid wardrobe. Buy new *quality* basics (timeless classics) and incorporate fun used pieces, such as bold items in unusual textures and colors. On the semiannual shopping trip, the latter can be traded at the thrift store (donate the colors that you grew tired of wearing and purchase a replacement palette, for example). If you patronize a charity shop, your business can even support a good cause!

Versatility

The Zero Waste lifestyle is about retraining ourselves to consume intelligently, just as it is about letting creativity bring excitement into everyday activities. In terms of fashion, I have found that a minimal but carefully thought-out wardrobe can actually highlight personal *style*. Versatility is simply the secret ingredient to making the most of a small selection. It starts by carefully selecting and purchasing items that can be worn many different ways: from a hike to a party, from the beach to a concert, from a sunny afternoon to a chilly night. One versatile dress can be twenty outfits, paired with diverse accessories, shoes, or layers.

Here are some tips on acquiring versatile pieces that can be applied to any event or season:

Color

- **Pick basics in neutral shades** (black, brown, gray, or navy, depending on your complexion). Khakis tend not to mix well with winter pieces (picture khaki pants with a black down jacket). Your base color choice should represent the permanent staples of your wardrobe, the pieces that you are least likely to replace on your next shopping trip.
- **Add a few colors and prints.** We tend to get tired of colored items and prints faster than neutrals. These should therefore represent the rota-

tional staples, the pieces that you use to add fun and zing to the wardrobe and are likely to replace on your next shopping trip.

- **Stick to one hardware/metal color.** Define the metal color that compliments your skin tone. Choose gold jewelry and accessories if you have warm tones (green veins under the forearms), silver if you have cold ones (blue veins).
- **Stay away from colors or patterns that are too casual.** Acid washes and tie-dye rainbows are restrictive; they cannot be dressed up for a formal event.

Materials

- **Choose cross-seasonal materials.** Tweed is too warm for summer, organza too light for winter. One pair of pj's should be light enough for summer, warm enough for winter, and decent enough to wear when staying as a guest at someone's house.
- **Favor medium-weight fabrics.** They can be layered interchangeably over or under other garments.
- **Pick fabrics that are neither too formal nor too casual.** Terry cloth, for example, is too casual and difficult to pair with dressier elements.
- **Stick with low maintenance.** Stay away from those materials that require hand washing or dry cleaning. Favor those that can be machine washed and tumble dried.
- **Favor leather and suede shoes** over canvas or mesh. They can withstand a wider variety of activities and harsher conditions; they are also dressier and can be worn all year around. Smooth leather can even be waterproofed using the recipe on page 132.

Cut

- **Favor fitted and medium fit for permanent staples.** They can be layered or worn alone.
- **Stay away from cuts that are difficult to layer** such as bat sleeves and mock necks.
- **Favor adjustable belts,** such as the braided kind. They can be fastened at the waist or worn loose at the hips and can accommodate variable thicknesses of clothing.

- **Look for multifunctionality in bags, too.** A removable strap can turn a daytime purse into a nighttime clutch, for example.

Repurposing

Infrequent shopping trips eventually lead to wear and tear, and a small wardrobe sometimes breeds boredom (especially as my biannual shopping trip nears). To remedy these predicaments, there is much to consider. Here is my A-to-Z list to rethinking, repairing, and extending your wardrobe's useful life:

Accessorize it: Hide a hole with a pin or a flower.

Borrow it: Use your kid's scarf, your husband's hat, or your mom's jewelry to spruce up an outfit.

Color it: Use natural dyes (see page 204 for color ideas) to give a white shirt a new look, a marker to cover a bleach spot, or leftover house paint to cover a stain with a strategic splash of color.

Darn it: Learn our grandmothers' handcraft to repair worn-out socks and sweater holes. Visit zerowastehome.com for a tutorial.

Edit it: Not liking a sewn-on design on a shirt, belt loops on a pair of pants, or pockets on a sweater? Removing them can make all the difference.

Felt it: A wool sweater can be felted down to fit a smaller size or to make another useful item. My girlfriend Rachelle taught me that the forearm can be cut to make an extra-small dog sweater (the cuff serves as the sweater collar; simply cut two holes underneath for the legs). It keeps our Chihuahua cozy in the winter.

Glue it: A dot of glue can save a pair of shoes.

Hem it: The height of a hem can completely change a garment. A dress can turn into a shirt, jeans into shorts (I use orange thread to follow the design elements of denim).

Improvise it: A chain belt can double as a necklace; a skirt with an elastic waistband as a tube top; a long top as a minidress.

Juxtapose it: Contrasts add zing to outfits and can revive an old garment. Pair worn with new, casual with formal, sporty with dressy, etc.

Knot it: Knot a shirt at the waist or wide pants at the hem to alter their fit and look.

Layer it: Layering can alter the visuals of a piece. Worn under a shirt, a strapless dress will appear to be a skirt, for example. But layering can also hide defects. When worn as a layer, a stained red shirt can add a touch of color under a sweater.

Mend it: Simply repairing a seam or sewing on a button can save a garment; but mending also encourages thinking out of the box. The elastic ankle of a worn-out sock can replace a ripped sweatshirt cuff (speaking from experience, no one will notice)!

Nip it: Adding darts to a shirt can both enhance the design of a garment and hide holes (or prevent them from getting bigger).

Organize it: Reorganizing or shuffling a wardrobe can provide a new outlook on its contents; changing the placement of a garment might simply highlight its potential.

Patch it: Stop holes from getting bigger at the knee before it's too late. Iron on patches at the knees (inside the pants) at the first sign of wear.

Question it: Google will tell you what to do with it. YouTube has some great tutorials on how to turn old T-shirts into dresses or men's shirts into skirts without sewing (one short video inspired me to experiment and wear a men's dress shirt fifty different ways).

Return it: If it still has a price tag attached, don't wait, return it to the store.

Shrink it: A clothes dryer can shrink your clothes to the perfect fit (it works especially well for those items that warn against using a dryer).

Trade it: Have a clothes-swapping party or use an online trading website.

Unravel it: Unravel old sweaters to make new ones; unravel buttons from worn-out clothing to substitute lost ones on wearable garments.

Vamp it up: Tired of your same old sandals? Vamp them up by replacing their ankle straps with ribbons and tying them into bows.

Wrap it: A skinny belt serves double duty wrapped around a wrist as a chunky bracelet; a scarf wrapped around the waist as a beach cover-up.

XYZ: eXamine Your Zipper; if the zipper pull is broken, use a paper clip, a chain link, or a ribbon as an alternative.

I learned how to sew at a young age and am capable of confecting my own outfits from fabric cuts, but I find it much easier, affordable, and eco-friendly to use my expertise in revising, altering, and reinventing those pieces that already exist in thrift stores instead. For example, my one pair of shorts comes from a boy's pair of suit pants. With only a few stitches, I have been able to save countless outfits by simply shortening a hem, adding an elastic band, or changing buttons. It does not take much time and does not cost much.

Collection

The superb quality of most vintage clothing is a reminder that clothes are, by and large, no longer made to last. The secondhand market provides an outlet for wearable discards, but when these wear out, they become the responsibility of the secondhand consumer. A thrift-shop enthusiast will inevitably be exposed to higher incidences of irreparable holes and tears than the average shopper (I wear out about three pieces of used clothing between shopping trips).

Recycling

At home, our efforts are limited to repurposing worn-out T-shirts into rags, grown-out socks into convenient dusters, old nylons into efficient shoe shines, etc. There is no need to collect more than is truly needed. The recycling job is best left to the professionals.

The Environmental Protection Agency estimates that about 97 percent of postconsumer textile waste is recyclable. Yet only 20 percent gets recycled because the consumer simply does not know it can be. When I was a child, I remember watching a wooden mill turn old bed linens into beautiful paper sheets at the Fontaine-de-Vaucluse, but I had forgotten about the class field trip until today.

Throughout the world, a small portion of worn-out textiles is currently being converted into rags for the construction, painting, and automobile industries; another percentage is shredded into flocking fibers for insulating, padding, upholstering, or soundproofing purposes. But the recyclers wish they could put their hands on all textile discards, including the extras that we simply throw away or hoard for the what-if.

Resale giant Goodwill, along with mobile recycling bins, accept both natural and man-made fibers of any brand for recycling. Those items that have holes, rips, and stains beyond repair can be boxed, labeled "rags," and donated to participating locations, where they are then dispatched to textile recyclers.

On the manufacturing front, Patagonia has been a leader, taking responsibility for the clothes that it manufactures, paving the way in setting up repair and recycling programs for its gear, sometimes even making new clothes out of old ones. If you need sportswear, make sure to seek out the brand on the secondhand market.

In the shoe industry, Nike provides the Reuse-A-Shoe program, which grinds *any* worn-out brand of athletic shoes into sports surfaces. With two active boys, we fully take advantage of this recycling opportunity and have dedicated a bin for this purpose (when it's full, we take it to a nearby participating location).

Compost

Little compost will occur in the bedroom or wardrobe, but depending on the type of composter at your disposal, consider composting the following items most commonly found in the bedroom or wardrobe:

- Bits or frays of cotton, linen, silk, hemp, bamboo, wool, and jute that are too small to be recycled
- Feathers from pillows
- Sweater pills (as long as they come from a natural fiber)
- Untanned leather, shredded into bits

Landfill

Trash cans clutter all rooms, including bedrooms. They often collect receipts, tags, and paper packaging (bags, boxes, tissue paper): buying used will most likely eliminate the latter; otherwise they can be refused on the spot or, at worst, recycled in the kitchen (which is already set up for collection). A bedroom does not need a can at all, and the lack of it certainly will discourage accidental discards.

A MOBILE WARDROBE

We rent our house on occasion; it funds weekends and holidays away. When time comes to vacate our home, we each pull down the carry-on bags we keep in our closets, empty our wardrobes into them, zip them shut, and go. Truthfully, I am sometimes tempted to add items to my inventory, but I stay on track by reminding myself of the creativity and the unforeseen benefits that my minimalism has afforded.

I have found that a grab-and-go wardrobe supports:

- **Efficiency:** It saves time by reducing shopping, minimizing storage activities, and speeding up decision making in the morning. It makes each piece easy to see, easy to match, easy to grab.
- **Energy savings:** It reduces laundry loads by encouraging wardrobe management. That is, learning to manage the number of pieces and the amount of times that they are worn (you consider wearing pieces again, instead of thoughtlessly throwing them in the laundry).
- **Economic savings:** A small wardrobe obviously lessens shopping and storage costs, but when packed in a carry-on for air travel, it also saves check-in fees.
- **Effortless travel:** It is lighter to carry and quicker to pack (no need to debate what to bring on a trip, you can bring it all).
- **Easy maintenance:** Staying on top of repair and stains is manageable.
- **Emergency readiness:** In case of an emergency, it is packed in a few minutes and easy to grab.
- **Ecology:** A large wardrobe usurps valuable resources; a small one doesn't.

Putting together the perfect, versatile inventory took time and practice. It took about two years to determine the right amount (not too much, not too little) and the type of pieces that suit my local climate, places I visit, and favorite activities. My wardrobe accommodates speaking engagements and private consultations, art making and outdoor hobbies (hiking, foraging, camping, traveling), household chores (weekly cleaning and laundering), social life, and preferred modes of transportation (walking and biking). The pieces I have chosen can be mixed and matched, dressed up or down, for any occasion. Nothing is left in a dark corner for the rare event. For me, the ideal closet is made up of pieces that can multifunction through the seasons (e.g., the all-purpose cover-up serves as swimsuit cover-up but also as a wrap or scarf in cold weather), and also fit my ever-changing activities. They say "you can tell a lot about a woman by the contents of her purse." My purse indeed represents the essence of my lifestyle. It is big enough to hold my computer but discreet enough for dressy occasions. The removable strap turns it from a daytime messenger bag to an evening clutch. The leather is black, durable, and easily maintained, therefore meeting my foraging and travel needs. It features a couple of zippered pockets, which eliminate the need for a separate wallet. Throughout the day, it carries my belongings from a client's home to a mountain hike to a cocktail party, without ever having to transfer my things (essentially cell phone, sunglasses, cash, insurance card, credit card, Multipurpose Balm, and handkerchief) into a different bag.

Obviously everyone's needs are different: if you work as a crab fisherman in Alaska or as a surfing instructor in Hawaii, your purse and the quantity and type of clothing in your wardrobe will greatly differ from mine. For illustrative purposes, here are the current contents of my closet:

Tops
- Blouse
- Striped long sleeve
- Basic long sleeve
- Embellished top
- Fitted tank
- Loose tank
- Thick sweater
- Lightweight sweater
- Cardigan

Dresses
- LBD (little black dress)
- Colorful dress

Bottoms

- Jeans
- Trousers
- Black skirt
- Colorful skirt
- Shorts

Intimates

- Convertible bra and seven matching undies (going commando requires more washes and is therefore wasteful)
- One pair of each: light, medium, and heavy socks
- One pair of tights
- Pajama set
- Swimsuit
- Two personal handkerchiefs

Accessories

- All-purpose purse
- Wool fedora
- Straw hat
- Belt
- Jewelry: statement ring, bracelet and necklace, and a pair of earrings
- All-purpose cover-up/scarf/shawl
- Sunglasses
- Leather gloves
- Carry-on luggage

Outerwear

- Blazer
- Leather jacket
- Overcoat

Shoes*
- Open-toe high heels
- Flat sandals
- Flat boots
- Colorful pumps
- Heeled bootie
- Slippers

* I store a portion of the Multipurpose Balm in a separate tin, which I keep on the shoe shelf to add shine to my polish-free toes when I wear sandals.

SHOE CARE

To dust, use a worn-out sock.

To remove salt marks, use the Basic Mix cleaner on page 137.

To polish, use worn-out nylons.

To protect, use the Multipurpose Balm recipe (see "Bathroom, Toiletries, and Wellness," page 102).

WATERPROOFING

DIRECTIONS

1. Melt 2 tablespoons beeswax and 1½ teaspoons oil in a double boiler (I use a small glass jar in an inch of water).
2. Brush onto leather. (The wax will streak the shoe as it cools during application. It might look scary but don't be alarmed. The streaks will disappear when you dry the shoe.)
3. Use a blow dryer and an old sock to work the wax into the shoe or boot.

Body Bronzer

A body bronzer is a great wardrobe addition for those who, like me, want to add a golden glow to their winter-white legs. Apply on the spot, when wearing dresses, skirts, or shorts, being careful not to stain your clothing!

COCOA BRONZER

DIRECTIONS

1. Moisturize the body parts to tan.
2. Dust cocoa powder using a large makeup brush (best for décolleté). Or, mix cocoa powder with your choice of bulk oil in the palm of your hands before applying (best for bare lower legs).

TEA BRONZER

DIRECTIONS

1. Steep 5 tablespoons black tea in ½ cup boiling water for 15 minutes.
2. Strain.
3. Use a spray bottle or a cloth dipped into the solution to apply.
4. Let dry and reapply to achieve your desired shade.

Note: This method requires more work and takes longer than cocoa but can be applied to all body parts.

5 *R*S CHECKLIST: 5 TIPS FOR THE BEDROOM

Refuse: Resist *trends,* embrace *style.*
Reduce: Stick to minimal furnishings and a small, versatile wardrobe.
Reuse: Buy secondhand clothes and repurpose to extend their useful life.
Recycle: Donate worn-out clothing to participating recyclers.
Rot: Compost your wool sweater's pills.

ONE STEP FURTHER

Most of the ideas that we covered in this chapter addressed the visible and tangible aspects of waste, but the following tips on energy, water, and time savings will complete (and further reward) your sustainable efforts.

Energy

- Switch your reading lamp's incandescent lightbulb to an LED one.
- Get books from the library or download them as e-books.
- Use a pumice stone, razor, or steel wool to remove sweater pills manually.

Water

- Water your bedroom plant with the leftovers of your bedside water.

Time

- Pick an easy bed-making style. For example, I fold and smooth our comforter halfway down the bed. That way, the bed airs and is ready to slip into.
- Place your hamper in the closet and undress next to it.
- Consider separate hampers for darks, whites, and dry cleaning.
- Night meds are best kept in the bathroom, where water flows and evening ablutions take place.
- Store your jewelry in the closet, near where you dress.

Housekeeping and Maintenance

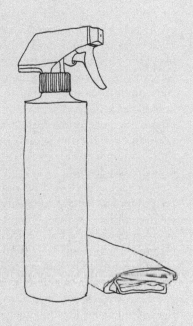

I gathered my skirt with one hand and let the other guide me down the polished stair rail to the clacking sound of the heels I'd borrowed from my mother. We were overnight guests at the estate of a family friend in Belgium, and in the grandeur, I pictured myself as an actress on the set of the series *Dallas*. At ten years old, I was already visualizing my dream home: a big house with a big staircase and a big lawn.

Twenty years later, Scott's hard labor had afforded my fantasy, but the reality was far from what I'd imagined: instead of wearing cowboy boots like Bobby Ewing, my husband was knee deep in our pond, pulling weeds, wearing shorts and diving booties. Gardening took most of our weekends, and a routine cleaning, an entire day. We hired a bimonthly housekeeper, but it stopped neither the kids' toys from spreading throughout the house, nor fingerprints from propagating across the large bay windows, nor dust bunnies from herding in the corners. Yet we accepted our home's time commitment and upkeep expenses as facts of life, the unavoidable cost of living our dream.

Relocating presented an opportunity to rethink our ways. With the adoption of voluntary simplicity, we came to ask ourselves: What do we want from life? Are we living it fully? We have one life to live and only so many hours in a day. Downsizing answered our questions. It gave us a chance to shift our lives from spending our free time maintaining our investments to doing things that we truly enjoy, such as spending time with our loved ones, indulging in a few hobbies, creating, and learning. After all, these are activities that I want to fully explore before I die . . . rather than spending my life cleaning those extra rooms, mowing an ever-growing lawn, or spending the fruits of my professional work to hire people to do those tasks for me.

In this chapter I will discuss how to simplify cleaning, laundering, upkeep, and gardening.

Over the years, powerful marketing campaigns have complicated our routines and led us to believe that different applications require different products. Over the generations, we have filled our gardening sheds, under-kitchen-sink cabinets, and laundry rooms with expensive and toxic products, forgetting our grandmothers' most powerful cleaning weapon. As inexpensive and nontoxic as their solution was, it can clean most surfaces, disinfect, and cut odors and grease around the home; it can dissolve lime, soap scum, and mold in the bathroom but also fight stains and sticky residues and even soften our laundry; in the yard, it gets rid of pests and weeds. I am referring to . . .

THE MAGIC OF VINEGAR

Although I have not been able to find vinegar in bulk (I purchase it in a glass bottle), I believe it to be an essential for the home and the garden. I use the following mix for most applications.

BASIC MIX

DIRECTIONS

Fill a spray bottle with 1 cup water and ¼ cup white distilled vinegar.
Note: For added scent, you can infuse the vinegar with citrus peels in a jar for a couple of weeks, prior to diluting it.

Here are examples of cleaning, laundry, pest, and gardening products that you can eliminate from your home by using vinegar instead:

Adhesive remover: Remove stickers by soaking them with warm vinegar. For gum, use an ice cube to remove the bulk of it, then warm vinegar to clean off residues.

Bathroom cleaner: Use the Basic Mix to dissolve soap scum and hard-water stains and simultaneously shine counters, floors, sinks, showers, mirrors, and fixtures. You can also dip a toothbrush in the cleaner to scrub grout joints and soak your showerhead in a bowl of vinegar overnight to remove lime buildup.

Color set: If a garment has proved to bleed in the wash, let it soak in vinegar before laundering.

Drain cleaner: Use a drain snake and plunger to clear pipes, then pour ¼ cup baking soda followed by ½ cup white vinegar. Cover until bubbling stops and flush with boiling water.

Eraser sponge (also known as Magic Eraser): Remove pen, pencil, or crayon marks from walls using a cloth or toothbrush dipped in straight vinegar.

Flower food: To extend the life of cut flowers, add a tablespoon of both vinegar and sugar to their water. You can also remove the white buildup on your vases by soaking them in undiluted vinegar.

Glass cleaner: Use a microfiber cloth if you have one—it does not require any other product but water. As a default, you can spray the Basic Mix onto windows, mirrors, and glass surfaces, then polish with cloth rags.

Herbicide (also known as weed killer): Simply kill weeds by spraying full-strength vinegar onto them.

Insect repellent: Spray where you do not want ants to come into your house (windowsills or door thresholds, for example). Versatilevinegar.org also recommends adding a teaspoon of white distilled vinegar for each quart bowl of your pet's drinking water to keep it free of fleas and ticks. The ratio of one teaspoon to one quart is for a forty-pound animal.

Jewelry/metal cleaner: To clean tarnished bronze, brass, and copper, apply a mixture of 1 tablespoon salt and ¼ cup vinegar, rinse with warm water, and polish with a soft cloth. For silver, soak the piece in ¼ cup white vinegar and 1 tablespoon baking soda, then rinse and polish with a soft cloth. For gold, simply cover with vinegar for one hour and rinse. Do not use on pearls.

Kitchen cleaner: Use full-strength vinegar to disinfect cutting boards. Use in lieu of your stainless cleaner or dishwasher rinse aid (simply substitute it in the dishwasher rinsing compartment). Use the Basic Mix to clean the sink, counter, and refrigerator (use a toothbrush to clean moldy joints). To clean the microwave, pour some Basic Mix into a cup and bring to a boil to cut odors and loosen food bits. To clean the oven, generously spray with vinegar, then sprinkle with baking soda and let sit overnight, scrape with a spatula, and wipe clean. To remove lime buildups in the coffeemaker, fill its water reservoir with water and ¼ cup vinegar, run it through, empty, and rinse. To remove unpleasant odors from the garbage disposal, your hands, or food jars, use straight vinegar. To remove tea or coffee stains from ceramic cups, soak in vinegar for a few hours, then scrub stubborn stains with baking soda.

Laundry booster: Adding ½ cup of undiluted vinegar to your rinse cycle will prevent soap buildup and yellowing, act as a fabric softener and a color booster, and reduce static cling.

Mildew remover and prevention: Use full-strength vinegar to remove mildew off most surfaces. To prevent mildew on a shower curtain, spray vinegar on the problem areas or add vinegar to your rinse cycle when you wash it.

Nicotine stain remover: Clean walls stained by nicotine with straight vinegar.

Odor neutralizer: Instead of covering up an unpleasant smell with toxic fragrances, address the source and air the space out. Then place a bowl of vinegar in the room to absorb persistent odors (e.g., in a newly painted room to remove paint odors, in a car to remove vomit stench, or in a kitchen to remove smoke odors).

Pet repellent: Spray vinegar where you do not want your dog or cat to chew, scratch, or urinate.

Quick mop: No need for disposable floor wipes; simply spray a microfiber mop with the Basic Mix and mop.

Rust remover: To remove rust from small items, soak them in undiluted vinegar for a few hours, scrub with a toothbrush, and rinse thoroughly. Rub steel wool on stubborn residues.

Stain remover: Pour vinegar on mustard, pen, pencil, or crayon marks, then scrub with a toothbrush to remove the stain and launder as usual.

Toilet cleaner: Spray vinegar, then scrub. For tough jobs, you can spray vinegar, sprinkle with baking soda, let sit, and then scrub.

Upholstery freshener: Lightly spray the Basic Mix on a cloth and wipe upholstery to neutralize odors, remove surface dirt, and boost color (first test in an inconspicuous area). The vinegar smell will subside, leaving a fresh scent. Wiping with a microfiber helps pick up pet hair.

Vinyl cleaner: Clean and shine no-wax vinyl linoleum floors with 1 gallon of water supplemented with 1 cup of vinegar.

Wood renewer: Mix equal parts vinegar and oil, and rub in the direction of the grain to remove water rings and scratches. You can also use the Multipurpose Balm (see page 102) as wood polish!

XYZ: eXamine Your Zipper. If a zipper does not run smoothly, spray vinegar onto it and run the zipper a few times to clear any blocking gunk.

Now let's go into depth about how to reduce waste and facilitate housekeeping, upkeep, and gardening.

HOUSEKEEPING

My brothers and I rolled our eyes every time our grandfather said: "*L'homme sera victime du progrès!*" ("Man will be victim of progress!") As an adult, I now understand the truth behind those words. Since disposability hit the market and entered our homes, our standards of cleanliness have gone extreme.

Pounded by advertisements for disposable products that promise a cleaner, thus healthier, life over reusable alternatives, our society has become increasingly germaphobe and finds reassurance in deliberately using and disposing of such products as paper towels, latex gloves, tissues, and antibacterial wipes. Absurd claims intended to win our buying power lead us to believe that we are filthy and under the attack of dangerous germs that we absolutely need to kill or at least avoid (an impossible feat) and that reuse is gross. "Regular washing of bathroom hand towels does not ensure clean hands" one company claims while trying to sell you its disposable hand towel. Industry professionals who find and create a market for every germ location, including that of our clean laundry, reinforce our perceived dependence on disposable and toxic products. But living up to these made-up standards is not only costing us the health of our planet— through resources depletion and disposal of single-use products—it is costing us our personal health, too!

According to Mother Nature Network, "U.S. consumers spend nearly $1 billion a year on antibacterial products that aren't necessary." Some carry Purell on their key chains; others look for dispensers in public spaces. Yet, as the Mayo Clinic warns: "Antibacterial soap is no more effective at killing germs than is regular soap. Using antibacterial soap may even lead to the development of bacteria that are resistant to the product's antimicrobial agents—making it harder to kill these germs in the future." We fight an invisible war that we do not fully understand, and by attacking it in full force, we are breeding the superbug.

Finding the right balance between squeaky clean and hygienic is a new necessity. It's important to understand that some germs are beneficial to our immunity and that antibacterial wipes and gels are not necessary. Simplify your housework by (1) embracing low-maintenance housekeeping methods, (2) streamlining your cleaning and laundry products, and (3) composting the leftovers.

Embrace Low Maintenance

Simplicity can be addicting. Once I fully understood the benefits of living in a small home and realized the time-saving potential, I scrutinized my daily activities for opportunities to simplify further. I looked for ways to automate my life as much as possible and limit chores.

Cleaning Methods

Today, straightening the house each morning takes five minutes; a deep cleaning takes two hours. With my Euro dance music in the background, I have turned my least favorite chore into a weekly workout; no need for housecleaners or gym subscriptions. Efficiency has even made time for generating more income from my business and spending more time with the kids. Here are some tips on making housecleaning painless:

- Adopt a minimal lifestyle. The less you have, the less needs to be picked up and organized.
- Assign a location and container for donations. Decluttering is an ongoing process; make it convenient to let go.
- Choose materials and surfaces that are easy to maintain. A leather couch, for example, lasts longer and is easier to maintain than an upholstered version; it can simply be wiped.
- Eliminate or condense flat surfaces as much as possible to reduce dusting.
- Keep the floor clear of furnishings as much as possible. Pick hanging fixtures over freestanding ones. Wall-mounted television, lights, or coatracks, for example, ease floor cleaning.
- Open a window or run the bathroom fan for at least twenty minutes

after you shower to reduce mold, and therefore reduce the amount of grout cleaning.

- Run the kitchen hood fan when cooking to reduce grease buildup, which is difficult to clean and collects dust.
- Install a shoe storage in your entryway and adopt a no-shoe policy inside to limit incoming dirt.
- Restrict your pet's access to certain rooms.
- Install an under-counter soap dispenser at the kitchen sink and fill it with liquid soap to conveniently wash dishes and hands.
- Install a gas insert in place of your fireplace: it not only burns cleaner and is more efficient (with programmable thermostats) than the wood-burning type, but it also does not require sweeping.
- Let plants cleanse the air for you. According to NASA research, the ten most effective plants are: bamboo palm (*Chamaedorea seifrizii*), Chinese evergreen (*Aglaonema modestum*), English ivy (*Hedera helix*), gerbera daisy (*Gerbera jamesonii*), Janet Craig (*Dracaena deremensis "Janet Craig"*), marginata (*Dracaena marginata*), mass cane/corn plant (*Dracaena massangeana*), Mother-in-Law's Tongue (*Sansevieria trifasciata "Laurentii"*), pot mum (*Chrysanthemum morifolium*), peace lily (*Spathiphyllum*), and Warneckii (*Dracaena deremensis "Warneckii"*).
- Store food in airtight containers such as mason jars to prevent pest problems.
- Clean the house from top to bottom. Dust first, clean floors last.
- Buy only dishwasher-safe goods for the kitchen to ease dishwashing.
- Run a full dishwasher instead of hand washing. It saves time and water. When your dishwasher needs replacement, scout the secondhand market for a drawer model. When one drawer is running, the other can be filled: it discourages sink pileups.

Laundering Methods

People tend to believe that a small wardrobe requires frequent laundering. Not true. Laundering once a week is possible if you are organized. The trick is taking measures to reduce washes and finding a detergent that meets your needs. Washing less will not only save you time, it will also extend the life of your garments and delay fading. In order to reduce laundering:

- Stick with minimal wardrobes to encourage wardrobe management, discourage multiple changes in one day, and reduce pileups.
- Pick fabrics that do not require special laundry care.
- When dry cleaning is necessary, choose a delivery service so you don't have to deal with pickups and drop-offs, and a provider that accepts or offers a reusable garment bag so you don't have to deal with the disposal of plastic sleeves. Recycle the metal hangers with your next pickup.
- Use your sense of smell and an occasional spot cleaning to wear something again before laundering.
- Assign laundry hampers to each bedroom (including one for visiting guests: they'll appreciate it).
- Encourage family members to treat stains on the spot. For example, a wine stain will easily come off in the wash if it is pretreated with salt immediately. Post a stain removal chart in your laundry room.
- Pick and stick with one brand and color of socks to eliminate sock matching. Scott loves the fact that he does not have to fumble around looking for matching socks at 6 a.m. before going to work.
- Opt for fabrics made from natural fibers to eliminate the surprise static shocks or the need for static guards in the dryer.
- Assign a napkin ring, a specific color, or a particular folding trick to each family member to differentiate dinner napkins and reduce their laundering.
- Assign a towel bar, a specific color, or a monogram to each family member to identify bath towels and reduce their washings.
- Delay sheet washing. In Europe, people air out their sheets between washes. The word *purifying* is even a synonym for *airing out* in French.
- Run only a full washer, and run all loads in one day to maximize physical efficiency.
- Fold laundry as soon as the dryer beeps, to reduce the need to iron.

Streamline Cleaning Products

Streamlining products offers many advantages. It allows you to address the toxicity of the products that you are accustomed to using, evaluate your true need for them, and adopt simple alternatives, all the while reclaiming significant storage space! But in the process, you will likely face a decluttering conundrum: What to do with the toxic products that you no longer want? Consider dropping them off at your local hazardous-waste facility (restrictions apply), giving them away (Freecycle or Craigslist, for example) to people who would purchase such products new anyway, or making an effort to finish them. Your time spent decluttering is, however, maximized if you make a decision on the spot and alter your habits immediately.

Here again are some questions worth considering when paring down housekeeping products:

- **Is it in working condition?** Can it be repaired? If your dustpan is cracked and cannot pick up floor sweepings efficiently, recycle it and purchase a metal one, which will last longer. Why waste time cleaning with a sponge that falls apart or a scourer that has become dull?
- **Do I use it regularly?** Products such as metal polishers are seldom used but take up valuable space under your sink all year round. Don't be afraid to let them go. Use my vinegar tips or google homemade alternatives when occasional products are needed.
- **Is it a duplicate?** The typical kitchen contains many different types of soap: dishwashing soap, hand soap, floor soap, pet shampoo, etc. But essentially, soap is soap! One natural type such as castile soap can do it all. No need for duplicates intended for specific uses.
- **Does it put my family's health in danger?** The Environmental Working Group advises to avoid products containing nonylphenol ethoxylates, 2-butoxyethanol, butoxydiglycol, ethylene or diethylene glycol mono-butyl ether, diethylene glycol monomethyl ether, or methoxydiglycol; to skip spray products that contain ethanolamines (MEA, DEA, and TEA) and "quats"; to beware of ADBAC, benzalkonium chloride, or ingredients with "-monium chloride" ... but who can remember such unpronounceable words? Simplify by segregating those with label warnings that include the words *poison, danger,* or *fatal* and bring them to your local hazardous-waste facility. Better yet, let them all go (along with your concerns) and trust and use only the vinegar alternatives and additional nontoxic alternatives mentioned below.
- **Do I keep it out of guilt?** Holding on to a product because of its high cost ("I paid a lot for this") or toxicity ("I feel bad throwing it away") does not justify keeping it. Its true utility, effectiveness, and impact on your health should be ruthlessly considered throughout the streamlining process.
- **Do I keep it because society tells me that I need one** ("everyone has one")? Maybe you own a laundry basket.... Could something else

achieve the same task? Maybe you could use your laundry hamper instead. If each closet is outfitted with a mobile hamper, it can not only collect and transport dirty clothes to the washing machine, it can also be used to sort and transport a pile of clean and folded laundry back to the specific closet.

- **Is it worth my precious time maintaining? Does it really save time?** For example, I personally found my vacuum cleaner to be counterproductive. By the time I'd lugged it out of the closet, untangled the cord, plugged it in, vacuumed, unplugged it, carried it up the stairs, and untangled the cord again—not to mention occasionally emptying the bag and repairing the belt—I could have swept my house twice. I eliminated it along with the floor robot, which needed tending more than it saved time. I have since enjoyed the time, energy, and money savings, not to mention the cleared closet space!
- **Could I use this space for something else?** If you iron only occasionally, you could protect a flat surface (the top of your dryer, for instance with a towel or ironing pad) and use it lieu of your bulky ironing board. Giving up your ironing board could open up wall space to keep your broom and mop organized and clipped to the wall.
- **Is it reusable?** Forget about paper towels, disposable wipes, and sponges. Consider reusable alternatives.

Reusable Cleaning Supplies

Implementing reusable alternatives is not only better for the environment, the money savings can really add up! I beat myself for not adopting them earlier.

- **Washable cloths:** I bought a stack of microfiber cloths when I first started greening my home. The microfiber's efficiency instantly eliminated my need for toxic cleaners, wipes, sponges, and paper towels. They made my transition to green cleaning effortless. That said, they are synthetic: cut-up T-shirts would make a better eco-friendly alternative in terms of their (eventual) disposal (cotton being biodegradable and widely recyclable).
- **Mop pads:** I find the apparatus used for disposable wipes easier to use that the traditional "mop and bucket" system, and it saves a great deal of water.

You can fit the mop head with a washable cloth or purchase microfiber pads, but other nonsynthetic alternatives include felt squares and crocheted cotton pads. Etsy.com, a handcrafting website, offers a great selection.

- **Broom:** Giving up our vacuum has made the broom our go-to tool for most floor and cobweb jobs. Natural materials for brooms include silk, corn, and coco fiber, and boar and horse hair. Ours is made of silk, but what I appreciate most about its design is the rounded edges of the head, which facilitate sweeping corners.
- **Heavy-duty metal scourer:** The stainless-steel mesh type lasts for years (maybe a lifetime) and has worked wonders in my house. We use it to remove sticker residue from glass and tough baked-on grime from stainless-steel surfaces. (Use in the direction of the grain.)
- **Scrub brush:** For washing dishes or scrubbing dried batter off the counter, a wooden brush made of natural fiber makes a good alternative to sponges or harsh scouring pads, and lasts longer. Some can even be fitted onto a reusable handle to keep your hands off the grime. You might also consider growing a loofah (see instructions on page 155) or knitting a scrubby from salvaged sisal twine. Unlike the synthetic scouring pads, all three options are 100 percent natural and compostable.
- **Toothbrush:** We find that an old toothbrush is perfect for cleaning hard-to-reach places such as grout and refrigerator joints. Since we purchase compostable toothbrushes, we compost them when the bristles are no longer effective.

Waste-Free and Nontoxic Product Alternatives

Downsizing has simplified our cleaning routine, but more important, it has helped to wean us off toxic chemicals commonly found in cleaning products. We no longer have to puzzle over the ingredient lists of our household cleansers to try to decode their potential impact on our health. But finding the right laundry soap for our household was honestly not easy and actually rather frustrating. Week after week, load after load, testing half a dozen eco-friendly detergents, including that of clay beads or soap nuts (which I considered growing in my backyard) brought disappointment to hopeful inspections, as grayed whites and grease-spotted darks poured out of my washing machine. An experiment sans detergent even proved to produce comparable results. Further dampening my environmental dedication, one that I discovered to remove stains happened to be packaged in a nonre-cyclable cardboard. For a while I wondered if living green meant learning to accept stains, until I found a system that worked for us.

Finding a laundry detergent that removes your household's stains and simultaneously satisfies your packaging restrictions is an individual affair, one that each household must define for itself. A detergent that works for one household might not work for another. I believe that eco-laundering with stain-free results depends on a few parameters: your household's washing machine (front load versus top load), water composition (hard versus soft), washing cycle temperature (hot versus cold), staining patterns (grease versus tomato, for example), garment material (synthetics versus natural fibers), and color (darks versus whites). And I found the same to be true with dishwasher detergents: results will vary with water softness/hardness and dishwasher brands.

After experimenting with brands and available bulk, here are the cleaning and laundering product alternatives that we have come to adopt:

Liquid soap

Castile soap is wonderful, and apart from dishwasher and laundry detergents, it can satisfy all your soap needs in the house! I use it to clean my dining chairs, floors, hands, dishes, and even the dog. A bar of it works great, but it simplifies my life dispensing liquid soap from my sink dispenser onto dirty dishes and hands. Liquid castile soap is quite expensive, so I make my own. I confess that this recipe does not cut grease as well as the Dr. Bronner's brand, but it works well enough for my needs. Scott reaches for the solid bar when he needs to wash bike grease off his hands.

LIQUID SOAP

DIRECTIONS

In a stockpot or bucket, combine 1½ cup grated soap with one gallon warm tap water, stir, and let sit overnight. Blend using an immersion blender and transfer into a gallon jar. Use in your sink dispenser for easy access.

Dishwasher detergent and laundry detergent

The majority of green detergents are either sold in liquid form in a plastic container or in powder form in a cardboard box lined with plastic. Inspect the box carefully before buying. I prefer supporting the brands sold in bulk when I can find them (they are not a common bulk item). Otherwise, I keep bulk ingredients on hand to make my own.

DISHWASHER DETERGENT

DIRECTIONS

In an airtight container, mix 4 cups washing soda (you can also use baking soda, though it's not as efficient), 1 cup citric acid (available in bulk at brewing-supply stores), and 1 cup sea salt. For best results, add vinegar to the rinse dispenser.

LAUNDRY DETERGENT

DIRECTIONS

In a tub, mix ½ cup washing soda (also known as soda ash or carbonate sodium), ½ cup grated unpackaged blue soap (using blue substitutes for the optical brighteners used in commercial detergents), and 3 quarts warm water. For best results, add vinegar to the softener dispenser.

Scrubbing Powder

We purchase baking soda in bulk and use it for medium scrubbing jobs, when our metal scourer is too tough and the bristles of our wooden brush too weak for the job (scuff marks for example).

DIRECTIONS

Transfer baking soda into a spice shaker. Spray water on the area to clean. Sprinkle the powder and rub the spot with a cloth.

Note: Alternatively, you can dilute the powder in a little water to make a paste and rub the area with a cloth.

Ironing starch

I seldom iron. The time and electricity usage is hardly ever worth it to me. We have applied the tips mentioned earlier to keep our clothes as wrinkle free as possible and reduce our need for it. However, we do use a dry cleaner to launder and give Scott's dress shirts a crisp finish for professional meetings. The company uses a nontoxic cleaning system and provides a reusable sleeve (which conveniently turns into a laundry hamper for transport). But when for some reason I do need to iron his shirts, I use a homemade ironing starch.

IRONING STARCH

DIRECTIONS

Combine 1 pint water and 1 tablespoon cornstarch in a spray bottle. Shake before using.

Housekeeping Simplified

That's all we keep around the house to clean and launder! When I run into a tough stain, I use lemon, salt, and the sun on unidentifiable stains; cornstarch or a paste of dishwasher detergent on grease stains; vinegar on mustard, pen, pencil, or crayon stains; cooking oil on tar stains; and hot water poured from a foot high onto berry stains (they disappear like magic).

The products that I have eliminated under the kitchen sink have made room for storing my colander conveniently, where I need it most.

Compost Your Leftovers

When we clean and launder, we are left with waste remnants (sweepings and dryer lint, for example). The compost is a great way to return those trivial resources back to the environment. Depending on the type of composter at your disposal, consider composting the following discards:

- Ashes from the fireplace* (wood ashes only)
- Contents of your shower drain
- Dead flies
- Dead flowers (see "The Magic of Vinegar," page 137, to make them last longer)
- Dead houseplants and their soil and clippings
- Dryer lint* (see pages 205 and 245 for fun ways to reuse it instead)
- Dust bunnies
- Feathers from pillows
- Floor sweepings
- Fur from the dog or cat brush
- Leftover dog chews (rawhide and unraveled cotton ropes)
- Loofah*
- Natural cleaning brush* (e.g., wood and silk or boar hair)
- Natural potpourri*
- Peels of the citruses used for cleaning or adding scent to your vinegar cleaner (page 137)
- Pet feces along with the layers of paper used to pick them up (purchase a separate composter or use the instructions on page 159 to make one)
- Sea sponges*
- Vacuum cleaner bag* or the contents of a bagless vacuum cleaner

UPKEEP

I've found staying on top of maintenance crucial to extending the useful life of our investments and avoiding consequent waste associated with repair and pest control products. But even the most dedicated conservation and

---

* Alternatives to discarding/composting these materials are covered throughout the book.

waste-reduction efforts will inevitably result in some trash. The quart-size jar of landfill waste that my family generates each year is mostly filled with bits of old electrical wiring, old bits of caulk, and fragments of rags used to clean up new applications of caulk, flakes of dried-up paint, and used paint rollers to cover their patches, etc. These are basically items that are necessary to keep our house safe from fire, water damage, or sheer degradation, which would otherwise lead to bigger problems and more waste. A Zero Waste home should strive to reduce the incidence of repairs by being proactive (embracing low-maintenance methods) and adopting waste-free alternatives to repair products.

Embrace Low Maintenance

Occasionally renting our house has been really helpful in keeping home and garden shipshape. Staying on top of repairs is facilitated if you implement these proactive methods:

- **Adopt a minimal lifestyle.** The less you have, the less needs repair, and the easier it is to stay on top of repairs.
- **Buy quality.** The great majority of the products we buy are no longer made to last. Discriminate against ephemeral crap. Spending more for quality pays off over time in repair or replacement costs. For example, if you select metal and wooden tools, they cost more at first but they'll last longer, look better, and can be repaired more easily.
- **Catch the breaks as soon as possible,** and repair before it's too late.
- **Save yourself the guesswork.** Make a rule to contact the manufacturer when something breaks. They can advise how to proceed with the repair, and often they'll send you the repair piece free of charge.
- **Keep your house exterior under control to avoid pest problems.** Remove wood scraps to avoid termites, and keep trees and vines off your house to avoid rodents.

Adopt Waste-Free Alternatives

Although home repair products and their packaging are hard to eliminate, some waste-free alternatives do exist.

Salvage yards, Freecycle.org, and Craigslist.org are great resources for locating used and leftover materials for small repairs and landscaping jobs, such as lumber, tiles, paint, pipes, and fencing. Local contractors might also be willing to donate discards such as an old window, siding, or bricks. You can obtain paint for small jobs from paint stores that sell mismatched cans from returns and color tests. Alternatively, some municipalities mix paint received through hazardous-waste collection programs and make it available to residents. Check with your local facility.

Some local hardware stores sell nails, screws, scrap wood, and specialty hardware (such as felt pads, turnbuckles, hooks, etc.) by the unit or weight (i.e., package free). Bulk availability varies greatly from store to store, but once you keep an eye out for it, you will find it in unexpected places (paint stores, country drugstores, for example). Make a mental note of their location for future purchases—and remember to bring a bulk cloth bag when buying small loose items.

Great examples of collaborative consumption, tool libraries are popping up across the country. They are also a great place to "store" and maximize the use of *your* equipment. They provide community members with access to a wide variety of tools. They loan hand and power tools for home repair, landscaping, and automotive work, free of charge. The tool library is structured on the book library model and often includes similar services such as limits, renewals, holds, waiting lists, and overdue fines. Check your city's availability. Otherwise, simply knock on your neighbor's door to borrow that tool!

GARDENING

While hiking one day, it struck me that I could not name any of the plants I was seeing. I wanted more from my hikes; I wanted to know all about the vegetation that surrounded me. So I signed up for an evening college botany class for six months to learn about our local flora with a focus on edibles. After completing my class and spending hours researching, I created an elaborate list of edible natives and made a plan to landscape our yard with them. Natives require less watering and, once established, no watering at all. They seemed to match our landscaping requirements perfectly. We went to a local native nursery, bought all available plants (about seven types, thirty containers), and planted them according to their instructions—but in the space of two months, they all died or got eaten by deer. What a waste of money, effort, and plastic containers!

We consequently decided to hire a professional to create a deer- and failure-proof landscape that was drought tolerant and low maintenance for our backs and schedules. Her expertise, although costly at first, has saved us time and money in the long run. The plants that Scott and I put in the ground as per her instructions have survived the deer and have met our land's restrictions and low-upkeep needs. We now keep our edibles within the confines of our balcony, and I keep my botanical knowledge strictly for hikes.

While planning a low-maintenance landscape is a question of personal choice (some of you might enjoy spending time in the yard), adopting waste-free alternatives, on the other hand, should be taken into consideration.

Embrace Low Maintenance

Scott no longer wears diving booties to maintain our yard. And you don't have to either if gardening is not something that you truly enjoy. Here are tips on how to keep your yard easy to care for:

- Select plants that do not require frequent trimming.
- Pick plants adapted to the region that do not require frequent watering. For example, you can replace your lawn with short native grasses. The look is amazing and does not need mowing!
- If you do keep your lawn, do not pick up the grass clippings. "Grass-cycling" returns nutrients to the soil. Mow your lawn when dry to avoid clumping.
- Spread mulch or fallen tree leaves once a year to keep weeds down.
- Spray straight vinegar onto emerging weeds. Don't wait for them to get out of control; keep a spray handy.
- Spray a solution of ¼ cup liquid soap to 1 gallon water at the first sign of fungus or pests, such as spider mites, to avoid bigger problems. You can also buy ladybugs to get rid of aphids.

Adopt Waste-Free Alternatives

In trying to tend to our land properly we often end up taking actions that have harmful repercussions. Our garden might smell pretty, but the resulting methane of the nearby landfill doesn't. How did we come to package compost or any type of dirt in plastic shrink-wrap? It seems to go against the simple rules of nature conservation. Wasteful gardening does not make sense and is unnecessary. Consider these alternatives:

- Locate bulk seeds. They are hard to find in nurseries. The bulk aisle of the grocery store is your best bet. Don't forget to bring your own bag.
- Start your seeds in an egg carton, thus reducing your plastic pot use and trips to return them.
- If you do purchase a plastic container from the nursery, ask if they'll take the container back for reuse. Many do.
- Give away plants that you no longer want or extra landscaping parts that you do not need such as rocks, fencing, irrigation piping, etc. Post them for free on Craigslist; they get picked up quickly, and it's a great way to get those nursery pots reused.
- Get your dirt, rocks, compost, etc., simply delivered to your home, or purchase them in reusable sand bags. We go to a garden center that has piles of mulch, dirt, rocks—we simply fill and get charged by the bag.
- Get your borders from the scrap pile of the lumber yard, clay pots from a salvage yard, and irrigation parts from farming- or plumbing-supply stores (where they are sold loose).
- If you compost at home, you can of course use it as a soil amendment. But some discards can be deposited straight at the base of the plant. Pee has proven to be the best amendment to our citruses, coffee grounds are good for acid-loving plants such as tomatoes, and the water and crushed shells of your hard-boiled eggs are a great source of lime. Our worm composter also provides a "worm tea" that conveniently comes out of a spigot. I dilute it with four parts water and use it to nourish my plant wall.
- Have too much harvest? Donate it to a soup kitchen, make it available to neighbors, post it on Craigslist, jam it, or freeze it.
- Save the seeds from your harvest for next year's planting.

- Keep a minimal tool selection. Select the best, and donate the rest to a garden club, a nursing home, or better yet, a tool co-op.

GROW YOUR OWN SCRUBBER

Loofah, a coarse, fibrous material, more commonly used in bathrooms or spas, can be grown in your own backyard! Also spelled luffa or lufah, the loofah is an annual vegetable, a South American native vine of the Cucurbitaceae family, and a "zucchini on steroids" look-alike. The tropical species thrives in warm weather but will tolerate cold climates if started indoors and protected from frost. When risk of frost has subsided, it can then be transplanted in a sunny location, preferably with a southern-facing exposure. A true climber, the plant will grow up to thirty feet on a trellis, fence, or the ground.

Immature fruit can be eaten, but waiting for the sponge is rewarding.

DIRECTIONS

1. Pick the vegetable when overripe and fully matured to a brown/yellow color. It will feel light in weight and its skin dry.
2. Crush and remove the skin.
3. Shake the seeds out.
4. Put the seeds aside for next year's seedling.
5. Soak the loofah or hose it off with a pressure spray to clean it.
6. Let dry on a rack in the sun.
7. Cut into desired shapes (a scouring pad, for example)

5 *RS* CHECKLIST: 5 TIPS FOR HOUSEKEEPING AND HOME MAINTENANCE

Refuse: Reject single-use and antibacterial cleaning products.
Reduce: Use vinegar and baking soda to clean.
Reuse: Adopt reusable cleaning rags, and make repairs with a borrowed tool.
Recycle: Purchase white vinegar in glass bottles for their recyclability.
Rot: Compost your dust bunnies!

ONE STEP FURTHER

Most of the ideas we covered in this chapter addressed the visible and tangible aspects of waste, but the following tips on energy and water savings will complete (and further reward) your sustainability efforts.

Energy

- Line-dry your laundry when possible.
- Wash and dry all of your loads in one day. The warmth of the dryer transfers from one load to the next.
- Clean your refrigerator filters twice a year to maximize its efficiency.
- Launder in cold water as much as possible.
- Use a rake instead of a leaf blower.
- When an electric bulb goes out, replace it with an LED.
- When you need to buy new batteries, pick rechargeable ones.

Water

- Drip irrigation uses 50 percent less water than sprinklers, and mulch retains moisture.
- Install a water-wise irrigation system, such as one with a precipitation gauge that adjusts watering automatically.
- Install a rainwater catchment.
- Check with your local authorities and, if possible, install a gray water system to recycle the water from your washing machine for landscape irrigation (for horticultural purposes only).
- Put a bucket in your shower to collect the cold water while your shower heats: use it to water a different part of the yard each day.

ZERO WASTE DOG

Zero Waste is a family affair. In our home, everyone is on board, and that includes our dog. Since we don't have a cat, I can't comment on feline issues specifically, but I'm sure you'll find that some of the tips below apply to cats or whatever other furry friends you have in your home.

Zizou joined our family about five years ago. We wanted a dog that would be small enough to not only fit in our small house but also accompany us everywhere we go, whether it is by plane, car, bike, or foot—we also chose his coat color to match the floor so that his shedding hair would not show.

We figured a Chihuahua would give us just as much love as a big dog. Zizou has been the answer to all our pet needs, and despite a rat's taste for street trash ("Rat Boy" is his nickname), he has more than exceeded our expectations of the breed.

When I told my younger son I was writing about Zero Waste dog and asked him what made Zizou Zero Waste, he replied: "Easy, he does not bring anything home."

While it is true that he does not bring any junk into the house, he does bring in loads of affection. Affection that we reciprocate. After all, what a dog needs most is love . . . and there is nothing more Zero Waste than love, is there?

Zizou does not need much, and in a society where, despite the recession, sales of pet products and services rose 5 percent in 2009 to reach $53 billion (sales are projected to reach $72 billion by 2014), we like to keep things simple, minimal, and Zero Waste for him, too:

- **Bed:** Our dog is spoiled and is allowed on the furniture, so he does not need a regular dog bed. He sleeps by the gas-insert fireplace in the winter, in a cozy chair, or on the warm wood deck in the summer, and on the kids' beds at night.
- **Toys:** He plays with a found tennis ball (good for running/exercising) and a rope chew (good for cleaning teeth). Dogs have faves. Pick a couple, and donate the rest to a shelter (they also accept old towels and

sheets, and sometimes empty prescription bottles). My mother-in-law makes a chew toy out of old socks tied together for her dog.

- **Grooming:** Once a month, we wash him with the Liquid Soap (see page 147) and clip his nails (compost).
- **Bowls:** We use the same canning jars that we use throughout the house, as food and water bowls. When we need to pack up and leave for a trip, I can just clip the jars shut and pack them up. I struggled to keep the floor dry around his drinking water using conventional dog bowls and a fountain, when all along I had the solution a few feet away. When he drinks from those jars, for some reason, he does not spill at all!
- **Food:** He licks our plates clean every night before we load them into the dishwasher, and we occasionally feed him food scraps. To supplement, we buy kibble in bulk, but the couple of times that I failed to find it (because the store was out) and bought a bag, I washed it and used it for thrift shop donations. (Since we refuse plastic and paper bags, we are always looking for alternate containers to carry donations.)
- **Treats:** We purchase treats from the bulk section of the local pet store.
- **Wellness:** If needed, we add garlic powder to his food for flea control—the garlic breath dissipates after a few minutes—and a capful of cider vinegar to his water to stop tearstains.
- **Walks:** On walks, we pick up his waste in paper from the recycling can. For a big dog, I would use a few sheets: for Zizou, a receipt will do.

According to my local water-treatment plant, flushing dog feces down the toilet is acceptable, but since flushing requires water, composting them provides a more eco-friendly alternative.

My Two Cents on Cat Waste

A parasite called *Toxoplasma gondii,* sometimes found in cat feces, has been linked to endangering sea otters. When flushed down the toilet, it survives the water-treatment process and is consumed by sea otters as it sinks to the bottom of the ocean. It is therefore not recommended to flush cat feces down the toilet!

BUILD A DOG WASTE COMPOSTER (NOT FOR CAT FECES)

DIRECTIONS

1. Find an old trash can with a lid. (You can stack two five-gallon paint buckets alternatively.)
2. Drill ⅜-inch holes all over the lower two-thirds of the sides of the container.
3. Using a utility knife or jigsaw, cut the bottom of the container.
4. Pick a sunny spot away from your foundation, vegetable garden, or compost.
5. Dig a hole deep enough for the container to fit in and its rim to come level with the surface of the surrounding soil (higher if you get snow in the winter).
6. Place the can into the hole.
7. Lay some rocks or gravel at the bottom of the can, then some plant clippings.
8. Cover with the lid.

APPLICATION

Dispose of dog waste, top with some leaves, plant clippings, sawdust, or shredded paper, and close the lid. Over time the feces will decompose. If the can fills up, you will have the choice to either: (1) pull up the can, cover the feces with dirt, and dig another location for your compost; or (2) let the feces decompose fully into a soil amendment to use on ornamentals (*not food seedlings or crops*), in which case a second composter is needed to receive new droppings.

Workspace and Junk Mail

On occasion, I am invited to give lectures about our lifestyle to universities. Questions usually follow the presentation. One of them particularly struck me:

"How do you expect students to do what you do? Unlike you, we're very busy," said one dubious student.

People indeed tend to associate the Zero Waste lifestyle with homesteaders and homemakers, and the purpose of my speaking engagement was to shatter these preconceptions, but the undergrad had arrived late to the session. Depictions of my home filled with jars and handmade products had confirmed this observer's assumptions: I was a housewife with too much time on my hands. "I am busy, too," I replied, flustered by the comment.

On my way home, I reflected on the true meaning of *busyness*. I remembered an episode of *Seinfeld* where George bluffed working hard. He used clever tricks such as acting stressed, sighing, and exposing a disorderly tabletop to give his boss the impression that he was deeply involved in his job. Busyness could be faked. It seems a fairer measure to evaluate our occupational contributions based on productivity level rather than how cluttered our desks are or how many minutes we have to spare. Today, we want people to know about (and sometimes pity) our crammed schedules to show that we are both important and fully engaged in life. Our culture associates being busy with being happy, fulfilled, popular, and hardworking, but being busy is not the same thing as being efficient.

Not so long ago, procrastination was my biggest enemy, but putting the effort into simplifying my life has actually made procrastination a thing of the past and maximized my efficiency. It certainly took active work to evaluate and control my productivity constraints. The first step was to streamline my office; the second, to eliminate digital clutter.

WORKSPACE

In our previous home, Scott and I worked from separate rooms. I turned the granny quarters (a bedroom, bath, and fully equipped kitchen) into an artist studio, and my husband repurposed a bedroom into an office that was so large, he added useless furniture (such as a lounge chair) to fill the voids. Located at opposite ends of the house, both workspaces were outfitted with a television, phone, printer, office supplies, refuse can, and task lighting. I could close his door when I could no longer stand the sight of his pile-scattered floor, and he could close mine to ignore the bulky picture frames that I had amassed over the years. When we moved to a smaller home we were forced to combine our workspaces. It took years of progressive stream-lining to realize that office sharing makes practical, ecological, and financial sense. Through the process, we eliminated duplicates and merged the equipment and office supplies inventories, leading to reduced overall heating and lighting costs and even allowing us to communicate sans intercom!

On a larger scale, the emerging trend of coworking is a great alternative. It abides by the same ecological principles of a shared home office but offers a social, collaborative, and supportive environment to the independent professional or small business. It also reinforces the separation between work and home. The simple act of getting dressed (and out of pj's) can have a positive effect on productivity! DesksNear.Me, and WorkSnug are websites that point to nearby locations.

In either case, home office sharing or coworking supports a flexible work style and justifies letting go of unnecessary clutter. I said farewell to all my picture frames, among other things. . . .

Simplicity

Albert Einstein once said, "If a cluttered desk is a sign of a cluttered mind, of what, then, is an empty desk a sign?" For me an empty desk is not a sign of an empty mind. A clear desk is a sign of a sharply focused intellect. Bare working surfaces—and I include my inbox and computer's desktop in this definition—mean that I am all caught up with trivial, miscellaneous tasks.

Work should be evaluated based on productivity. A workspace should maximize it.

Maximize efficiency by evaluating the contents of your office space. Here are some questions worth considering when decluttering:

- **Is it in working condition?** Donate broken electronics through an e-waste drive. Test your writing instruments; discard those that do not work anymore. If your favorite pen is one of them, contact the manufacturer about refills or repairs.

- **Do I use it regularly?** We often hold on to professional books for the occasional reference, but they take up valuable space and collect dust. Donate them to your local library, where you can reference them as needed and where they benefit the community. You can also sell them on Amazon. From experience, I can attest that your old schoolbooks can generate some surprise income!
- **Is it a duplicate?** How many pens, pencils, and highlighters does one really need? Probably one of each. Better to have one good pen than three dozen cheapies. Through my simplifying business, I have seen homes filled with dozens of free business and hotel pens. Help stop the free pen madness: refuse and stop taking them! Donate supply duplicates (folders, pencils, etc.) to the local public school or a small thrift store, where they are sought after at the beginning of the school year.
- **Does it put my family's health in danger?** Home laser printers emit particles that have been linked to respiratory problems, asthma, and some cancers and can create ozone and nitrogen oxides, which can cause headaches, nausea, and dermatitis. Consider relocating yours. When evaluating art materials, look for an AP seal, which means that ACMI (Art & Creative Materials Institute) has rated the product nontoxic. Dispose of toxic ones through your local hazardous-waste facility. For example, consider discarding rubber cement and superglue, which respectively contain heptane (or hexane) and cyanoacrylate, both of which give off toxic vapors. Refer to the homemade glue recipe at the end of this chapter.
- **Do I keep it out of guilt?** Corporate gifts and company logo-wear clutter our offices out of guilt over not being a team player. Will you really ever wear your company's "2010 Sales Conference" T-shirt again? Most likely not.
- **Do I keep it because society tells me that I need one ("everyone has one")?** Most offices are outfitted with whiteboards and use highlighters. **Could something else achieve the same task?** Dry-erase markers work as well on mirrors as they do on whiteboards; a mirror also has the added bonus of reflecting light and gives the illusion of a larger space. Colored pencils can easily replace highlighters and have the added bonus of being erasable!

- **Is it worth my precious time dusting and cleaning?** It's not the physical award, plaque, or diploma that matters; it's the actual achievement. Take a picture; recycle its material; save yourself some dusting.
- **Could I use this space for something else?** Many of the homes that I consult engage in a common practice: saving electronics packaging. Keeping these boxes does not add to the long-term value of their original content, but they take up a lot of space and collect dust over the years. Recycle them; reclaim their space. They are not worth storing "just in case."
- **Is it reusable?** Staples are now considered essentials of home offices, yet they are disposable. Donate your stapler and choose one of the reusable and more sustainable alternatives to paper fastening mentioned below. You probably already have some paper clips around.

Reusability

If you don't allow disposables in your home office, you will naturally learn to either do without or adopt a reusable alternative. Disposables need to be replenished. By eliminating them you simplify not only your inventory but your shopping, too.

Writing Utensils

Most people buy office supplies in bulk to save money, but while economy-size bundles save packaging waste, they encourage wastefulness and disposability. In addition, the sales and marketing tactics of the big-box office-supplies stores leverage this bundled packaging for the most trivial office supplies in order to stimulate consumption. You can't buy just one pencil eraser top; you are forced to buy a bagful. To purchase singles visit your local stationery store: you can often buy just what you need, unpackaged. In the long run, it saves money.

- **Pen:** Today, the most reusable pen is a fountain model fitted with a piston or converter and refilled with bottled ink. The most sustainable pen is the one that already exists. Search eBay for secondhand pieces.

Another alternative is to choose a stainless-steel refillable ballpoint pen; however, these cartridges come in packaging and end up as waste.

- **Pencil:** The most durable and reusable pencil alternative is that of a refillable mechanical pencil in stainless steel, but the leads are sold in plastic cartridges. Until manufacturers sell leads in a recycled cardboard box, newspaper pencils (versus wood) are the most Zero Waste alternative. Make sure to pick an eraser-free model (purchase a natural rubber eraser separately) so you can compost it when it is too small to write with.
- **Whiteboard markers:** Whiteboards (or mirrors) are a reusable alternative to large paper pads for collaborative brainstorming. Use refillable and nontoxic markers. AusPen offers an array of colors.
- **Highlighters:** Not only can their felted tips lose their integrity and dry out, when highlighters no longer work, they are designed for the landfill. Colored pencils can serve the same purpose and last longer. As mentioned earlier, they also have the advantage of being erasable and their leftovers and shavings compostable. Again, an eraser-free newspaper model is today's most Zero Waste alternative.

Shipping

Shipping inevitably generates carbon emissions and produces packing waste. To lower the former, use ground mail; to lower the latter, request recyclable material from your shippers. Reject bubble wrapping, Styrofoam, and plastic bags, and propose alternatives such as paper or cloth. Mail leads to a host of unsolicited products, and even the most proactive efforts will result in unwanted plastics, sometimes in the form of bubble mailers, sometimes in the form of plastic tape.

Therefore, when you mail, make sure to:

- **Reuse packing material.** Dedicate a space for some of the boxes and envelopes that you receive and reuse them instead of using new ones. If you must buy new, choose newspaper-padded envelopes in lieu of bubble mailers. Shredded paper is also a wonderful alternative to bubble wrap.
- **Use paper tape** (alternatively string) to fasten your parcels. I confess that it was a hard switch for me. There was something comforting about

protecting my shipping addresses behind waterproof plastic tape, but I have not used plastic tape for years, and all my packages have arrived to their destinations.

- Hand-write destination and return addresses directly on the mailing package. As a default, use a return address stamp instead of stickers; the latter leaves you with a nonrecyclable backing sheet destined for landfill; stamps last longer. We will cancel the pesky charity-themed address labels in the Junk Mail section.

- If you must send an invitation or a greeting card by mail, choose a postcard (see the "Holidays and Gifts" chapter). It not only saves posting fees, it also is smaller than a regular card and does not require an envelope. For mailing normal-sized one-ounce letters within the United States, purchase a roll of Forever stamps: they don't need additional postage when postal rates increase (in other words, they do not "expire').

Supplies

- **Fasteners:** Staples are disposable and therefore a waste of resources. Paper clips serve the same purpose but are reusable. Choose paper clips instead of staples, or fasten your papers with a staple-free stapler. I choose the former for their recyclability and availability. They seem to enter homes on their own from the kids' school. They can be purchased in bulk by weight at select stationery stores (remember to bring a cloth bag!), but your need for them should diminish as you adopt the paperless alternatives mentioned below. To secure a couple of sheets together, I also use this folding trick: (1) line up the pages, (2) fold their corner back, (3) tear (or cut) a couple of notches in the middle of the fold, and (4) fold the resulting small flap forward.

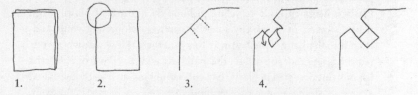

1.　　　　2.　　　　3.　　　　4.

- **Ink cartridges:** Making a real effort to adopt paperless alternatives can eliminate the need for a printer altogether. Otherwise, printing when absolutely necessary and in "draft" mode will extend the life of your cartridges. You can then get them refilled at stores like Walgreens and Cartridge World.

- **Media storage and sharing:** CD-Rs are disposable, and although CD-RWs are rewritable and therefore reusable, memory sticks and external drives are more efficient and last longer. However, cloud storage does not require supplemental hardware, automatically syncs files, provides access to them from anywhere (including any computer or your phone), and facilitates sharing. Consider using such free services as GoogleDrive or Dropbox.

Collection

In our old life with separate offices, Scott and I both had trash cans, none dedicated to recycling. Paper, food, pictures, plastic bags, packaging, all commingled in the same basket and shared a ride to the landfill. In those days we associated recycling only with food packaging. Today, we not only have turned our shared waste bin into a recycling one, we also have designated a drawer to collect such items as Tyvek envelopes (you know, those envelopes that look and feel like paper but cannot be torn) that come unsolicited in the mail for reuse. As mentioned before, it is best to refuse these as much as possible before considering recycling.

Recycling

- **Paper and cardboard:** The biggest recycling receptacle in an office will most likely collect paper, but if you follow my junk mail reduction and paperless tips below, you can achieve zero paper waste!
- **Plastics:** Most curbside recycling pickups do not accept plastic bags, plastic sleeves, or Tyvek envelopes. Proactively requesting your senders not to mail any is the best way to avoid them. However, when your request is ignored, you can set the materials aside for reuse or check the list of items accepted in plastic bag collection bins such as those offered at grocery stores, as many accept more than grocery bags. Alternatively, you can send Tyvek envelopes for recycling (see "Resources," page 271). Such parcel stuffers as bubble wrap (no tape attached), packing pea-

nuts, or Styrofoam (entire pads only) are accepted at participating UPS stores for reuse. Alternatively, you can call the Plastic Loose Fill Council's Peanut Hotline (1-800-828-2214) for the names of local businesses that also accept them for reuse.

- **Electronics:** Spend money on upgrading your system instead of buying a new one. Donate computers, printers, or monitors (any brand) to a nonprofit or participating Goodwill location for refurbishing (some charities repair them and give them to schools and nonprofit organizations). For unrepairable cell phones and miscellaneous electronics, locate a nearby e-waste recycling facility or participate in a local e-waste recycling drive, or make a profit by selling them on eBay for parts. Best Buy collects remote controllers, wires, cords, cables, ink and toner cartridges, rechargeable batteries, plastic bags, gift cards, CDs and DVDs (including their cases), depending on store locations.

Compost

Little compost will be created in the office, but depending on the type of composter at your disposal, consider composting the following items:

- Paper tape such as water-activated tape
- Parcel twine (untreated cotton, sisal, or jute)
- Pencil shavings (contrary to popular belief and misuse of the term, pencils do not contain lead, but graphite, which does not pose a threat to your compost)
- Shredded paper*, which is a nightmare for recyclers to separate if you have a mixed recycling can, but it can be a carbon source to your compost pile!
- Leftover homemade glue (recipe below)
- Leftover papermaking pulp (recipe below)
- Leftover pencils (newspaper and unpainted wood bits only)

---

* Please refer to "Shipping," page 166, for an alternative to discarding/composting this material.

Landfill

Ditch the trash can. Use it as a receptacle for your Goodwill donations. A Zero Waste office should be mainly about paper management, possibly elimination.

DIGITAL DETOX

Today, true alone time has become a rarity; as a result, our ability to concentrate and be productive suffers.

We're connected 24/7 by landlines, cell phones, voice mail, email, texting, instant messaging, and social media. When used indiscriminately, our smartphones and tablets take our interactions to the meat counter, to the post office line, and on the bus. At home, we are connected at the dinner table, in the bathroom, and in bed. We like to think that our time is fully utilized when we multitask; we try to be two places at once, in both the physical and digital worlds. On a car ride, movies, tweets, and electronic games have replaced the simple pleasure of watching the countryside go by.

There is such a thing as being too connected. Overusing digital devices is not only environmentally draining (requiring the latest electronics and massive server farms running nonstop to keep trivial pieces of information available), it can also be detrimental on a human level. It distracts us from living in the moment, from enjoying real life; it discourages person-to-person contact and face-to-face connections; it can expose our every move and steal our privacy. Notably, nonstop entertainment robs us of alone time, crucial for independent thinking, appreciation, and gratitude—and maybe even happiness.

While social media can be a useful business marketing tool, I found that on a personal level it made me feel unfulfilled and discouraged with my life. Sometimes I felt as if I were involved in an unspoken contest I was destined to lose. My "friends" were more popular than I could ever be, with more tweets, more achievements, and more expertise. Social media made me revisit the worst insecurities of my high school days that I thought I had buried twenty years ago.

When we took steps to simplify our lifestyle, we not only evaluated belongings and screen times, we also evaluated friendships. We identified and focused on those that brought positivity, happiness, and strength to our life and allowed the others to fade away. This streamlining exercise made us appreciate the quality of the true friends we had. What was the point of spending precious time tending digital acquaintances to the detriment of our real-world ones? I realized that life was too short to fret about unsatisfying, meaningless online relationships. Reinforcing the bonds that we cherish and living in the moment with the people we love have since become family priorities. I no longer feel pressured to belong to social networks; those that I really care about know how to get in touch with me.

Social media, and more generally the web, are the bane of a procrastinator's existence. But it's not hard to identify and do away with digital time wasters. Deleting my personal Facebook account was the first step to simplifying my digital life and increasing my productivity. Here is the complete list of steps that I have taken and you might consider:

- **Delete personal social media accounts;** I kept business ones that provide specific benefits. I also limit postings to the essential, and synchronize accounts for maximum automation.
- **Keep a list of web-related tasks** and block Internet time for them, to avoid sidetracking and aimless surfing.
- **Turn off my cell phone** when I work and use Google Voice to send voice mail transcripts to my email inbox.
- **Set times to check emails** thrice per day (instead of all day or every time they come in), concisely reply only to those that require a response. I always strive for an empty inbox and use it as a to-do list: Once an item has been acted upon, I file or delete it.
- **Keep my computer desktop clear,** and streamline personal folders and my favorites on a regular basis.
- **Work in an inspiring setting** and sometimes escape Internet access. My favorite place to work is probably my deck, where procrastination is limited to observing nature: squirrels leaping about in the oaks or a hummingbird buzzing around our Meyer lemon buds. But when I approach a writing deadline and am striving for maximum productivity, I have found that I work best in cafés or parks, where my landline does not ring and Wi-Fi is not set.

When used in moderation, electronic devices can save time and increase knowledge and efficiency, while mobile ones enable us to work in fabulous settings. But letting go of their digital clutter is an environmentally sound step to take since it maximizes available storage, memory, and speed, and therefore decreases the need to upgrade, consume new technology, or unnecessarily crowd those ever-growing server farms.

Do you remember the last vacation where you deliberately restricted your use of electronics or were forced to do so for lack of Internet access? You came back rested, marveled at how easy it was to disconnect. You can retain that vacation feel year-round by restraining your electronics use!

For me an empty tabletop, email inbox, and computer desktop mean that I have tackled my to-do list, that I have eliminated distracters and reasons to procrastinate. These are areas that I can control; junk mail is much trickier.

JUNK MAIL

At one point in my life, I ran to the mailbox for the season's new Pottery Barn catalog. Back then I was drawn to the publication's home organizing ideas and take on seasonal decorations. Unlike other free publications, such as the *Penny Saver,* which went from the mailbox straight to the recycling can, I would carry the catalog into my home and add it to a basket full of paid subscriptions. Magazines and catalogs seemed to come in faster than I could flick through them, but I kept only the latest issues, and this specific catalog helped me fantasize about every Hallmark celebration ahead. I drew inspiration from the catalog, confecting replicas of the felt pumpkin for Max and Léo's trick-or-treating or tying ornaments to doorknobs for Christmas. I browsed the company's idea of perfection for five years before plunging into my first purchase (at the store, not through the catalog): a set of faux-fur blankets to keep our heating bills down the first winter that hit our small home.

Today, I wonder . . . How many trees on average did home-goods retailers stuff in my mailbox to make a deal? I do not exclusively blame the business(es) for using such wasteful marketing methods. For as long as I received the catalog(s) without actively doing something to stop it, I was just as responsible for perpetuating the junk mail practice.

When I started simplifying my life, I evaluated daily tasks and noticed that my letterbox took more time out of my day than seemed reasonable. A typical trip to the mailbox involved separating mail, taking some to the curbside recycling bin, transporting the rest into the house, laying one stash on Scott's desk (bills and statements), another on the kitchen counter (restaurant and grocery ads), and another in my studio (kids' activities). Regardless of destination or content, the totality would eventually end up back on the curb, right next to the mailbox where it originated, to be either trashed or, at best, recycled. Once I started paying attention to paper management in my household, I saw junk mail was a problem. So, long before we cared about reducing our household waste, we took steps to prevent unwanted mail from landing in our box.

I quickly found eliminating junk mail to be a frustrating task. You can't imagine the array of defenses I heard: "You can recycle it." "It creates jobs." "Paper is a renewable resource." "It's only a small piece of paper." "It's made out of recycled content." I was once even told: "I care about the environment; I am vegetarian, you know." Looking beyond the excuses, I eventually started to understand how junk mail worked. I found that the community education catalogs are mailed using my tax dollars! The Environmental Protection Agency reports that Americans as a whole receive close to 5 million tons of junk mail every year; over 44 percent enters the waste stream before it has ever been opened or read.

It takes time and work to eradicate junk mail. I no longer run to my mailbox to look for the latest home goods catalog; now I count how many mail pieces I have landed and have to fight. The number has declined over time, but I still receive a couple of pieces per week, the origin of which is usually indiscernible. Eradicating junk mail is a just cause: in the long run it saves time, money, and resources, not to mention frustrations. To declare your own war on junk mail, first, be proactive:

- Give out your contact information only when absolutely necessary. Product warranty cards, for example, are not required but are used to collect data about your consumption habits and target direct mail. When you must provide personal information, write or say: "Do not rent, sell, share, or trade my name or address."
- Remove your address from personal checks.
- When moving, opt for a temporary change of address. The permanent one is shared with local marketing lists.
- Go to DMAchoice.org to stop direct mail.
- Go to OptOutPrescreen.com to stop credit card and insurance offers.
- Go to YellowPagesOptOut.com to stop receiving the phone directory.

Now, examine the contents of your mailbox. Starting today, attack each item as it comes in. Become a junk mail detective.

- **Commercial catalogs:** Go to CatalogChoice.org (they cancel catalogs for you) or call the catalogs directly. I opted out and I have never been happier with my personal sense of decorating and celebrating.
- **First-class mail:** Do not open the unwanted letter. Its postage includes return service; you can write "Refused—Return to sender" and "Take me off your mailing list" on the front of the unopened envelope. I keep a pen in my mailbox for that specific purpose.
- **Mail addressed to the previous resident:** Fill out a U.S. Postal Service change-of-address card for each previous resident. In lieu of a new address, write: "Moved, no forwarding address." In the signature area, sign your name and write "Form filled by current resident of home [your name], agent for the above." Hand the form to your carrier or postal clerk.
- **For standard/third-class presorted mail:** Do not open those that mention "return service requested," "forwarding service requested," "change service requested," or "address service requested." These postages also include return service, so here, too, you can write "Refused—Return to sender" and "Take me off your mailing list" on the front of an unopened envelope.

  Otherwise, open the letter, look for contact info, then call/email/write to be taken off the mailing list. These items typically include promotional flyers, brochures, and coupon packs. Make sure to also request that your name or address not be sold, rented, shared, or traded.
- **Bulk mail:** Inexpensive bulk mailing, used for items such as community education catalogs, allows advertisers to mail to all homes in a carrier route. It is not directly addressed to a specific name or address but to "local" or "postal customer," and is therefore most difficult to stop. A postal supervisor told me that my carrier had to deliver them and that he could take them back when refused, but since the postage does not include return service, the mailman would simply throw the mail away with no further action. The best way to reduce the production of such mailings is to contact the senders directly and convince them to either choose a different type of postage or adopt Internet communication instead. In the case of community-born mailing, one could also persuade his/her city council to boycott the postage preference. But ideally, the U.S. Postal Service would not even provide this wasteful option.

If these steps are too much for you to handle at once, you can let 41pounds.org or CatalogChoice.org handle the bulk of it for a fee. And when your best efforts fail at stopping a specific mailing, you can resort to the U.S. Postal Service's PS Form 1500: It declares that "Under the *Pandering Advertisements Statute,* 39 USC 3008, if you are the addressee of an advertisement, and consider the matter (product or service) that it offers for sale to be 'erotically arousing or sexually provocative,' you can obtain a Prohibitory Order against the mailer." Don't let big words intimidate or stop you; your opinion of "sexually oriented" material is at your sole discretion and will not be questioned. Today this USPS form may be our last recourse against the peskiest junk mail.

A PAPERLESS WORLD

There is no doubt that our society is going paperless. E-books are emerging as a replacement for books, tablets for schoolbooks, apps for grocery lists. Here are some of the things I have done to transition to paperless, organized in alphabetical order:

Assign a file or paper tray to collect single-side printed paper for reuse.

Boycott paper sourced from virgin forests and reams sold in plastic.

Cancel magazine and newspaper subscriptions; view them online instead.

Digitize important receipts and documents for safekeeping. Digital files are valid proofs for tax purposes. Download CutePDF Writer to save online files without having to print them.

Email invitations or greeting cards instead of printing them (see "Holidays and Gifts" chapter).

Forage the recycling can when paper scraps are needed, such as for bookmarks or pictures (for school collages, for example).

Give extra paper to the local preschool.

Hack the page margins of documents to maximize printing.

Imagine a paperless world.

Join the growing paperless community.

Kill the fax machine; encourage electronic faxing through a service such as HelloFax.

Limit yourself to print only on paper that has already been printed on one side.

Make online billing and banking a common practice.

Nag the kids' teachers to send home only important papers.

Opt out of paper newsletters.

Print on both sides when using a new sheet of paper (duplex printing).

Question the need for printing; print only when absolutely necessary. In most cases, it is not.

Repurpose junk mail envelopes—make sure to cross out any barcode.

Sign electronically using the Adobe Acrobat signing feature or SignNow .com.

Turn down business cards; enter relevant info directly into a smartphone.

Use shredded paper as a packing material, single-printed paper fastened with a metal clip for a quick notepad (grocery lists, errands lists), and double-printed paper to wrap presents or pick up your dog's feces.

Visit the local library to read business magazines and books.

Write on paper using a pencil, which you can then erase to reuse paper, or better yet, use your computer, cell phone, or erasable board instead of paper.

XYZ: eXamine Your Zipper; i.e., your leaks: attack any incoming source of paper.

And when all else fails, you can make paper or a recycled notebook . . .

HOMEMADE OFFICE SUPPLIES

PAPERMAKING

Technically, this should be named "paper recycling," since we are not making it from wood pulp, but calling it "papermaking" helps us to avoid confusion with curbside recycling. This stationery comes in handy when a physical card is needed (i.e., accompanying a money gift or greeting someone without Internet access) and makes a great teacher's gift (especially when made from the stack of papers sent home from school).

Window screening mesh (It is sold by the yard at your local hardware store)

Tacks

Frame(s): Choose a frame with a flat front. The size of the frame will define the size of your paper. I use a 3.5" x 5" frame for small cards and postcards, an 8.5" x 11" for letters (this size has the advantage of doubling as an envelope when folded). It also needs to fit flat into your tub, so plan accordingly.

Felt squares: They need to be larger than the size of your frames and can be made from felted sweaters.

Tub: I use a stainless-steel tub from a restaurant-supply store.

Papers: For maximum conservation, choose paper that has been printed on both sides.

Seeds, lint, or dried flowers (optional)

Large sponge: I prefer sea sponges for their natural composition, but an absorbent cloth can work just as well

DIRECTIONS

1. Tack the window screening mesh tightly onto the frame.
2. Line a table with felt squares.
3. Tear small pieces of paper into the tub and fill with water (I like to let it sit overnight to give the paper time to soften).
4. Using an immersion blender, blend the soaking paper into a pulp. At this point, you get an idea of the color of the finished product (a few shades lighter than your pulp), and you have the option of adding seeds (for "plantable" paper), lint from your dryer, dried flowers, etc.
5. Dunk the frame flat into the pulp, and lift to drain.
6. Flip the frame onto a felt square and immediately absorb as much water as you can off the mesh with the sponge.
7. Delicately remove the frame (the pulp should stick to the felt).
8. Line dry over your plants (the felt will drip on them and no water will be wasted).

9. When dry, peel the paper sheet off the felt and iron if needed. **Note:** When you're done (i.e., the pulp is too thin to make paper), you can compost the leftovers.

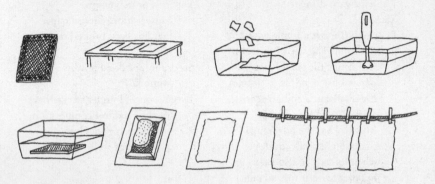

RECYCLED NOTEBOOK

I occasionally make one of these notebooks with the kids' school papers for jotting down notes and drawing. I have found the size to be perfect for travel and the binding strong enough to last through the year.

MATERIALS NEEDED

Fifteen sheets single-side-printed letter-size paper

Two sheets single-side-printed letter-size colored paper (optional)

Nail and hammer

String and needle

DIRECTIONS

1. Fold all sheets in half with the printed side inside.
2. Pile them up facing in the same direction, and placing the optional sheets top and bottom.
3. Using a nail and hammer, punch holes at regular intervals along the *open side* of the stack.
4. Starting at one end and using the threaded needle, pass the string intermittently through the holes.

5. Turn the book over and pass the string through the same holes, but from the underside, ending where you first started.
6. Tie a knot.

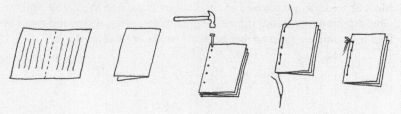

Growing up, I watched my dad use milk to affix labels onto wine bottles. Today, I use it to glue paper on another piece of paper or glass, but when I need a stronger hold or a paste for big projects, I use the following recipe.

DIRECTIONS

1. In a small saucepan, bring ½ cup water to a boil.
2. Slowly whisk in 1 tablespoon white flour and 1 tablespoon cornstarch.
3. Cook over low heat, stirring constantly until thickened.
4. Remove from heat and dilute with one tablespoon of white vinegar.
5. Store in a small glass jar and apply with a natural bristle paintbrush.

Note: Dries clear and works on wood.

5 RS CHECKLIST: 5 TIPS FOR THE WORKSPACE

Refuse: Say no to the business cards, goodie bags, free pens or pencils, junk mail, and wasteful shipping materials.

Reduce: Choose quality writing utensils; you will more likely keep track of them.

Reuse: Repurpose shipping material and single-printed paper.

Recycle: Throw into the recycling bin only paper that is printed on both sides.

Rot: Compost shredded paper and pencil shavings.

ONE STEP FURTHER

Most of the ideas we covered in this chapter addressed the visible and tangible aspects of waste, but the following tips on energy, water, and time savings will complete (and further reward) your sustainable efforts.

Energy

- Use smart power strips on your equipment to eliminate phantom energy consumption. Since this did not work for our system, we have strategically plugged our equipment into power strips that we turn off at the end of the day.
- Trade incandescent lightbulbs for LED ones (CFLs contain mercury and become a health hazard when broken).
- Restrain yourself from needlessly copying others on your emails, limit the size of attachments, and simplify your Internet signature to reduce the size of your emails and the energy needed for servers to run and store them.
- Set your computer to energy-saver mode; do not use a screen saver but have your computer go to sleep when idle. On my PC, there is also the option of turning off the display as needed with the touch of a button.
- Get a laptop, if buying a new computer. It is more energy efficient. Consider buying the floor model: it is not only cheaper, it comes sans packaging.

Water

- Empty leftover drinking water into your plant.

Time

- Patronize the local office-supply store.
- When running errands and making deliveries, plan your route to maximize right-hand turns.

Kids and School

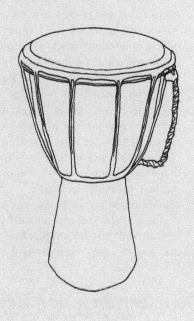

No Zero Waste discussion about kids would be complete without asking these questions:

Where does waste originate? When something is manufactured? When we throw it away? Or when we create a new resource-dependent life?

According to the U.S Census Bureau, the world counted close to 2.5 billion inhabitants when my mom was born; today, we have reached the 7 billion mark. At this rate, overpopulation is imminent and probably our biggest ecological threat. The Earth simply cannot survive such growth. Unless we change our reproduction and consumption habits, our planet will conclusively neither be able to provide the resources needed to sustain human expansion nor absorb its waste (whether it be solid or gaseous). Aware of these environmental implications, a number of young couples choose either not to have kids or adopt instead. While I find such discipline to be commendable, I understand that it is not easy for every loving pair to abide. Ironically, my kids and their future is what led me to rethink my ways, conserve, and ultimately write this book. To have kids or not is a personal choice that I wouldn't dare judge. After all, I have two boys myself! But beyond this fundamental question, it has become essential that for the sake of the survival of our children and that of our children's children, we:

1. **Reconsider** the idea of raising large, blood-related families. Beyond "replacing ourselves," can we adopt instead of breed to increase family size?
2. **Protect** ourselves against surprise pregnancies. Of the contraceptive methods available to us today, tubal ligation and vasectomy are the least wasteful and among the most effective options. IUDs, which are the least wasteful of the nonsurgical alternatives (lasting up to twelve years), are also "the most inexpensive long-term and reversible form of birth control you can get," according to Planned Parenthood. Diaphragms and cervical caps are adequate reusable options, too, but gel (which is inevitably sold in packaging) is needed for them to be effec-

tive. Call your local Planned Parenthood to get specific information about these methods.

3. **Teach** our kids (i.e., future generations) to care for their environment and conserve resources; teach them to live simply and thrive within a life rich in experiences versus one filled with stuff. The earlier we train them, the better, since young minds are fresh, uncorrupted, and receptive. But it's never too late to get started! Regardless of age, don't doubt your kids' ability to grasp and absorb new principles.

I am not a professional parenting adviser and I don't presume to tell you how you should or should not raise your kids. A Zero Waste household, however, inevitably involves the children. Adopting this lifestyle has affected our family life and guided our parenting. The tips I share in this chapter are what I've learned through our experience. Clearly, every parent has to decide what's best for his or her family. But there are some simple, really practical ways to deal with, for example, helping your kids make good choices about food.

Other parents often tell me that they cannot envision embracing the Zero Waste lifestyle because their kids are too attached to packaged brands. I believe that parents often use their kids as a pretext not to change their own habits. "How did your kids give up Oreos?" asked one hesitant mother.

When making the transition, it's helpful to focus less on the foods to be avoided (packaged and processed) and more on the loose and fresh ones waiting to be discovered in the bulk bins and at the farmer's market. Kids are innately simple. They are content as long as their modest needs are met, regardless of labels. Adults are the ones who attach importance to brands and condition children to care about them. Bulk cereal or homemade cookies will satisfy them just as well as the packaged kinds, if they are offered the opportunity and encouraged to try them. Similarly, the goal is not to deprive your child of toys but to let go of the unloved ones in order to make the favorites easy to find. "Simplification is not just about taking things away. It is about making room, creating space in your life, your intentions, and your heart," writes Kim John Payne, author of *Simplicity Parenting*.

Working parents also often tell me that they are too busy with their jobs to change their lifestyle and adopt Zero Waste alternatives. But what is their overtime work really funding? While employment is needed to sustain life, the amount of work in many cases depends on the parameters that parents set for their family and the social pressures that they succumb to. Outfitting one's life with the biggest, the latest, and the fastest, most expensive gadgets requires a certain earning level to afford them. In contrast, the Zero Waste lifestyle supports consuming less and therefore reduces a household's cost of living, which translates to less work, increased family time, and more home-cooked meals. Getting adjusted to a new standard of living and finding balance between true needs and economic sufficiency takes time, but adopting voluntary simplicity has an immediate impact on finances.

Slowing down our consumption has slowed down my family's life overall, and the increased time that Zero Waste's efficiency has afforded me has completely changed my interaction with our boys. A composed, pleasant mom has replaced the erratic, stressed-out mom I used to be. Of course, there are exceptions, but in general, thoughtful parenting decisions have replaced impulsive ones. I just wish I had started earlier. Our children's lives seem to roll by at the cadence of a Charlie Chaplin movie. Before we know it, they learn to walk, dress themselves, take themselves to school, and then they leave home. Every day, our fear, joy, and love for them remind us how precious life is. How quickly their childhoods slip away if we don't set aside family time, take time to hug, cuddle, and play! Quitting the rat race for the off-beaten path of simple living definitely makes room for savoring life's precious moments.

Our Zero Waste path has been gradual and our kids did not notice many of the changes until we pointed them out. Today, their lives blend with their friends', and that of our family with the neighbors'. We eat, play, work, sleep, and sometimes argue like everyone else. We simply differ in that we let Zero Waste principles guide our decision making and create strong family bonds by finding solutions to the obstacles that we sometimes encounter. I can't foresee whether my kids will rebel against their upbringing (as most kids do) and/or stick with the Zero Waste lifestyle when they leave our home. But I do feel confident about the conservation ethic that we are instilling in them.

Here are the lifestyle elements that facilitated our kids' transition and that we still use today:

- **Set a routine and establish traditions:** These encourage stability and organization in a household, define a family, and provide kids with a healthy sense of belonging, anticipation, and confidence (knowing what to expect).

- **Encourage togetherness, say no:** Socialization is important, but too many social engagements, sleepovers, and extracurricular activities rob us of quality family time. Learn to say no to invitations and overscheduling; balance social activities with family gatherings. Dinnertime, for example, represents an opportunity to share concerns or ideas regarding the lifestyle, and craft making is an ideal time to bond (see the "Arts and Crafts" section, page 202, for ideas).
- **Turn the TV off, limit digital media:** Both are programmed to grab kids' attention to the point where they become unresponsive zombies. These media are too easy to turn on, too difficult to turn off. Eliminating or limiting them opens time for reading, commercial-free movies, and more important, unstructured play and the exploration of creativity. It makes room for quality family time and discussions. Turning off electronics also protects our kids from the wall of ads that conditions them to want what they do not have and find dissatisfaction with what they do.
- **Bring awareness:** Your local library is a haven of wealth. Borrow movies and books with an underlying environmental message. Use them as an educational support to explain ecological issues and how our actions can impact the health of the planet. Point to the importance of change, and discuss how the smallest effort can have a positive impact on the environment.
- **Connect with nature:** Encourage outdoor activities, so kids learn to appreciate and protect nature. Teach them to be good scouts and leave a place better than they found it. Once they are connected with the environment, ecological explanations and the need for Zero Waste make sense. Hiking, camping (see the "Out and About" chapter), geocaching, bush crafting, canoeing, biking, swimming in lakes and rivers, and building forts in the forest or sand castles on the beach are great ways to immerse them in natural surroundings and teach them basic survival skills. Additionally, foraging and vegetable gardening further reinforce human-earth connections.
- **Grocery shop together:** It goes without saying that grocery shopping is easiest without kids. But you can occasionally take this opportunity to point out seasonal produce, teach about eco-shopping (such as finding local products by looking at their origin), and let them pick favorites from the bulk section.
- **Get them involved:** Include the kids in family life as much as possible. When age and location permit, you can send them to the ice cream

store to fill a jar (they can fill it with their favorite flavor), include them in your volunteering or campaigning activities (such as organized trash pickup events as covered in the "Getting Involved" chapter), and let them participate in everyday activities such as cooking and cleaning. These activities build their confidence and provide memorable, hands-on experiences.

- **Give the gift of experiences:** Privilege gifts your kids can *do* over gifts your kids can own. Refer to the gift ideas proposed in the "Holidays and Gifts" chapter.
- **Encourage independence:** Do not dictate, but guide. Allow them to make their own decisions outside the home. Kids often worry about peer pressure. Don't expect them to necessarily adhere to Zero Waste practices in a social setting. Teach your kids to be autonomous. Parental hovering is helpful to neither the kids nor the parents. Finding balance, on the other hand, allows your children to blossom at their own tempo.
- **Play!** The best way to get a message across is through play, when kids are happy and receptive. Board games or sports provide excellent opportunities to bond. But spontaneous playfulness is equally important. Keeping a good sense of humor and occasionally incorporating surprises into the routine can brighten a grim environmental or family situation. Keep it light, make it fun.

TOYS

Unless limits are set, a household with children can easily get inundated with toys. Their volume can really get out of hand, taking over not only a child's bedroom but living room, hallway, bathtub, garage, and yard. An afternoon of hard play can turn into a sea of brightly colored plastics spread across the floor and end in arguments about cleaning it all up. Who is really to blame for such a mess? Who is the origin of long cleanups and subsequent quarreling? The kids, for taking their playthings out, or the parents, for permitting so many into the house?

Several years ago, when the kids ignored my requests to clean up and did not start gathering their things before I could count to three, I brought a large trash bag into their room and slowly filled it with their scattered toys. Although I used this method only a couple of times, it proved to be highly effective in motivating the kids to tidy up. But as we adopted Zero

Waste, the tactic proved to be unnecessary. The kids themselves rave about the fact that since we have embraced simplicity, cleanup is no longer an agonizing chore nor a source of conflict; the organizational system in place, combined with their small amount of toys, make it quick, easy, and painless. I believe this difference to be the most palpable benefit of their personal Zero Waste journey.

To get and stay organized (and limit the risk of injury slipping on a toy underfoot), we'll take a look at the toys to favor (selection), those to eliminate (simplicity), then how to organize them (organization), and how to keep them under control (refusal).

Selection

Not all playthings are created equal. Some promote the exploration of innate senses more than others. Ironically, the ones that are marketed to promote our kids' development rarely do so. Instead, it is the barest of designs that often sparks our children's inspiration. It is the simplest of objects with which they will create a relationship. Provide access to the recycling bin, they will craft; provide cloth, they will design clothes; provide branches, they will create shelter; provide pots, they will open their first restaurant; provide lids, they will form their first band.

The materials you select for your child's toys are just as important as their design. Plato said, "The most effective kind of education is that a child should play among lovely things." Provide beautiful toys; they will likely care for them. Materials such as wood, metal, and cloth not only bring beauty into your child's play, they also develop his or her sense of touch and texture; they survive the test of time better, are generally healthier, and can more easily be repaired. Compared to a hollow piece of plastic, a piece of solid wood can be glued with nontoxic compounds or nailed, for example.

When decluttering the toy chest, keep your child's age and needs in mind and favor nonplastic, simple items that promote:

- **Creativity:** Building blocks and craft materials (see the "Arts and Crafts" section)
- **Imagination:** Miniature characters, farm animals, knights
- **Imitation:** Fun clothes, hats, purses, gloves, heels, rag dolls, kitchen accessories

- **Rhythm:** Harmonica, maracas, triangles, hand drums, xylophone, ukulele, recorder
- **Social interaction:** Board games, cards, pickup sticks, dominoes, stacking wood, puzzles, puppets
- **Outdoor activity:** Rope, recycled tire or wood swing, bike, leather balls, skateboard, metal bucket and shovel, fishing equipment

Simplicity

Through the homes that I have helped organize, I've found that children's attachment to toys is often a reflection of what we parents have instilled in them, and it manifests itself in two common ways. First, their toy selection is frequently a collection of items we wish we had had as kids. When we brag about these toys ("How lucky you are to have a remote control car, I never had one"), our hopes and dreams therefore become our kids' burden to let go. Second, the language that we use to describe our own attachment to stuff can influence their reasoning. When we use pretexts to not let go of a personal item, such as "my friend gave it to me," "it cost a lot of money," or "I might need it later," our kids will most likely use a similar jargon to justify keeping an object. "Santa gave it to me" is a recurring excuse.

When decluttering, be true to yourself and your child's needs; ask these questions and respond to them in all honesty:

- **Is it in working condition? Is it age appropriate?** In a regular household, the number of broken and outgrown toys often equals that of working ones. Cars with missing wheels, board games with lost pieces, and dolls without heads commingle with working items. Putting aside those to grow into, donating outgrown ones, and discarding broken ones will immediately reveal your child's true toy selection.
- **Does your child use it regularly?** A full toy chest is like an overstuffed wardrobe. Faced with too many choices, your child keeps selecting the same ones, a phenomenon that the psychologist Barry Schwartz calls the paradox of choice, a paralysis induced by too much choice. Determine your child's favorites and put aside unloved items to be donated, reintroduced later, or swapped with a friend.
- **Is it a duplicate?** In an effort to instill a love of reading, we commonly outfit our kids' bedrooms with an array of books that they quickly out-

grow and that over time bow their bookshelves. These books not only require a substantial budget and considerable amount of space, they also often hinder our children from evolving at their own reading pace and even limit their reading selection. Apart from reference, religious, and a toddler's handful of nighttime favorites, your local library is better suited to store your child's collection and provide him or her with an unparalleled selection. Had we purchased all the books that our kids have read since adopting the Zero Waste lifestyle, our financial savings would be significantly less than they are today.

- **Does it put my child's health in danger?** Make your child's health a priority, and let go of PVC toys (plastic number 3), which contain malignant phthalates. Similarly, a collection of stuffed animals collects dust and may breed asthma-causing allergens. Pick a favorite or two, to facilitate laundering. Also, unless your craft material carries ACMI's AP seal (i.e., nontoxic), be wary of its toxicity.

- **Do you or your child keep it out of guilt?** Put aside feelings associated with the benefactor and/or cost of the toy evaluated. Let your child's true needs and well-being guide his or her toy selection instead.

- **Does your child keep it because society tells her that she needs one** ("everyone has one")? An array of electronic devices is marketed toward children, but many of them, such as portable gaming devices, portable DVD players, readers, etc., serve only single, restricted purposes. **Could something else achieve the same task?** Let go of the extras and stick with a single multipurpose device, such as a laptop or a tablet, which has the added bonus of exposing your child to digital advances and providing computer proficiency.

- **Is it worth your precious time dusting and cleaning?** While some children have a natural propensity to collect, for other children, these collections are often started and encouraged by their parents. For example, if we catch our child's interest in a given object, we are likely to add to it at birthdays and holidays. Collections are not only the epitome of consumerism, but large ones acquire an incredible amount of dust. Can your child's collection be sold to fund a favorite activity instead?

- **Could your child use this space for something else?** For example, train tables may be part of a child's room decor. Yet they are bulky, their high sides are restrictive, and their function limits a child's ability to create his or her own playing space on the floor. The space could be used for a multipurpose play area like a rug, or if space permits, a regular table instead.

- **Is it reusable?** Party favors are ephemeral. Made to last only a couple of uses, they are considered disposable (and make kids cry when they break). Gather those that you have and give them away to people who would buy them. Also refer to Refusal below to stop them from coming into the house again!

Note: Used toys, in good condition, can be donated to a shelter or a pre-school; new ones put aside for Operation Christmas Child (see page 272); and books donated to a public library or school.

What About Video Games?

Scott and I used to think that there was no place in our home for video games. Having succeeded in removing TV from our lives, we thought we could also prevent access to gaming, and for years, we resisted our children's pleas. However, over time our restrictions led our boys to seek their video game fix elsewhere—at their friends' houses or the neighbors'—to the point where they were spending more time in other homes than their own. It became clear that despite our best efforts, and unless we relocated to a remote area, gaming was unavoidable. If one of the principles of Zero Waste is to boost human relations and interactions, then there is a place for video games within the lifestyle, given that sustainability parameters are respected and socialization boosted:

- Buy console and games used.
- Use rechargeable batteries to power the remote controls.
- Scrutinize games for their age appropriateness (visit commonsense media.org for recommendations) and, if possible, select those that foster physical activity.
- Set time limits.
- Restrict usage to multiplayers (i.e., games that are played with a partner).

Organization

Now that we have decluttered, it is time to organize so that toys are easy to access and cleanup is effortless:

1. **Separate toys into groups.** Groups might for instance include dolls, pretend, wood blocks, music, games, etc.
2. **Assign each toy group a bin,** preferably one that is made of a see-through material, such as steel mesh.
3. **Label each bin accordingly.** Instead of words, a simple drawing will help toddlers easily identify the contents of each bin. The label can be a ribbon.
4. **Stick to the predefined number of bins.** Apply the rule: if one comes in, one goes out.
5. **Keep a close eye on age appropriateness.** Donate, swap with friends, or put aside outgrown toys for a younger sibling. You can also sell them to fund age-appropriate replacements. Consider buying used from the thrift store, garage sales, Craigslist, or eBay.
6. **Inform grandparents and friends** about your simplification efforts to limit material gifts. Refer to the "Holidays and Gifts" chapter for tips.
7. **Teach your child** how to refuse.

Refusal

Kids can be the recipients of an incredible amount of extras: toys gifted by grandparents, paperwork sent home by the teachers, and party favors given by friends can quickly accumulate and exponentially increase with each additional child in your household.

It's no wonder moms are professional organizers' biggest business. However, unless new habits are formed, the best organizing efforts cannot realistically put an end to clutter. The more that comes in, the more that needs organizing. The key to staying organized is not to hire special services, install more shelving, or buy additional containers. Rather, you need to find a way to cope with potential gifts, to stop stuff from coming in the first place. Managing the deluge of stuff that makes its way into your home is essentially about refusing.

As we've discussed, clutter-busting tactics start outside the home.

Remember that whatever stays out of the home won't need to be addressed later. In a Zero Waste home, the kids' most important assignment is to think twice about bringing things in. Teach them that some objects are not made to last but to rapidly break and lead to tears when they do. Teach your kids to be proactive, to distinguish between something of worth and something that will quickly become waste, and to say no before it is too late. Refusing comes with its challenges. In a society where accepting has become the polite norm, refusing can appear to go against the grain of good manners. But it's up to us modern parents to teach our kids that it's okay to politely decline a well-intentioned offer. The fear of being different is almost universal and especially pervasive in children. Refusing requires tremendous courage, but kids build lasting confidence when they meet challenges like this, and they become examples for others.

Our boys find it difficult to say no to free candy, but they have learned that they lose interest in party favor toys after five minutes, after which the favors add to the clutter (i.e., stuff that they will be responsible for picking up from the floor) and eventually the landfill. They surprise the hostess and make a lasting impression when they turn them down: from the water noodle at a pool party (we don't have a pool) to coloring sets (Max is a teenager)! Proved to be the kids' most significant area of involvement within our Zero Waste lifestyle, refusing has also empowered them to make independent decisions.

Ever since marketing geniuses realized kids' powerful influence on their parents' purchasing powers, they have become an easy target for advertisers. And it starts as soon as they are born! They are welcomed into the world with a vinyl diaper bag stocked with formula, coupons, diapers, and OTC samples. Here are the types of freebies to look out for:

Activity pouch on airplanes
Buttons and pins
Crayons and coloring place mats from restaurants
Disposable sample cup from the grocery store
Erasers and pencils with eraser tops
Fireman hat from a visit to the fire station
Goodie bags from county fairs and festivals
Hair comb from picture day at school
Infant goods from the maternity ward
Junior ranger badge from the ranger station and Smokey the Bear

Kids' meal toys

Lollipops and candy from various locations, such as the bank

Medals and trophies for simply participating in (versus winning) a sporting activity

Noisemakers to celebrate New Year's Eve

OTC samples from the doctor's office

Party favors and balloons from birthday parties

Queen's Jubilee freebies (for overseas travelers)

Reusable plastic "souvenir" cup and straw from a diner

Stickers from the doctor's office

Toothbrushes and floss from the dentist's office

United States flags on national holidays

Viewing glasses for a 3-D movie (why not keep one pair and reuse them instead?)

Water bottles at sporting events

XYZ, etc.: The big foam hand at a football or baseball game or Band-Aids after a vaccination or various newspapers, prospectuses, and booklets from school, museums, national parks . . .

I am not suggesting that your kids refuse them all. It would require superpowers to do so. But I am hopeful that they will consider the disposal and impact of taking these objects. You'll be amazed at how much clutter they can stop from coming in! Often, you can make it easier on your child by being proactive. For example, you can consult the organizing parent of a birthday party and request that your child not receive a favor (mention that you are working on decluttering your home).

WARDROBE

I have found a minimal wardrobe for my children to be as beneficial as a small toy collection.

Prior to simplifying our lives, Max and Léo owned three times the amount of clothes they have today, and the majority would end up in the wash each weekend. Throughout the week, their dresser dispensed clean T-shirts and shorts if they splashed water on a top, if they spilled juice on a bottom. The "dirty" discards found their way into the hamper or more often were dropped on the floor. A sock worn in the morning and then lost under the sofa in the afternoon automatically led to reaching for a replacement pair. Jackets and hats disappeared as fast as I could buy them. It's as though I had allowed their closet to become a dispenser of disposable, single-use products. Today, their simple wardrobe allows them to manage their inventory throughout the week, to care for what they have, and to be responsible for the occasional loss. They no longer thoughtlessly change throughout the day, and they don't lose their jackets (as often) as they once did. Minimal wardrobes have significantly decreased my weekly washings and the purchase of replacements.

To adopt a small wardrobe for your child:

- Evaluate your child's weekly clothing needs, dependent on age and activities, and stick to a small, controlled quantity.
- Include his or her favorite pieces, and favor dark apparel for its stain-concealing properties.
- Teach your child to undress next to the hamper to avoid floor pileups, and if he or she wears light colors, provide two hampers to foster laundry separation and time savings.

When the time comes to replace outgrown pieces, clothes-swapping websites facilitate exchanges between parents and are a wonderful way to save money, but they come with a heavy carbon footprint associated with packaging and shipping. When available, pick a local thrift shop instead, and remember to bring a shopping list! Take your child shopping if he or she shows an interest in style. Not only will it allow them to pick what they like, it also offers a great opportunity to point to the originality and low price tag of secondhand clothes (less money spent on clothes means more to spend on a vacation) and, more important, provides practice for their future purchases. Kids who grow up buying secondhand clothes are more likely to continue the tradition as adults.

For illustrative purposes, here are the contents of each of my boys' wardrobes:

- **Fall/winter:** four pairs of pants, seven long-sleeve shirts, one dress shirt, one pair of long pj's, a stocking hat, and gloves.
- **Spring/summer:** four pairs of shorts, seven short-sleeve shirts, one collared shirt (polo or button-down), one pair of swim trunks, one pair of flip-flops, one pair of short pjs, and a summer hat.

- **Year-round:** seven pairs of socks, seven undies, one pair of sneakers, a hoodie, a waterproof Windbreaker, a down jacket, and a carry-on.

Please refer back to the "Bedroom and Wardrobe" chapter for more tips on shopping and disposing of outworn or outgrown pieces.

THE DIAPER CONUNDRUM

Our kids were long out of diapers before we went Zero Waste, so making an eco-decision about this topic is not something I had to do. That said, a Zero Waste chapter on kids would not be complete without a note on them, given that they can represent the most wasteful aspect of children's pre-potty-training years.

Sadly, there is no one-size-fits-all solution to the eco-diaper conundrum, once product manufacturing, local restrictions, and disposal requirements are all taken into account.

The manufacturing process of conventional disposable diapers involves the use of a nonrenewable resource (petrol) and of chlorine. At home, they release malignant VOCs (volatile organic compounds), and when they are thrown "away," they contribute to our growing landfill, releasing methane into the environment and never decomposing. According to the EPA, disposable diapers account for 2.4 percent (by weight) of the total landfill waste.

But recently, countless brands have come up with "green" options to counter the wasteful disposal of conventional diapers—biodegradable, compostable, flushable, reusable diapers have popped up on the market. Which ones to choose? Be wary of green claims; know all the facts and then pick the method that works best for you. Here is my two cents on available options:

- **Biodegradable diapers:** Just because a product is marketed as biodegradable does not mean that it will, in fact, biodegrade. For a material to biodegrade, light, water, and oxygen must be present, but in general, a packed landfill doesn't provide those conditions. In *Garbology*,

Edward Humes describes a landfill core sample collected by students from the University of Arizona: guacamole, hot dogs, and newspapers from twenty-five years ago came out intact! So don't count on biodegradable diapers to decompose in a landfill.

- **Flushable liners (and wipes!):** Flushing away seems like a good idea, but again, where is "away"? The liner goes down the pipes, travels to the water-treatment plant, and if it hasn't had time to completely disintegrate before it gets there, it clogs filters, for the facility to deal with. When I took a tour of our local water-treatment plant, the staff was adamant: "Do not flush anything down the toilet apart from bodily waste and toilet paper, nothing else, and that includes products sold as flushable." While manufacturers of these products do advise not to flush them down a septic tank, I would go further in recommending not to flush them down a sewer system.

- **Compostable diapers:** Compostable means that if we provide adequate conditions, then the diapers can simply disappear! Now that sounds like a great idea, but what do you do with the poo? Unless you set up a special human waste composting system, neither it nor the dirty diaper can be composted at home or through an advanced municipal composting facility like the one in San Francisco. Companies selling such products mention this in the fine print only. These diapers are simply not meant for your common backyard compost, because it does not get hot enough to destroy the feces' pathogens.

- **Cloth diaper service:** The major environmental concerns here are related to the laundering and transporting of the diapers. These services use extensive amounts of water and chlorine bleach to keep their products sparkly white, not to mention a fleet of trucks to get diapers to and from homes.

So what would I do? As with every other environmental conundrum that I face, I would consider the 5 Rs in order. If I had a baby at home, I would reduce by implementing elimination communication (EC), a technique that can get a baby diaper free before his first birthday (see "Resources"). I would reuse by using cloth diapers and washing them at home (you can practice EC with or without diapers). I am a firm believer in reuse, so this option would fit my ethics nicely. Clearly, this option requires manual labor, and might result in more frequent diaper changes (cloth not being as absorbent as the disposable counterparts), but it is a challenge I believe I would be willing to take to reduce landfill waste.

But again, everyone needs to choose the option that works best for their family, and this solution is not perfect for everyone. My girlfriend Robin, for example, cannot do this because her condo rules won't allow her to use the common laundry facilities for washing reusable diapers. Instead she chooses to rot by subscribing to a local compostable diapering service, earth-baby.com, which offers pickup and delivery. It's costlier but the next best thing after cloth!

SCHOOL

Back to school doesn't have to be all about buying dozens of blank notebooks that market the latest summer superhero blockbusters or bulk quantities of disposable pens that will end up floating at the bottom of your kids' backpacks. Back to school can be about meeting new friends, devising creative ways to avoid the supply spend-a-thon, finding new lunch ideas, and choosing fun activities for your kids.

Supplies

When I was a child, school was barely over, and I already looked forward to the first day of school. Later, I came to dread the start of my kids' new school year, in apprehension of the loads of incoming papers and laminated projects, and the many unrecyclable items that I do not purchase for our home but am obligated to buy for their classrooms. While teachers have very kindly respected our personal request not to send home unnecessary papers and not to laminate our children's work, their supply lists, on the other hand, are still a source of frustration. In a perfect world, teachers would coordinate their lists and agree to a limited inventory. For example, they would choose a common binder to serve a child's needs from kindergarten through fifth grade. Today's picky requests—two-inch zippered binders for some, half-inch unzipped for others, plastic dividers for one, multicolored cardboard for another—hinder reusability and add unnecessary expenses for parents. Ideally, teachers would also keep reusable year-end supplies for new students or donate them to either their colleagues or the local thrift shop. Better yet, manufacturers would offer nontoxic stainless refillables of modern staples such as markers, and teachers would limit their demands to those available and reuse them. Until that dream comes true, here is how to tackle the supply list with Zero Waste in mind:

1. **Streamline the list:** Consult last year's leftovers and update the list accordingly with truly needed items: your child probably already has the amount of requested pencils (or mechanical pencil refills) and markers—and maybe you can volunteer to provide reusable wipes instead of the disposable kind.
2. **Shop your home office:** Simple requests such as a "black pen" are most likely available in the drawer of your desk.
3. **Scout the local thrift shop:** Office supplies are too trivial for large thrift chains to bother selling. Small thrift stores, on the other hand, are a great source for secondhand binders, dividers, and sometimes even school paper, markers, pencils, and color pens.
4. **Patronize the local stationery store:** When you're looking for items that you did not find in the prior locations mentioned, a small local business can provide the right amount (one instead of a box of ten), unpackaged (sold loose). Refer to the "Workspace and Junk Mail" chapter for tips on how to select products.
5. **Check eBay:** The website is ideal for very specific items, such as a scientific calculator.

Lunch

Many parents consider homemade lunches to be a time-consuming, creativity-exhausting inconvenience. Are they worth our time?

Packing Zero Waste lunches offers more than the obvious environmental and financial relief. It offers a valuable alternative to school-provided meals. While our society's growing obesity and diabetes rates skyrocket, a home-packed lunch is a way for parents to get a measure of control over and insight into what their children are eating. If you feed your kids a balanced, varied, and wholesome diet, you'll eliminate the need for vitamin supplements to compensate for deficiencies. The Zero Waste principles will also reduce the ingestion of processed foods (and absorption of the chemicals leaching out of the packaging materials). Of course, once they walk out the door, we can never be sure exactly what and how much our children consume, but those kids who bring their lunch packs home are more likely to shed some light on their actual food intake and preferences, and parents can adapt lunch ingredients accordingly.

Making lunches can be a chore; creating one that adheres to healthy and Zero Waste principles is intimidating to many. But when Zero Waste pantry methods are in place, it is relatively easy and stress free. Storing pantry and refrigerated foods in clear glass containers makes choices visible; adopting a pantry rotation system can stave off boredom and limit options on any given day, consequently hastening decision making. Enlisting your kids to help make lunch can save time, too! And it augments the chance they'll like (and therefore eat) their meal. It also offers a valuable opportunity to instill self-reliance and healthy nutrition habits, valuable principles for their future health.

Here are examples of steps you can take to facilitate your children's involvement and add interest to their meal:

- **Cut:** Precut hard-to-slice items such as baguettes. Leftovers such as pizza or quiche can be cut into bite sizes.
- **Dip:** Provide a dip such as tamari sauce, yogurt, hummus, or mustard to flavor raw vegetables.
- **Portion:** Subtract small portions (i.e., half cup of yogurt) from regular sizes (a pint) and transfer into smaller containers.
- **Reheat:** Warm up leftover pasta or rice dishes and store in a thermos.
- **Roll:** Fashion slices of deli meat, seaweed sheets, and lettuce leaves into wraps.
- **Shape:** Cut veggies into sticks, rounds, squares, or stars (use the trimmings in a chopped salad).
- **Skewer:** Use turkey lacers as toothpicks to make mini-skewers. You can dull the ends by filing them if you judge them too sharp for your child.
- **Slice:** Offer toasted baguette slices as an alternative to crackers. Some fruits, such as oranges, are also more attractive and convenient to eat when sliced.

To pack a healthy lunch, my children follow simple packing guidelines. They combine, and not duplicate, ingredients from each of the following categories. All are available in either loose or unpackaged form, and when possible, we buy organic. In order of importance (i.e. amount), they pick:

1. **Grain** (favor whole wheat when possible): Baguette, focaccia, buns, bagels, pasta, rice, couscous
2. **Vegetable:** Lettuce, tomato, pickles, avocado, cucumber, broccoli, carrots, bell pepper, celery, snap peas
3. **Protein:** Deli cuts, leftover meat or fish, shrimp, eggs, tofu, nuts, nut butters, beans, peas
4. **Calcium:** Yogurt, cheese, dark leafy greens
5. **Fruit:** Preferably raw fruit or berries, homemade apple sauce, or dried fruit
6. **Optional Snacks:** Whole or dried fruit, yogurt, homemade popcorn or cookie, nuts, granola, or any interesting snack from the bulk aisle

To pack a lunch, there is no need to purchase or store a specialized container. You most likely already have all the necessary elements: a reusable container, kitchen towel, and optional fork and spoon. Although many parents would prefer a stainless steel container for their little ones, I find that our glass jars have worked well for Max and Léo, with no breakage to date; I believe that kids are capable of caring for breakables if given the

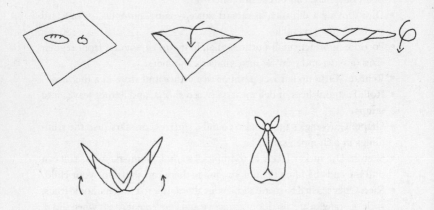

opportunity to do so. The container can then be wrapped along with a baguette sandwich and a piece of fruit in a kitchen towel, Furoshiki-style. Furoshiki is the Japanese art of wrapping in cloth. Shown on page 200 is the technique we use to wrap lunches; instructions on how to wrap other shapes are available at furoshiki.com/techniques. As opposed to standard lunch bags, the towel serves many functions: protective layer for transport, carrying handle, place mat, and napkin all in one!

Extracurricular Activities

Our children's lives can be cluttered with more than extra toys; enrolling them in a maximum of extracurricular activities has become commonplace. Why do we book our kids' time so tightly? Does it benefit them?

Although working parents sometimes legitimately use after-school activities as child care and as an alternative to TV and video games, enrollment decisions are often driven by a mix of parental emotions: hopes of discovering a precocious talent or developing our child's simple interest into competitive excellence; regrets of not pursuing a childhood dream ourselves; self-doubt we can feel when we see other parents overscheduling their children; fear of not exploiting our kids' full potential and somehow limiting their future as a professional football player or Harvard grad. Although well intentioned, foisting this stew of emotions on our kids and booking every minute of their time only creates stress, robs them of family time, and hinders their natural development.

Unstructured play allows kids to enjoy the outdoors, create their own world, cultivate their imaginations, and figure out who they want to be regardless of parental aspirations. Free play provides valuable time for them to evolve at their own rhythms and find autonomy. When provided a chance to be bored, they find ways to occupy their mind, to solve problems, and to join a world where nothing is expected of them, where they control their abilities, limitations, and achievements.

We parents all want what's best for our kids, and we are all free to raise them the way we like. But I must say that Scott and I love what this lifestyle has done for our family beyond waste reduction, and I hope that many more families will get to discover the benefits of balancing extracurricular activities with unstructured play.

ARTS AND CRAFTS

Arts and crafts offer an ideal opportunity to bond with our children, develop their fine motor skills, and instill in them valuable conservation and do-it-yourself aptitudes. Plus, they make a great after-school activity!

But you might be thinking: Doesn't "living with less" hinder creativity?

Before embarking on this lifestyle, I associated minimalism with creative austerity. Yet I have found the opposite to be true. Seven years ago, I had an inventory: hundreds of frames, dozens of unpainted canvases, gallons of paint, countless brushes, and loads of miscellaneous art materials stored in the studio. I was proud of my clientele and the recognition that my work was getting. But I also remember being frustrated at my lack of creativity. When we moved, we let go of many of our belongings, including those related to art making. I donated some to schools and friends, shared some through Craigslist, and brought some to Scrap (a reuse shop for artists). As I let go of potential/unfinished projects and seldom-used materials, I let go of frustrations and expectations. I realized that the unused art supplies had been nagging at me. They were just sitting there, waiting to become something better, something artful, something amazing, something that would allow me to vanquish my fears and exceed my abilities. With the Zero Waste lifestyle, these anxieties have vanished and have been replaced with the satisfaction of finding alternatives to disposability. I discovered that creativity need not be limited to the canvas, that opportunities to create abound all around us. For example, reinventing leftovers for dishes, and repairing have been sources of creativity, and our yard, compost, and recycling, of materials. Since the latter keep recurring and are always on hand, the kids and I do not need to collect or store them but simply reach for them when needed. Just as "the clothes do not make the man," I believe that the art supplies do not make the artist. It is not a wealth of supplies that gave van Gogh's work power, but rather his vision and execution. After all, "creativity is inventing, experimenting, growing, taking risks, breaking rules, making mistakes, and having fun" (Mary Lou Cook); none of it depends on supply inventory. Art and art making are highly personal—but I must say that Zero Waste has sparked a creative fuse in me that I had not realized before.

With the rise of the green movement, crafts are experiencing a rebirth.

Many eco-minded parents use crafting as a reason to collect materials, as a way to divert rubbish from disposal and sometimes justify consumption habits ("It's okay to buy a plastic bottle; I can use it to make a bird feeder"). Making crafts from salvaged materials has become a known waste-busting tactic. Yet many of the projects presented through the media contradict Zero Waste principles. They use toxic supplies (e.g., strong glues) or support the use of materials that we should refuse in the first place (e.g., plastic bags); they propose the construction of items that we do not need or employ processes that turn a material that is recyclable into one that will no longer be. Be aware that reuse is potentially a clutter instigator and craft making a waste producer.

Here are some things to keep in mind when you want to do some Zero Waste crafting with your kids.

- **Supplies:** No need for large amounts of fancy supplies; a few suffice. Try water-based paint, colored pencils, twine, scissors, homemade glue (see recipe on page 179), and supervised access to a toolbox. Supplies should be neither wasteful nor toxic. Purchase them from a small thrift store or an art store, where you can buy them by the piece (just the right amount, unpackaged). Also consider their future disposal. For example, although popular with children and teachers, today's markers are neither reusable nor recyclable: use paint, pastels, and pencils instead. Look for the nontoxic AP seal on labels, and consider homemade watercolors (see instructions below).
- **Materials:** Direct your child to your household's available discards for materials. Use landfill, compost, and recycling items on hand (no need to store them year-round for the eventuality): cheese wax, washed butter wrappers, wood scraps, twigs, dryer lint (see instructions below), worn-out clothing, felted sweaters, paper that is printed on both sides, and parcel boxes are great resources. On the very rare occasions that we struck out (teachers requested magazine cutouts), our neighbors happily provided.
- **Purpose:** The objective of crafts generally fits in one of four categories: repair, fabrication, embellishment, or artistic exploration. The latter is particularly important to the development of a child (experience materials, texture, and color), but as he gets older, technical instruction can introduce him to practical crafts. For instance, darning, woodworking,

sewing, and knitting become valuable skills for repairing or creating functional items. Suggesting the construction of something useful to you, your household, a deprived individual, or nature not only limits decorative clutter, but the conservation, survival skills, and benevolence that he gathers through the process empower him, too. For instance, fabric scraps or felted wool sweaters can be made into quilts to keep the needy warm; wood scraps into a bee house to provide mason bees with a healthy nesting site and encourage their reproduction (see instructions below).

- **Process:** Consider the end of the life of the craft. Will it be recyclable or compostable once completed, or will the addition of materials convert it into eventual landfill waste? When using recyclable or compostable materials, pay attention not to permanently mix materials (synthetic glue on wood, for example), so that the finished product can retain its compost or recycling properties. Ephemeral alternatives in craft making particularly enhance Zero Waste efforts. For example, sand sculptures, candle making, table decorations (as those described in the "Kitchen and Grocery Shopping" chapter), or play dough (see instructions below) encourage creativity and temporary creations, not collections and landfill waste.

WATERCOLOR DYES

COLORS

Blue/purple: huckleberries, blueberries, grapes, red cabbage, wilted rose petals, wine, squid ink

Red: beets, red elderberry, strawberries, cherries, raspberries

Yellow/orange: pomegranate or onion skins, golden beet, yellow turnip, celery leaves, carrot tops or root, turmeric

Green: peppermint, spinach, artichoke leaves

Brown: coffee, tea, red onion skins, soy sauce, compost tea, walnut hulls and husks, bark and dried leaves (from nontoxic plants), charred toast, cuttlefish ink

Black/gray: blackberries, octopus ink, wood charcoal, almond charcoal (see kohl recipe on page 99)

- Use liquids "as is" or boil to reduce them to achieve the desired color intensity.
- Cover solid materials with water, bring to a boil, and reduce until color intensity is achieved. Strain or filter (depending on the size of your material).

APPLICATION

- To use as watercolors, add ½ teaspoon salt and ½ teaspoon white vinegar per ¼ cup of liquid and store in small glass jars.
- To dye Easter eggs, submerge them in the simmering bath.

DRYER-LINT PUTTY

INGREDIENTS

3 cups dryer lint	2 tablespoons salt
2 cups water	¾ cup flour

DIRECTIONS

1. In a pan, soak the lint in water and salt.
2. Add flour and stir over medium heat until dough is formed.
3. Remove from heat and let cool.

APPLICATION

Use alone or on a form as you would papier-mâché. (Grease your mold with cooking oil or Multipurpose Balm on page 102.) The paste takes a few days to dry into a very strong material. Summer and sun are best for this activity.

Note: You can also use dryer lint as a fire starter (see "Out and About" chapter, page 245), as stuffing material (rag dolls or quilts), or to supplement your homemade paper (see "Workspace and Junk Mail" chapter, page 177).

Don't worry, the house will not attract stinging honeybees.

MATERIALS NEEDED

4" x 6" untreated wood scrap of
    8 to 12 inches
Pencil
Ruler

Drill
⁵⁄₁₆-inch drill bit
Sandpaper

DIRECTIONS

1. Draw a grid of 1-inch intervals on the widest side of a wood block.
2. Drill each intersection to the depth of 3½ inches (mark the drill bit).
3. Smooth out the holes with sandpaper.
4. Hang on a fence or tree, in a south-facing location, sheltered from the wind, between 3 and 6 feet from the ground.

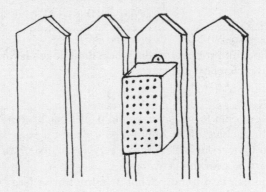

PLAY DOUGH

INGREDIENTS

2 cups plain flour

2 cups water

1 tablespoon cooking oil

1 teaspoon cream of tartar

1 cup salt

DIRECTIONS

1. Combine all ingredients in a pan.
2. Stir over medium heat until a dough forms.
3. Cool and store in a jar.

5 *R*S CHECKLIST: 5 TIPS FOR KIDS AND SCHOOL

Refuse: Reject freebies, extra school papers, and lamination.

Reduce: Streamline toys and after-school activities.

Reuse: Buy secondhand clothes and school supplies.

Recycle: Make crafts out of compostable or landfill materials.

Rot: Compost your crafts.

Holidays and Gifts

We should not blindly follow traditions—there's no learning in that. We need to understand them.

—Overhill Cherokee Indian saying

Holidays are very personal. Everyone has their own familial traditions and perhaps religious observances. In no way should Zero Waste living diminish your enjoyment of the holidays or impinge on important traditions. That said, Zero Waste principles have changed the way our family celebrates. Since the average American generates 25 percent more waste per week between Thanksgiving and Christmas than during the rest of the year, it's the first place to question whether aspects of your celebration could benefit from simplification.

CHRISTMAS

When Max and Léo were toddlers, I mapped out holiday fantasies for them. Each year, I planned for months to exceed the previous year's festivities, and hoped for our best Christmas ever. I always kick-started the season with a trip to the art-supply store to scout fancy paper and scrapbooking materials in order to handcraft our family's greeting card. The elaborate design had to outdo my previous ones; the forty cards took a week to complete and were mailed out the first week of December. The seasonal preparations also included inflating our Christmas decor and adding lights to our existing collection to ensure that our house outshined our neighbors'. Each time, the size of our tree increased; each time, I purchased new ornaments to decorate it. Throughout the year, I bought various gifts on sale and gathered them in a dedicated cupboard. But as the holiday neared, I ramped up my expenditures, looking for more, including stocking stuffers from the dollar store. It was not quality but quantity that I was after. I spent hours paper-wrapping countless and oddly shaped presents; I planned feasts and outfits for both Christmas Eve and Christmas Day. Advent was basically filled with activities aimed at psyching us up for the "big day." My quest for unbeatable excellence was a source of a lot of stress. Still, I considered myself a dream maker and worried about meeting expectations— expectations that I had created for myself, I now realize.

The long-awaited moments were short lived. They vanished into memories as we fought with the sea of discarded wrapping paper and ribbons, queued for returns, looked for storage for new possessions, and dealt with the mountain of post-holiday trash. We hoped to see our waste swiftly disappear from the curb by stuffing our sixty-four-gallon container as much as possible, but the load usually required subsequent pickups.

Nonetheless, the inconvenience was quickly forgotten as post-holiday sales appeared in the stores. In January, I bought ornaments at a discount and welcomed greeting card ideas in anticipation of next year's celebration. A pop-up tree decorated with hand-sewn family pictures would certainly top the beaded ornament I had sent to friends and family that year! Striving to be a step ahead of everyone else was a symptom of the addictive consumerism we'd fallen into.

Simplifying our lives led us to evaluate our consumption habits and face the enormity of our wasteful holidays. It triggered reflection. Were my efforts aimed at satisfying my children or my competitive cravings? What principles was I instilling in my boys? What was I setting them up for? For bigger and better, year after year? I sure did not grow up that way! As a child, I anticipated receiving gifts, and Santa did drop by our house, but with modesty and consistency. While I have forgotten what he brought, beyond the baby doll, Barbie, and secretary desk that I used for years, I do recall never expecting an outperformance. I just hoped he would come again. What I recollect most vividly are the simple traditions. Every year, I looked forward to decorating a small tree (a couple of days before Noel), singing "Douce nuit, sainte nuit" at mass, and sitting at a beautifully decorated table, indulging in the annual shellfish platter, foie gras toasts, and my grandmother's crêpe suzette, to the clinking sound of champagne flutes and the glow of the candles that my mom would save for the special night.

Traditions, rather than the objects stuffed into my shoes (in France, we use shoes instead of stockings), filled my memories. I came to wish for the same simple appreciation of the holidays for my children. But how could I reverse the traditions that I had established? How could I lower the expectations that I had set? As much as keeping up with the Joneses was no longer an option, alternatively, changing our ways seemed like an impossible feat. Our first attempt at a simplified Christmas felt like I had invited the Grinch into our home. Weaning the children off the fantasy that I had imposed on them took a couple of years, but eventually they got used to our pared-down rituals, and as a result of the change, we all reconnected with the true meaning of the holidays: family togetherness and genuine cheer.

Through the implementation of Zero Waste principles, my holiday frenzy (cooking, shopping, parking, mailing, etc.) naturally subsided. Dropping the wasteful, stressful, and complicated activities has opened time for more meaningful traditions, based on one simple guideline: Be kind to ourselves and to others. Here is how:

1. **Avoid the mall** and refuse to take part in Black Friday (make it your "buy nothing" day and go hiking instead). It not only keeps everyone's stress level down, it is good for your carbon footprint (less driving and reduced demand for new stuff), wallet, and creativity. Refer to the "Gifts" guide below for alternatives to mall purchases.
2. Include **"acts of kindness"** in the holiday schedule. Helping in a homeless soup kitchen, volunteering at the local food bank, writing a thank you card to someone whose services or efforts you appreciate (the friendly baker, for example), singing carols in the neighborhood or at a senior home, participating in a gift drive, or putting together a box for Operation Christmas Child (see "Resources") bring compassion to the season.
3. **Host one or multiple simple "holiday cheer" gatherings.** I found that just one afternoon of baking can go a long way. I make large batches of several types of cookies for Scott to share at work and the kids to offer as teachers' gifts and to host small get-togethers, such as afternoon cocktails with my girlfriends, a coffee hour with my walking group, a mulled-wine evening with the neighbors, and spiced-cider playdates with the kids' playmates. A minimal effort for maximum impact. No wasted flour there!
4. **Keep traditions simple.** Streamlining cooking, shopping, decorations, and card making eliminates stress for everyone. Slow down and enjoy the season!

Decorations

As you might expect, our Christmas decorations went through a decluttering process like everything else in our life! Since our holiday cheer has not suffered from the process, but instead benefited from it, it was well worth the effort.

Here again are the questions to ask yourself if you are looking to simplify that area, too:

- **Is it in working condition?** For example, broken light strings should not linger in your decorations inventory. Repair them (kits make it easy to identify the faulting bulb and replace it). Otherwise, home improvement (some online) stores across the United States and Canada accept old, broken, or used incandescent holiday light strings for recycling.
- **Do you use it regularly?** Consider the fact that Christmas decorations (as with any holiday decorations) get used only once a year. Let go of the ones that you do not systematically use, year after year. Anything that you have not used in the last year or two, consider donating.
- **Is it a duplicate?** How many Christmas trees or ornaments does a household really need to celebrate the holidays? Probably one tree with just a few ornaments that allow the tree's beauty to come through.
- **Does it put your family's health in danger?** Artificial trees are generally made with PVC, and scented candles commonly contain phthalates-based fragrances, both of which release harmful chemicals into the air. Consider discarding these unsafe items and replacing them with healthier alternatives mentioned in this chapter.
- **Do you keep it out of guilt?** At one point in time, some marketing genius had the idea to launch a "my first Christmas" ornament. I received one as a gift when Max was born and although it was not something I would have purchased, I felt obligated to keep it for my child because the packaging called it a "keepsake." When I simplified my life, I learned to put the heirloom guilt aside (see "Conclusion"). Take control of your tree, keep only those pieces that you love, let go of the pieces that you would not have bought for yourself. And remember: only you (not a friend, a relative, or the brains behind a successful marketing campaign) should determine your family keepsakes.

- Do you keep it because society tells you that you need one ("everyone has one")? For years, we purchased a Christmas tree like everyone else. But when we could no longer bear to cut one down, we came to wonder: Could something else achieve the same task? We have since used our six-foot-tall patio topiary. Because it is not something we had seen done elsewhere, it seemed weird at first to decorate a bush instead of a tree. Yet, today, we could not imagine doing otherwise. Consider reusing a potted plant that you already have or purchasing one that can become your yearly alternative to the Christmas tree.
- Is it worth your precious time dusting and cleaning? Unless you live in a year-round Christmas village, holiday dishes take up precious real estate all year, for only a few hours of use. They also take time to clean before using and store afterward. Your time during the holidays is precious, use it wisely. Consider donating those items that require special care every season.
- Could you use this space for something else? Donating your holiday housewares (dishes, glasses, towels, etc.) and the life-size reindeer that sleeps in the attic will open up space and make everyday or functional items easier to store, reach, and find, in your home.
- Is it reusable? Disposable, themed paper napkins, plates, and wrapping paper are a waste of money, and the reusable alternatives are so much prettier.

Our inventory, which filled a tall garage cupboard and grew yearly, now fits neatly into one bin and does not expand over time. Resisting the temptation to add to it hasn't been hard. As we unpack and rediscover our holiday decorations every year, we always find that we have enough; we add oil votives and edibles to complete our decor. It's simple and fun to confect a gingerbread house from scratch, string a garland of popcorn (for birds to enjoy post-holidays), and adorn the table with seasonal produce. Putting these garnishes together offers an opportunity to slow down and bond with your family.

REFILLABLE OIL VOTIVE

Small heatproof container: You
can use a glass votive or reuse
an empty votive tin.

Wire: Choose stainless steel to
avoid rusting. Gauge can vary
but needs to be strong enough
to hold your wick up and
flexible enough to twist around
a nail. I use a 19 gauge wire.

Thick nail

Wick: Strips of braided cotton
scraps (twine or needlepoint
thread work well). A wick
will also last longer if soaked
in a strong salt solution and
thoroughly dried.

Olive oil or leftover cooking oil

DIRECTIONS

1. Wrap the wire around the nail to create a ¼-inch-long spring,
then twist to take the shape of the bottom of your container.

2. Pass your wick through the spring, exposing ¼ inch of the wick
above the spring, and rest the apparatus in the bottom of your
container.

3. Fill the container with your choice of oil up to the top of the
spring (the wick will be sticking out).
4. Light it. When the oil level runs low, pull the wick up another
¼ inch and refill the container with oil.

Note: I keep six of these handy and use them throughout the house, when we have company or a reason to celebrate. Also be aware that using leftover cooking oil will not smell when burning, but it will when you blow out your wick. You can prevent the scent from taking over your home if you simply take your votives outside to blow them out.

Greeting Cards

I was so accustomed to sending out a greeting card each year, it took some time to get over the fear of not meeting expectations.

Card exchanges provide an excuse to reconnect with relationships that time has managed to neglect; they offer an opportunity to lighten up an elder person's day; and they satisfy my curiosity, as each year, I look forward to seeing how distant family members have changed. The materials commonly used in the manufacturing of greeting cards and the shipping associated with mailing them can add up to a hefty carbon footprint. And unfortunately, since there is currently no recycling in place for photo paper, anything printed on it is destined to end up in the landfill (so is the backing of the stamp used to mail them).

Electronic delivery is a good alternative to alleviate environmental impact. It's true though that especially when blasted to a huge list, these greetings lose their charms. I believe that a thoughtful greeting card should take both ecological and human factors into consideration. Electronic can replace physical delivery when done right.

Regardless of delivery method, what makes a greeting special is personalization. A long recipient list makes it tough to make each card special. As discussed in the "Workspace and Junk Mail" chapter, I believe that fewer stronger relationships are more enriching than many weak ones. Can you look at your list and eliminate the contacts that do not bring positivity to your life? With a minimal recipient list, personalization is achievable. Whether you choose to send an email or a *real* card is up to you, but a personal message (maybe explaining why you value the friendship) will surely make your greeting meaningful. If you choose to send electronic greetings, make sure to embed them in the body of an email (versus annoying links) and address each message separately (no CCs or BCCs).

To minimize our ecological footprint, I traded weeks of crafting solo for collaborating with my boys to design a digital video or image, which we individually email with a personalized note. But this method is not for everybody. If you have difficulty transitioning to electronic greetings and prefer to stick to paper, give these options a consideration:

Picking materials:

- Reuse the cards that you receive to make new ones.
- Make cards from paper scraps (refer to the instructions on page 177), and consider adding seeds to your paper pulp to make your greeting "plantable."
- Choose recyclable materials when purchasing new cards, and choose recycled paper made from 100 percent postconsumer waste.
- Pick a small-size stamp

Eliminating the need for envelopes:

- Choose or create a postcard-type greeting card. You'll save on mailing costs, too!
- Use a small piece of paper tape or dot of glue (see glue recipe on page 179) to seal a common bifold card; address and affix stamp on a blank side.
- Use a trifold newsletter template; address and affix stamp on a blank side.

Disposing of the cards that you receive:

- Store them for reuse if you plan on sending cards the following year.
- Remove any photo paper and add them to your curbside recycling.
- Send them to St. Jude's Ranch, an organization that rescues abused children. The used cards are redesigned to support their cause. See the "Resources" section to find their address.

Thoughtful greetings are not one size fits all. The elder members of my family, for example, prefer a verbal delivery. It does take longer than an email or card, but avoiding the mall opens time for such indulgences.

Alternatives to cards or emails (i.e., voice your greeting!):

- Make a phone call.
- Set up an Internet video chat or conference.
- Make an impromptu visit.

OTHER CELEBRATIONS

The Zero Waste philosophy can naturally be extended to all celebrations. Celebrations do not need to be wasteful; on the contrary, their significance is highlighted when waste is reduced. Across the board, I happily dropped unsustainable traditions and the burden of storing manufactured decor. I've widely adopted new, edible traditions instead, and I've found that celebrating and decorating with food is fun and universally appreciated and can adapt to any decor or season. Find my tips for four typically wasteful holidays below. I haven't covered everything on the calendar, but you can use your imagination to adapt to the occasion and to your tastes and traditions.

Valentine's Day

Where I grew up, Valentine's Day was reserved for lovers (i.e., grown-ups involved in an intimate relationship). But when I moved to the United States, I discovered a whole different meaning behind this holiday. During Max's first year of preschool, the teacher instructed clueless parents like me to go to the local drugstore, buy a dozen valentines (I had never heard of such things, and did not even know what to look for), and address one to each classmate. I (a grown woman) would write love cards to twelve toddlers I barely knew. Although I did not quite grasp the point behind duplicates of impersonal and commercial valentines, picked out and signed by other moms, I did come to realize that Valentine's Day in American schools does not celebrate love but rather appreciation for fellow pupils. Eager to embrace the American culture, I participated in the school activity for years. Each year, the boys came home with a plastic bag filled with wrappers, half-eaten candies, and crumpled cards. When asked about his favorite card, my son bluntly replied, "I don't know . . . I just want the candy." The whole lot lay in the trash can by day's end.

Love and appreciation for fellow pupils are legitimate reasons to celebrate, but the celebration doesn't have to be drowned in red heart-shaped junk, dust-collecting stuffed animals, and tree-munching cards.

Valentine's Day does not need to be a wasteful event. To make it a sustainable one, consider one of these two options:

- Suggest an eco-friendly valentine exchange to your child's teacher. How about organizing a cookie exchange in lieu of overlooked valentines? Or what about "creating one inventive, recycled, or edible valentine to be exchanged randomly"? Ms. Dunn, Max's fifth-grade teacher suggested, "Take care, take time, and make something you yourself would like to receive."

- Welcome alternatives to paper valentines. Consider edibles instead. Heart-shaped cookies, homemade pretzels, birdseed cakes, candied flowers (whole violets or pansies or rose petals), oranges with nesting hearts carved into the white pith, and chocolate treats from the bulk aisle are all viable alternatives.

HEART PRETZEL

Makes 2 large pretzels (or 4 small ones)

INGREDIENTS

1 teaspoon dry yeast	**For the dipping solution:**
¾ cup warm water	4 cups hot water
2 cups flour	½ cup baking soda
½ teaspoon salt	
1½ teaspoons sugar	Coarse salt

DIRECTIONS

1. Dissolve dry yeast in water.
2. Add remaining ingredients and knead until smooth and no longer sticky.
3. Separate into 2 pieces and roll each one into a long and thin log and shape into a heart (join extremities at the top).
4. Combine hot water and baking soda in a bowl and dip each pretzel in the solution.
5. Sprinkle with coarse salt.
6. Bake at 425°F for 15 minutes or until browned.

Easter

When we speak of Easter, regardless of religious beliefs, we automatically think of eggs and the Easter bunny (or in France, we think of chocolate fish and church bells). But what excites me more about that holiday is the period that precedes it: Lent. Although I do not consider myself a religious person, I recently found that Lent satisfies my spiritual needs and presents an opportunity. It sets aside a forty-day period to test a sustainable idea, or to evaluate a personal attachment to a habit. Often we fear trying something simply because we fear commitment. But the time limitations of Lent provide you with parameters. Your project has an expiration date. I find that this yearly challenge, scheduled at the end of winter, breaks my routine and makes life exciting!

I am by no means suggesting that you convert to Christianity, but that you regularly set aside a time to try something new every year. The possibilities are infinite and offer a chance to give up (or even perhaps to add!) something for the period of time and to discover something new about yourself. Pick something that you can test for forty days. If you eat meat every day, going vegan overnight is bound to fail. Maybe cut out red meat or incorporate one meatless dinner into your week instead. Here are more ideas to get you thinking: try veganism if you are already vegetarian; grow herbs in a sunny window; give up coffee; buy local (be a locavore); try a Zero Waste alternative, such as giving up a packaged good or paper towels; try the "no-poo" method; shop with jars; act on every piece of junk mail you receive; turn the TV off; take navy showers; go on a walk every day; use public transportation; cycle to work; give up the car entirely; don't buy anything new; wear one dress for forty days or a men's shirt forty different ways.

Easter marks the end of my experiment. Maybe I will choose to permanently implement change in my life, maybe not.... But I can be proud of myself for sticking to it!

Now, time for the Easter egg hunt! Scott says the bunny drops them by. I say church bells do. Each year, we prepare and hide two types for our boys: a dozen hard-boiled (dyed per the instructions on pages 204–5) and a dozen surprise eggs.

For the surprise eggs, it is best to stay away from refillable ones, many of which contain lead, and instead opt for felt, fabric, or wooden eggs. Considering our region's wet weather around Easter, our family opted for a dozen of the wooden alternative. We simply fill some with money, others with treats found in the bulk aisle: malt balls, jelly beans, salted or chocolate-covered nuts, etc.

After the hunt and before brunch time, our hard-boiled eggs turn into devils. We munch them, and they disappear!

DEVILED EGG RECIPE

INGREDIENTS

12 hard-boiled eggs	Milk
1 cup grated parmesan cheese	Salt and pepper
1 tablespoon mustard (see recipe, page 70)	Paprika

DIRECTIONS

1. Peel the hard-boiled eggs and cut them lengthwise.
2. Carefully scoop the yolks out of the whites into a bowl. Set the whites aside.
3. Mash the yolks with the remaining ingredients and enough milk to create a paste.
4. Season to taste.
5. Using a spoon, scoop the mixture back into the white halves.
6. Dust with paprika.

Halloween

I experienced my first Halloween at the age of eighteen, shortly after my move to the United States, when I escorted the children for whom I was the au pair on a trick-or-treat outing. I remember that night vividly. I had never heard of the holiday before, but I could tell from the decorations and the anticipation in the air that the celebration was a big deal. As I struggled to make sense of the terms *trick-or-treat* and *jack-o'-lantern,* I accompanied Laura Ingalls, a little bee, and Batman from one lit house to another and blended in with the crowds. Never had I experienced a night filled with such communal enthusiasm, colorful dressing, and glowing light! I could not wait to share details with my mom the following day: "Wow, the Americans know how to celebrate!" I exclaimed over the phone.

Little did I know then that I would celebrate Halloween again with my children! Every year, I look forward to rediscovering the glowing atmosphere and conviviality that marked my first experience. I love coming up with creative ideas for costumes, seeing the excitement that lights the kids' faces, and sharing good times with friends.

Stress associated with environmental concerns took much joy out of my first Zero Waste Halloween, though. Had I embarked on Zero Waste without kids, I could ignore that the wasteful holiday even exists. But with our children wanting to share their trick-or-treating with their friends, we compromised and came up with guidelines that satisfy both their social life and our lifestyle. In a Zero Waste world, the celebration would be a noncommercial, waste-free, treasure-sharing, costume festival . . . For now, here are ideas on keeping Halloween as sustainable an event as possible:

Costumes

- **Use what you have on hand.** In my mind, homemade costumes always prevail. They demonstrate creative thinking and sometimes craftsmanship, and usually steal the show for their uniqueness. The Internet is a wonderful source of inspiration, and with just a few pieces of cardboard, sheets, fabric scraps, and the makeup recipes (see pages 99–103), you can achieve a memorable costume. Léo's friend Camilla once dressed as a present; all she used was a cardboard box and a ribbon!
- **Shop the thrift store.** When a lack of time, ideas, or materials limits homemade outfits, the secondhand store is a wonderful source of costumes and supplemental accessories. After Halloween, you can donate your costume back to the charity to reduce home clutter and make it available to others; make sure to bundle and label the attires' elements together to facilitate the charity's work and sale.
- **Host or participate in a costume swap.** A Zero Waste household ought to make seldom-used items, such as Halloween costumes, available to the secondhand market. But if you have some from years previous, you can swap them with friends or participate in an organized event (see "Resources").
- **Rent.** If you are after a fancy costume, renting is the way to go!

Trick-or-Treat

Hosting

I am not at all against the trick-or-treat tradition. The freebies are, after all, the force behind the consistent turnouts. But I am opposed to recent efforts aimed at replacing sweets with trinkets. Trinkets consume valuable resources and many of them are not recyclable. Edibles, on the other hand, are delicious, and they disappear once consumed. Hosts can limit Halloween waste if they stay away from keepsakes that are bound to clutter children's rooms, and choose to give out a single consumable (something that can be "used up") that is preferably not packaged, or packaged in paper or cardboard. Here are items to consider:

Food: A box of organic raisins, a whole fruit (like mandarins), a licorice root stick (I loved to chew on these as a kid), or any candy sold in a cardboard box, such as Milk Duds, Dots, and Junior Mints. Consider healthy items if possible.

Nonfood consumable: Money, a bar of soap, an eraser-free newspaper pencil, or packets of seeds.

Going

Trick-or-treating is Halloween's most anticipated activity, but without limitations, it can be a source of much incoming waste. Talk to your children and agree on a set of rules that satisfies your principles without spoiling their fun. The 5 Rs offered an invaluable guideline to defining our rules. Here is how we choose to trick-or-treat:

- **Refuse plastic trinkets.**
- **Pick in order of preference:** (1) unpackaged consumable, (2) consumable packaged in cardboard or paper, (3) candy wrapped in plastic. While the majority of trick-or-treat items currently fall in the third category, this simple guideline empowers the child to make a thoughtful decision, and therefore take a vote on (i.e., support or reject) a packaging practice.
- **Sort the candy.** While I do not support frequent candy eating, I personally do not mind my children enjoying a few pieces that time of the year. Con-

sequently, once their bounty comes home, they can keep any candy from categories one and two, but pick only ten from the third one. The sorting and trading has become a fun post-Halloween tradition with our boys.

- **Recycle the wrappers.** The plastic wrappers of the ten pieces selected will be sent to TerraCycle along with those opened during the outing (our kids are only human), when we fill a box, as mentioned on page 50 in the "Kitchen and Grocery" chapter. We simply recycle the paper and cardboard wrappers through our curbside recycling.
- **Donate the surplus.** Our kids have the choice of donating their candy to (1) a local nursery home, (2) a business that offers candy to their clientele, (3) a shelter, (4) a soup kitchen or local food bank (while these prefer nutritious food donations, the candy makes a treat for the upcoming holidays), or (5) a dental office that participate in the Halloween Candy Buy Back (which sends them to the troops). By choosing and personally delivering their candy to one of these outlets, the kids feel good about themselves too!

Decor

No need to store life-size mummies in your garage all year; a collection of pumpkins in addition to candles (see oil votive recipe on page 215) set in deep jars and strategically placed off the beaten path of trick-or-treaters keep decorating minimal and ephemeral. The pumpkins can be roasted or steamed for the cooked flesh to be used in seasonal recipes or frozen in jars for future meals. With the recipes below, what's left of your decor are roasted pumpkin skins in the compost or the birds' feeding bowl. When hosting a party, many recipes can be made with bulk or produce ingredients to add spice to a spooky decor for the night. A watermelon can be carved into a brain and meringues shaped into bones, for example.

Here is how to make the most of your pumpkin:

Using a Whole Pumpkin: Tureen, Soup, and Topping!

Once Halloween is over, your decoration can turn into a dish. Sugar pie, baby-bear, or red kuri pumpkins are best for this purpose, so purchase your Halloween decor accordingly.

TURN RIND INTO A SERVING DISH

DIRECTIONS

1. Wash the pumpkin.
2. Depending on the variety of pumpkin that you picked (shape and size), cut in half to make bowls or cut the top open to make tureens.
3. Using a spoon, scrape the seeds out and reserve in a bowl of water.
4. Bake the pumpkin upside down in a baking dish with an inch of water, at 350°F for about 30 minutes, or until a knife can be inserted into the cooked rind. Be careful not to overcook: it should be firm enough to hold the soup.
5. Run under cold water to stop the cooking process.

TURN SEEDS INTO A TOPPING

DIRECTIONS

1. Separate the seeds from the strings attached to them and compost the strings.
2. Remove excess moisture with a kitchen towel.
3. Toss in oil or melted butter, salt, pepper, and spices of your choice.
4. Spread on a baking sheet and bake at 300°F, stirring occasionally, for 45 minutes or until golden brown.

TURN FLESH INTO SOUP

DIRECTIONS

1. Scrape as much flesh as you can off the roasted pumpkin, including the top, as evenly as you can, without piercing the rind. Reserve.
2. In a large saucepan, sauté diced yellow onion in olive oil and butter until tender.

3. Add the pumpkin flesh.
4. Cover with stock: alternatively use water and a bone.
5. Season with salt, pepper, and nutmeg.
6. Bring to a boil, reduce heat, and simmer for 30 minutes to blend flavors.
7. Using an immersion blender, blend until smooth.
8. Add heavy cream or half-and-half (optional).
9. Adjust seasoning to taste.

TO SERVE

1. If necessary, trim a sliver off the bottom to improve the balance of your tureens or bowls.
2. Pour the soup into them.
3. Top with a few drops of olive oil and the roasted seeds.
4. Serve with toasted and buttered baguette.

Thanksgiving

I grew up without exchanging valentines or dressing up for Halloween or enjoying a Thanksgiving feast. But this day holds a special place in my heart, and if I were to observe only one holiday a year, this would be the one!

While the historical facts celebrated at Thanksgiving raise an ethical dilemma for some, the holiday holds more significance than the remembrance of the Pilgrims' first Thanksgiving. I find that it embodies the Zero Waste lifestyle beautifully.

Thanksgiving reflects simplicity and celebrates modest times. It does not require a manufactured decor. Leaves, acorns, pinecones, squash, or corn kernels found in the bulk aisle make fantastic table adornments.

Thanksgiving commends us to take time off from our busy schedules. Once a year, it encourages families to gather around the dinner table and share common pleasures: cooking, eating, storytelling, and sometimes recipe sharing and football watching.

Thanksgiving calls for reflection and thankfulness. Regardless of hardships, it incites us to find something to be grateful for in our lives. The French do not celebrate such tradition, but my cynical side likes to imagine how our complaining nature would benefit from a little appreciation.

Thanksgiving meals can be made using unprocessed bulk ingredients, and the leftovers can be enjoyed in sandwiches, casseroles, or soups (see "Bone Soup" recipe below). Although the next day is officially Black Friday, the embodiment of consumerism, it is unofficially considered a national Leftovers Day! What better way to offer gratitude and celebrate family than to spend the day making soup rather than at the mall elbowing other consumers to try to get the best deal on a TV.

BONE SOUP

DIRECTIONS

1. Bringing a turkey home Zero Waste–style is easiest if it is purchased whole from the producer or a small market and placed into a large container (a canner, for example), or cut up at the butcher shop to fit within a smaller one.
2. Break up a leftover poultry carcass into large pieces and place in a pot.
3. Cover with water and bring to a boil, then reduce the heat and simmer until the meat has loosened off the bones.
4. Remove from heat and let cool.
5. Remove skin and bones (you can reserve the bones and grind them to make bonemeal, a great source of phosphorus for your garden's soil).
6. Skim the fat off the stock's surface.
7. Add leftover vegetables, gravy, and stuffing.
8. Bring to a boil, reduce the heat, and simmer for an hour.
9. Season to taste and enjoy!

GIFTS

We sometimes give gifts out of obligation, sometimes out of pure goodness of the heart. But regardless of motive, what we give should be the product of thought and consideration. Coming from a Zero Waste household, your gifts should reflect your values. A Zero Waste present is a great opportunity to let your friends know about your waste-reduction efforts and inspire them to follow your lead. Here are a few ideas of gifts that follow the Zero Waste principles.

Experiences

The Zero Waste lifestyle is all about filling life with experiences versus stuff. A gift of experience will become neither a keepsake nor a source of clutter to others. An *experience* gift is not only kinder to the environment but the memories attached to it are likely to last longer! Each Christmas, our boys receive a monthly subscription to a surprise family activity (SFA). Throughout the year, we take part in twelve activities that we have never tried before. Some cost money, others are free, but Scott and I always keep them secret until we get to them. Listening to the kids' most extravagant guesses is priceless.

Among activities that we have enjoyed as a family, here are examples that do not involve consumption and could be offered in the form of a gift certificate (preferably digital or paper) or actual entry ticket:

Attending the ballet, the opera, a concert, a comedy show, a sports game, or the taping of a TV show

Backpacking to an overnight refuge; batting in cages; biking to a nearby town for lunch; bowling; boating; bungee jumping; bird-watching

Crabbing

Dining in an unusual restaurant: teppanyaki-style Japanese restaurant, Korean barbecue, Swiss fondue

Exploring a museum (check your local library for free passes!), a theme park, an aquarium, or a zoo; eating bugs (the ones we ate were chocolate covered!)

Fishing

Gold panning; geocaching; golfing; going to the movies

Horseback riding

Ice skating

Joining a club

Karting; kayaking; kite flying

Laser tagging

Making something; motorcycling; mushing (dog sledding); mushroom hunting (contact your local mycological club for outing schedules)

Nightclubbing

Overnight at a hotel with a pool, on a houseboat, in a tree house

Paddleboating; parasailing; picking fruit; playing in an arcade; picnicking in an unusual place

Quenching a thirst at a cool pub

Rollerblading; riding a Ferris wheel

Sledding; skiing; sailing

Taking tea at the Ritz; touring around in a Segway

Unplugging at a beach club; unicycling

Visiting a farm, a dude ranch, a recycling facility, or a factory

Watching a drive-in movie

XYZ, etc.: Zip-lining, indoor climbing or skydiving

Your Time

Time is money and makes a respectable present. It can be offered in the form of an IOU (i.e., a coupon) or as an impromptu visit.

Professional expertise: A plumber could offer to repair a leaky faucet, an electrician a faulty connection. I can offer decluttering and Zero Waste consultations.

Manual labor: Planting a tree, painting a room for a new baby, fixing a deck, leaf raking, lawn mowing, babysitting. These are particularly great for kids to give. For example, one sibling could take another sibling's chore for a period of time.

Visit: When distance keeps us away from our parents or grandparents, a spontaneous visit is sure to make them happy. Why not offer the gift of your presence?

Services

Professional services can be offered in the form of gift certificates and are wonderful ways to pamper someone: mani-pedis, facials, massages, a gym subscription, etc.

Digital Gifts

When used wisely, digital gifts can reduce waste, keep safe priceless memories, and facilitate long-distance communication. Consider offering online subscriptions to games, magazines, newspapers, or video streaming (such as Netflix or Hulu), e-books, iTunes, cloud file storage, photo scanning or video digitizing (transfer home VHS videos into digital files, for example), or Skype credit vouchers.

Consumables

Packaged in a reusable jar, which you can embellish with a ribbon, twine, or designs using the grocery shopping kit's washable crayon (see page 55), consumables are universally appreciated. See recipes in this book for inspiration. Among infinite possibilities, examples include:

Edibles

Homemade: Cookies, jam, mustard, pickles, quince paste, crystallized flowers, mulling spices, red wine vinegar, hot chocolate mix, liqueurs, infused oils

Bulk/unpackaged: Honey, cornichons, olives, maple syrup, toffee pecans, chocolate malt balls, gummy bears

Beauty Products

Homemade: Soap, scrub, balm, tooth powder, mascara, eyeliner

Bulk/unpackaged: Clay mask, soap, lotion, bath salts, massage oils

Household Products

Homemade: Paper, candles using leftovers, home-dried seeds, homegrown plants

Cash

One present that is always appreciated and fully reusable is cash! Online origami tutorials can teach you how to fold bills into an array of shapes, including suggestive ones that give a hint on how to spend the money, such as a "dime-in-a-ring" (diamond ring), a cat, a dress, a shirt, an airplane, or a toilet. These folding tricks are sure to impress your recipient!

One present that makes people feel good is a charitable gift card. JustGive.org allows the giver to purchase an electronic gift card of a chosen amount, which the recipient can then spend on the charity of his choice (and the choices are many)!

Secondhand Goods

Shop your home: Get over the taboo. There is nothing wrong with regifting or giving something that you already own as long as you know *for sure* that the recipient needs and will appreciate it! Consider as resources those items that you do not use or have set aside to donate (because they are)! Shopping your home not only saves time and money, it is an ecologically sound (and, in many parts of the world, a well-accepted) practice.

Shop the secondhand market: Thrift stores, garage sales, flea markets, consignment shops, Craigslist, Freecycle, Play-It-Again Sports, eBay, etc., are wonderful places to look for specific items, such as books and sporting equipment, on someone's wish list. When surfing eBay's goods, make sure to select the "used" box under the search options, and when purchasing, make sure to request paper or cardboard shipping materials, and if possible, ground shipping.

Note: If you are embarrassed to tell your recipient that your gift is *used*, just use the term *vintage*. The words essentially mean the same thing, but *vintage* has the more charming connotation.

Buy New

Buying new is the last option for the Zero Waste household, but it is sometimes inevitable when used options are not available. Look for durable, reusable items that are made locally from sustainable materials using sustainable practices, packaged minimally, and preferably not packaged at all—Ugh. So many rules. Buying used is so much easier! Eco-friendly products are the rage these days, and make acceptable gifts, but only if the gift is truly needed and desired. Otherwise it is bound to become clutter and a waste of resources. No need to offer a reusable stainless bottle to someone who already owns one, or something made of recycled materials if the recipient already has a version of the object. Aside from obvious choices, which include refillable bottles and shopping totes, consider family-bonding board games, foraging books, cloth gift bags, reusable-battery chargers, etc.

Being Proactive

Zero Waste starts outside the home, and relies on much proactivity. In terms of receiving gifts, here are some guidelines:

- Let those with whom you exchange gifts know that you abide by Zero Waste principles and prefer experiences to more stuff.
- Timing is everything. Let them know before they bother to gather/buy objects for you. It is easier for a child to refuse a party favor ahead of time than on the spot.
- Offer givers (grandparents, playmates' mothers) concrete gift examples, such as those mentioned above. Easy and inexpensive suggestions include gift certificates for the movies, the local ice cream parlor, or iTunes. Digital (versus a plastic gift card) is always preferable.

Gift Wrapping

A Zero Waste gift isn't complete without the right wrapping. Naturally, the most Zero Waste wrapper is none at all (hostess gifts, for example, do not require one) but if you want your present to be a surprise, consider these alternatives to common wrapping materials:

- Purchase or make **reusable gift bags** from fabric scraps (sheets, shirts, jeans, pockets, etc.). You can even redesign a lone sock into a gift card pouch, pillowcases into large present wrappers. These will encourage your recipient to reuse your gift bag and avoid store-bought wrapping paper (a present within a present)! Choose or make them with a fixed tie or ribbon to eliminate the need for loose ones.

- Purchase or make **Furoshiki squares** (any size will do, but I found a twenty-eight-by-twenty-eight-inch square to be most versatile) to artfully wrap your gifts in fabric. Sheets, curtains, or saris are great materials to make your own. As previously mentioned, easy-to-follow instructions are available at furoshiki.com/techniques, but below is my favorite way to wrap a bottle. The elaborate knots and tucks of this wrapping art also eliminate the need for a loose ribbon. Make sure to include instructions or show your recipients how to use them, so they can reuse them, too.

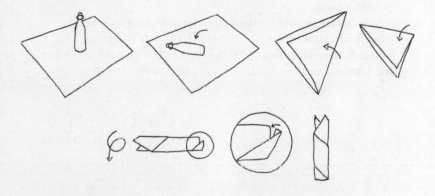

- Use a **gift to wrap** another. A T-shirt, a sweater, a kitchen towel can wrap just about anything and serve a double duty (a gift and wrapper in one). Consider using one of the kitchen towels that you deem "too pretty to use."

- Reuse **what you already have**, if lacking the previous wrapping alternatives: wrapping paper from gifts to you, papers from your recycling bin (your kids can quickly paint some designs on them), children's artwork, newspaper cutouts (if you still receive a newspaper), or shipping materials (box, brown paper, or an envelope turned inside out). If wrapping is done right, tape is not necessary. Twine, thread, and fabric scraps made of natural fibers can be used to secure your wrapping material, used again by your recipient, and even composted when they are no longer usable.

- **Label** your present only when necessary. If you are going to a birthday party or a wedding, there is no need to write the name of the recipient. For Christmas, labeling ensures that presents do not end up in the wrong hands. In this case, write the name of the recipient directly on the material, using a washable crayon (refer to the grocery shopping kit on page 55). Otherwise, make a gift tag from a tree leaf or anything in your recycling bin, cut into a small rectangle.

5 *RS* CHECKLIST: 5 TIPS FOR HOLIDAYS AND GIFTS

Refuse: Reject Halloween trinkets when trick-or-treating; pick consumables instead.

Reduce: Streamline your holiday decor; embrace edible decorating.

Reuse: Trade, borrow, rent, or buy a used Halloween costume.

Recycle: Send holiday cards and Halloween candy wrappers for recycling.

Rot: Compost your Easter eggshells and your pumpkin tureen.

Out and About

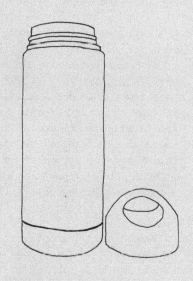

The Zero Waste lifestyle can (and should) extend well beyond your home's boundaries. As you will quickly realize, the methods used to tackle waste outside the home very much follow those applied inside; they boil down to one common principle: preemptive action.

Of course, life is full of surprises, with unforeseen events and spontaneous occasions that you don't want Zero Waste to spoil. But when we are aware of the activities in advance, we can use that information to consider the waste potential and then act accordingly. Before leaving the house, consider your day: Grab a coffee mug on your way to the café, a reusable water bottle to a hike, or a drinking glass to an art, beer, or street festival. Pack a plate and flatware if you plan on attending a community potluck or a pancake fund-raiser. Take a reusable toothpick if you plan on tasting samples at the grocery store or the farmer's market. BYO requires some thinking ahead, and on rare occasions, your efforts will prove to be unneeded. For example, some coffee shops offer ceramic alternatives. But in most cases, these actions will save a precious resource from being discarded. Better to be prepared and pleasantly surprised than frustrated and disappointed.

Besides extending conservation efforts, applying Zero Waste outside the home also provides an invaluable opportunity to share your knowledge outside your household and may even inspire others.

EATING OUT

The Zero Waste lifestyle shares many values with the Slow Food movement. It welcomes methods used to facilitate and cook a homemade meal, the ingredients of which can be healthier and less wasteful (in terms of origin, packaging, portion control, and leftovers) than in most eateries. Consequently, you dine in restaurants less, but it does not mean that you "eat out" less . . . because you can picnic more!

Restaurants and Takeout

Last year, the occasion of an SFA (secret family activity) prompted us to go to a Korean barbecue restaurant, an eating style that the kids had yet to experience. The four of us gathered around a hot table and stared at an extensive menu, unable to make a decision. Based on the advice of our friendly server, we opted for the "dinner special," which promised to accommodate four people. When an overabundance of meat, fish, and veggies were delivered, and barely fit on our table, we had clearly ordered way more food than we could gulp in one sitting. To avoid using the plastic containers provided by the restaurant to pack leftovers, we tried to stuff ourselves so as to "not waste" the food in front of us. Accepting a throwaway container to save a compostable item (i.e., food) from disposal was out of the question; it could not possibly make up for our misjudgment or the reusable container we had failed to bring along.

As I shoved a forkful of spiced pork into my mouth, conflicting thoughts came to fill my mind: Does pushing myself beyond satisfaction really count as "saving food"? Is it worth making ourselves sick just to avoid bringing a container home? When I was completely stuffed, I surrendered to the waitress's offer to pack it up. Too full to embark on an ecological debate, I blurted out: "Not in plastic, though, I am allergic to it." Although she had never heard of such an aversion, she accepted it with grace (probably better than she would have taken a conservation lesson) and reached for a sheet of foil instead. Not ideal, but better than plastic. Maybe I should have been more honest and explained why I did not want to use a plastic container; maybe the restaurant owner would have changed his restaurant practice— or maybe not. Whatever the case, it was an effective stopgap measure. After all, it is virtually impossible for a restaurant to dispute one of their patrons' health conditions.

Here is what to consider when eating out at restaurants:

- **Shopping is voting and dining is voting, too!** Patronize restaurants that use sustainable practices and offer local, organic fare. Frequent restaurants that support waste-reducing efforts; boycott those that do not. Haste makes waste. Generally, fast-food joints create more waste.

- **Avoid leftovers.** Order only what you can eat. Share large portions, or order French-size individual portions. The French do not use doggie bags because the portions served do not produce leftovers. Happy hour, tapas, and Japanese-style dining share a common waste-busting tactic: the portions are small, are generally intended for sharing, and can be ordered as needed.
- **Use only the condiments that you need.** Just because it's free does not mean that it did not take resources to produce.
- **Turn your water glass upside down** when you are no longer thirsty, to avoid unnecessary water refills.

Here is what to consider if you have restaurant leftovers or if you order takeout:

- **Bring your own containers:** we keep a jar in the car for this purpose.
- **Favor wax paper, cardboard, or aluminum** if you failed to bring your own container. Often, a simple paper napkin or clean handkerchief will do.
- **Refuse Styrofoam at all costs;** maybe explain that you are allergic . . . Its production and disposal are not only detrimental to the environment, its chemicals leach into our food and harm our health.

Restaurants expose their customers to not only a plethora of food and container waste but also wasteful serving accessories. These unsustainable practices have spread across the dining spectrum; they are not unique to the obvious fast-food joints. Although we did not use these disposables until recent times, today most of us expect a mixed drink to be served with plastic stirrer and cocktail napkin, a pizza box with a stacker, a sub sandwich with a flag toothpick, an ice cream cone with a wrapper, a cafeteria tray with an advertisement liner, a shellfish plate with a disposable hand wipe, a sandwich to-go with a swaddle of napkins and condiment packets. Do these extras enhance your dining experience? The thought of their impact on the environment brings sadness to mine.

When we order, it's common to ask what ingredients make up a dish. It's not out of the question to also ask: How is it served? What disposables are involved? Does the glass of water come with a straw? Because I do not need one.

Here are examples of disposables to watch out for and refuse when dining out:

Ashtray: Consider quitting.

Bakery wrappers: Have the baked goods deposited in your hand or handkerchief.

Chopsticks: Request reusable flatware.

Doilies: You can surely do without.

Espresso cups: Bring your reusable insulated mug.

Fake grass on the sushi platter, flags on the sub sandwich: Request none.

Guest towels: Wipe your hands on your handkerchief, your clothes, or a cloth roll towel system (or an air dryer if there are no other Zero Waste options).

Hot cups and lids: Bring your reusable insulated mug.

Ice cream cups and taster spoons: Choose a cone instead and trust your taste instincts.

Juice or water cup and lid: Have it poured into your reusable bottle.

Kids' spill-proof cups, coloring sheet, and crayons: Bring your own.

Lemon wraps: You can surely do without.

Mixed-drink stirrers: Stir it (or have your bartender do it for you) with flatware.

Napkins: Use your handkerchief.

Olive picks: Clean fingers will do.

Pizza stackers, otherwise known as a pizza box lid holder or white table in the middle of the pizza: So what if some cheese got on the box?

Quiche pans: Order something else; make your own quiche at home.

Restroom seat covers: Squat!

Straws: Order drinks without.

Toothpicks: Wait to get home to tackle your dental hygiene.

Utensils: Boycott plastic or bring your own (see flatware set in Picnics below).

Verrine: If a disposable plastic version shows up on your plate, propose glass alternatives instead.

Wipes: Wash your hands.

XYZ, etc.: Coffee stirrers (request a reusable spoon), lobster bibs (tie a cloth dinner napkin around your neck or tuck it into your shirt's collar), muffin liners (how about a pastry instead?), popcorn bags (fill your own cloth bag), steak markers (trust the staff), sugar packets (use a dispenser or ask for a bowl of sugar), tray liners (don't they wash the trays?), etc.

We can maximize our impact and eliminate our waste by being proactive and refusing these single-use items at the time of ordering. But if they sneak into your dining experience, propose reusable alternatives to the business owner (or suggest that they simply be eliminated) and point to the financial savings! The more we as customers act, the sooner we can phase these disposables out.

Picnics

The Zero Waste lifestyle inspires us to spend time outdoors to connect with nature, and what better occasion to do so than picnicking! Picnics present us with an unparalleled opportunity: to escape the demands of home, breathe fresh air, and absorb some vitamin D. During the working week, it provides a refreshing break; during the weekend, a reason to get together with friends. No need to sweep your floors for company; nature is the perfect place to entertain! Kids can run around away from electronic sources of entertainment and find creative ways to occupy themselves.

Picnicking is inexpensive and healthy, and doing it in compliance with Zero Waste is easy, assuming that you have adopted the grocery shopping methods covered earlier in the book.

To make it easy to grab and go anytime, we keep a picnic bag in our pantry stocked with: shatterproof plates, cups, and bamboo flatware sets wrapped in a napkin for each member of the family.

We also bring this picnic set to communal buffets and camping trips, and the flatware on flights.

When ready to go, we add:

- A few jars of whatever antipasti ingredient you might have in the refrigerator, such as cheese, salami, leftover pizza, roasted peppers, marinated mushrooms, cornichons, hard-boiled eggs, roasted tomatoes, olives, pickles (see recipe opposite). Shop the olive bar for ideas.
- Nuts.
- Fruit.

- A frozen baguette.
- A reusable water bottle and a bottle of wine.
- A blanket.

If I bring a prepared dish along, I wrap it in a towel, Furoshiki-style. (I also use this method to bring a dish to a potluck.)

BREAD-AND-BUTTER PICKLES

This is an easy recipe that we have found to be a great complement to our picnics. Recipe will fill one quart-size jar.

INGREDIENTS

5 cups sliced pickling cucumbers (about 5)	1 cup cracked ice
	¾ cup apple cider vinegar
1 sliced onion	¾ cup sugar
4 teaspoons coarse salt	Spices of your choice

DIRECTIONS

1. In a large bowl, mix together cucumbers, onion, salt, and ice.
2. Put a weight on the mixture for several hours. I use a plate and heavy jar.
3. Drain the mixture.
4. In a medium pot, combine the drained cucumber mixture, vinegar, sugar, and spices of your choice. For example, my

last batch included ¼ teaspoon cumin seeds and ⅛ teaspoon celery salt.

5. Bring to a near boil and turn off the heat.
6. Fill sterilized jars with pickles and liquid. The recipe will fill 1 quart-size jar.

Note: For long-term storage, you can boil the sealed jar for 10 minutes to can them. I personally don't. Instead, I refrigerate them and they disappear within a month.

CAMPING

We abuse land because we regard it as a commodity belonging to us. When we see land as a community to which we belong, we may begin to use it with love and respect.
    —Aldo Leopold, in his book *A Sand County Almanac*

Camping is not for everyone. The discomforts and dust are big barriers for many, including my mother in-law and my grandmother. But for those who can rise above the slight inconveniences, outdoor adventures can offer many advantages.

Whether you are drawn to Zero Waste for financial, ecological, or simplifying reasons, camping exemplifies and puts into practice many aspects of the lifestyle.

Camping provides a change of pace, an opportunity to experience a life with less. It strips away modern amenities and bluntly points to true necessities, the totality of which fits in the trunk of a car, or a backpack! It is a great exercise in reevaluating our attachment to things and habits. In the great outdoors, we loosen our standards of cleanliness and accept that dust is a fact of nature, that water should be conserved, that showers, tooth brushing, and makeup are not necessary in the grand scheme of subsistence. We momentarily let go of these luxuries to appreciate them more upon our return to civilization.

Camping also promotes togetherness and makes for an amazing family-bonding activity. Setting up camp, fetching water, preparing food, and cleaning dishes present rare occasions to collaborate. And it opens up time to play—football, music, cards, charades. It's rare to have this opportunity to team up in our day-to-day life. The walls that separate us at home disappear, making room for togetherness while camping. It is an ideal way for parents to teach their children a respect for nature, along with survival skills, such as fire making, fishing, foraging, and woodworking.

The most important aspect of camping is that it allows us to be in direct contact with the environment. As we join the world of raccoons and rabbits, watch a gopher build his burrow, hear coyotes howl at night, and wake up to the repertoire of a mockingbird, we can "see land as a community to which we belong."

Sadly, camping has changed. Not so long ago, campground sinks would attract an after-dinner rush of people lining up to wash dishes. I remember stressing out about beating everyone else to the washbasin. Today, however, throwaway dinnerware and water containers have replaced the reusable kind; overflowing waste bins have replaced the conversations at the sink. Camping is a fantastic activity to enjoy the environment, but camping wastefully is disrespectful, counterintuitive, and contradictory. It disregards the importance of nature, our graceful host. May we "begin to use it with love and respect."

Camping doesn't have to be wasteful. Simple preemptive tactics can make it a sustainable activity. Here are ideas to consider . . .

Waste-Free Camping Methods

- **Food:** The methods covered in the "Kitchen and Grocery Shopping" chapter and the tips mentioned under Picnic, above, provide alternatives to food packaging waste. Keep food in shopping reusables (glass, bottles, jars, or cloth bags) to reduce waste. Backpacking meals can be purchased in the bulk aisle, too. Snacks such as trail mix, nuts, and beef jerky (sold loose in liquor stores) can be stored in cloth bags, along with oatmeal and dry mixes such as curry lentil soup, corn chowder, chili, refried beans, and split pea and black bean soups which can then be rehydrated with hot water.
- **Water:** Refill containers instead of buying disposable water jugs and bottles. If you are backpacking, carry a water filter to purify water from lakes, rivers, or snow.
- **Cleaning:** A bar of castile soap to clean (dishes, body, hair, etc.), a metal scourer to scrub, a rag to wipe, and a towel to dry are all you need to keep campers and dishes clean. You can also wash greasy/oily dishes

with ashes (the combination of ash and oil creates a primitive soap) and scrub using sand or dirt.

- **Gas:** Although a nonrenewable resource, gas burns cleaner than wood or charcoal . . . but it results in an empty canister. You can connect a propane camping stove, manufactured to work with one-pound disposable canisters, to a refillable tank (such as those used to fuel gas barbecues) using proper connector hoses and adapter. You can also use a tank to refill a one-pound canister, using a special brass coupler.
- **Wood:** Many parks have restrictions on gathering firewood, so purchase wood before leaving home. In the United States, many state and national parks sell cut wood in cling wrap, but outside these parks, you can find it in convenience stores, sold in cardboard, or bundled in twine and for cheaper!
- **Recycling:** Sometimes even the best conservation efforts result in a few recyclable items (bottles of wine or beer, for example). Recycle at the campground or carry it out with you. While one-pound propane canisters are not recyclable (for safety reasons), butane canisters are. Empty ones must be rendered safe and punctured along the base, using a punch can opener, prior to recycling (please use caution in doing this: make sure the can is *completely* empty).
- **Composting:** Sometimes even the best conservation efforts result in a few compostable items (eggshells or orange peels, for example). Trench composting is an easy and convenient way to return your scraps to the ground when you left your worms at home. Simply dig a hole about twelve inches deep, deposit the compostable material, and cover with soil. We also use this trick when we travel and do not have access to a composter.
- **Repairs:** Don't throw away your tent over a split pole! It can be repaired via TentPole Technologies (visit TentPoleTechnologies.com for shipping instructions) or replaced via your tent's manufacturer.

Camping Products Alternatives

- **Mosquito repellent:** Spray vinegar or rub lavender flowers onto your skin.
- **Earplugs:** Soften a marble-size ball of cheese wax between your hands and stick in your ears for a peaceful night. If you have a snorer in the family, you know why you need these.

- **Table lighting:** Solar lamps are great but they are hard to find used. Refer to instructions on page 215 to make oil votives from scratch. You can also use an antique oil lamp, which you can fuel with cooking oil (olive oil is odorless) and outfit with a homemade braid using cotton scraps.
- **Fire starter:** Make your own by stuffing dryer lint (or sawdust) into the cups of an egg carton and topping them with melted beeswax, leftover candles, or cheese wax.
- **Waterproof matches:** Dip the heads of cardboard matches individually into melted wax. (Favor cardboard matches to refillable lighters, lighter fluid being a petroleum-based product.)

TRAVEL

When I was sixteen, I met a couple at a dinner party who had just completed a trip around the world. Ears wide open, I gave each of their stories my full attention and inquired about their favorite country, food, and people. At night, I lay in bed gazing at the ceiling, recalling their stories, picturing myself in exotic settings: exploring the savanna and trekking the jungle. I dreamed of patting an elephant, riding a camel, and diving with sharks. The travel bug was born.

I was lucky to wed a man who shared my aspirations to discover the world, and together we realized our travel fantasies. We tailored our wildest dreams to a low budget and took a six-month trip around the globe. We started out with huge stuffed backpacks. Clothes for both warm and cold climates, several pairs of shoes, books, and accessories weighed on our shoulders. Once in India, the packs weighed on our conscience, too. In the context of the savage poverty, our loads seemed disproportionate and out of place. Our extras became embarrassing luxuries. We edited our belongings down to the necessities (the clothes we wore, a change, bathing suit, and hat) and gave the rest away in exchange for grateful smiles. We learned that it is not what you possess but what you experience that makes life interesting. The trip opened our horizons and expanded our overall knowledge; it changed our preconceptions of faraway cultures and gave us a new outlook on life; later, it became a great source of inspiration for future works of art and Zero Waste alternatives.

What we failed to appreciate at the time was how pleasant and guilt free flying was when we were clueless about its ecological impact.

Carbon Footprint

The Zero Waste lifestyle is full of positivity: the money savings, the time gains, the health benefits, the multipurpose lip balm. The environmental awareness you gain, however, brings one great disappointment if you are a traveling enthusiast: the carbon footprint associated with flying.

Air travel is here to stay, and in our ever more globalized society, many relationships depend on it. But while we wait for genius scientists to discover clean alternatives, its carbon footprint is a huge issue. To fly or not to fly . . . is up to the individual.

On my end, I have come to accept the consequences of marrying and emigrating out of my country. When we chose the United States as our residence, we committed to a life of international phone calls to stay in touch with my family, and flights to visit my native land. Verbal communication alone would neither allow our kids to immerse in the French language nor give them the benefit of my mother's hugs and kisses. I know that I can adopt the Zero Waste lifestyle for as long as I live, but I also know that I must see my family. Flights are an unavoidable part of my bicultural life.

We are all responsible for adopting sustainable balance in our lives within regional limitations and personal needs. Carbon offsets offer an alternative to compensate for the detrimental ecological implications of travel, but carbon reduction should initially be applied to the entirety of your travel plans:

- **Reduce the frequency of trips.** Videoconferencing can substitute for business meetings, for example.
- **Reduce the distance traveled.** Can you stay local?
- **Consider transportation alternatives** to get to your destination. In many countries traveling by train is faster than flying.
- **Choose direct flights,** if you must fly.
- **Pack light.** With the tips that we covered for a Zero Waste wardrobe, it should be easy.
- **Stay in central locations** within walking distance of amenities.

There is no Zero Carbon way of flying, but there are steps we can take to reduce solid waste on the flight.

Disposable Flights

As the excitement of a vacation or the stress of a business meeting monopolizes our energies (i.e., "I have other things to worry about"), conservation ideologies are often put aside at the airport. We accept disposability as a sheer fact of traveling: the water bottle that is purchased before checking in, discarded at the security checkpoint, bought again a few minutes later, and replaced by another shortly after boarding. That's a lot of water, a lot of plastic, and a lot of waste in the space of an hour. There is more: the overflowing waste receptacles at the gate, the empty beverage container left on the bathroom counter, the takeout containers left on the ground, and the newspapers and magazines left on the waiting lounge seats. Your flight attendant offers you a drink, opens a single serving, pours it in a plastic cup filled with ice, and serves it with a cocktail napkin. When she comes around for seconds, she pours your new order in a new plastic cup with new ice and a new cocktail napkin. During the flight, your cups join the remains of half-eaten snacks, dirty napkins, and food wrappers.

At home, the outcome of our recyclables depends on many variable factors: it relies on the dedicated and joint efforts of manufacturers, consumers, municipalities, haulers, and MRFs (see "The 5 Rs" chapter). But the fate of the food and beverage containers, uneaten food, blankets, pillows, headphones, magazines, socks, and sleeping masks at a flight's destination is even more complicated given the rules and regulations of airlines, airports, customs, and health and security agencies. In the end, little winds up getting recycled at all. According to a report by the Natural Resource Defense Council (NRDC), "The U.S. airline industry discards enough aluminum cans each year to build fifty-eight Boeing 747 airplanes . . . and enough newspapers and magazines to fill a football field to a depth of more than 230 feet." Unfortunately, the waste problem is tangled and implicates many entities, and little collaboration is taking place to devise conservation solutions. But while we patiently wait for corporate and federal change to happen, there is much that the consumer, i.e., the traveler, can do, with a little preparation.

Here is what to pack to minimize your flight's solid waste:

- A reusable stainless-steel canteen (insulated, if you plan on consuming hot drinks)

- Your phone's earphones
- A wrap to use as a blanket or pillow
- Dry snack in a cloth bag
- Reading material: A library book, an e-book, or preowned magazines from the local thrift store
- A clear, reusable, waterproof pouch to store toiletries for their journey through safety checks (durable alternatives to flimsy ziplock bags are available)

For long-haul flights, add:

- A meal in a jar or stainless-steel container (or a sandwich in a towel)
- Your picnic bamboo flatware wrapped in a cloth napkin
- Optional: pillow (a neatly rolled jacket can serve as an alternative)

Grocery Shopping While Traveling

Once you have arrived at your destination, you can apply Zero Waste grocery shopping in using the same principles as those utilized at home and covered in the "Kitchen and Grocery Shopping" chapter. Wherever your travels take you:

- Familiarize yourself with the recycling and composting guidelines of the area.
- Locate a farmer's market to stock up on local produce.
- Use my smartphone app, Bulk, to locate package-free sources in the United States or Canada.
- Look for items sold loose in grocery store aisles, such as produce and buns.
- Look for specialty stores, such as bakeries or butchers.
- Use the cloth bag(s) and the jar(s) that you brought on the plane; as a default, purchase items sold in glass and reuse their containers to buy loose.

Most important, enjoy your trip!

Participating in Collaborative Consumption

While a part of me wishes that I were still naive about the impact of flying ("ignorance is bliss"), there is one aspect of Zero Waste traveling that I wish Scott and I had discovered earlier in life: renting our home when we are gone.

Participating in collaborative consumption, as discussed on page 23, makes complete environmental and financial sense. It makes those assets that sit unused for periods of time available to others. In the context of traveling, this "sharing" principle covers car rentals, house swaps, and short-term rentals. And it is capable of providing great financial relief to your travel plans—if not lucrative leisure!

While house swapping is an easy way to participate in collaborative consumption, we have found that renting out our home, on a short-term basis, provides us with more freedom of choice, as we are not limited to staying where the swapper lives. These short-term rentals also afford the advantage of being potentially profitable if you stay in a hotel or rent another home that is more affordable than yours. For example, if you camp, you can pocket a nice return.

The idea of renting our home was Scott's. Though I perceived it as a stroke of genius at the time, I now believe that it was his personal rite of passage to material independence. Throughout our journey and the implementation of the many alternatives that I shared with you in this book, we slowly learned to detach ourselves from our material possessions and to see stuff more as utilities. Today, we do care for our furnishings because we want them to last longer, but phrases like "I love my bed" have been replaced by "I can rent my bed," and taboos related to opening our home to "people we do not know" have been lifted. For us, the rental's security deposit provides enough of an assurance.

Minimalism is not crucial in participating in this activity, but voluntary simplicity naturally led us down this path and makes it easy to vacate the home. For example, clearing our space of the few personal items takes only fifteen minutes. Each of our four small wardrobes includes a carry-on suitcase. When renters are scheduled, we pull the bags down, fill them with our clothes and toiletries, zip, and we're out the door. It's that simple.

If you closely followed the tips provided in this book, you, too, can easily rent your home when you are gone. The first time requires preparation, but it is well worth the effort!

Here are ten steps to renting your house and making a profit while you're gone:

1. Create labels for the various ins and outs of your home. For example, we labeled our "compost" receptacle, to eliminate confusion with a trash container.
2. Type and print your "Home Operating Guide." Provide details regarding the operation of the heating, cooling, and entertainment systems, list contact phone numbers, include a map of the town, etc. We added Zero Waste operating pointers to our guide.
3. Contact a property manager or pick a friend to welcome renters during your absence and take care of any issues that may arise.
4. Find a housekeeping service to (a) clean your home and (b) wash and change linens between rentals.
5. Make duplicates of house keys.
6. Take pictures of your home in broad daylight.
7. Sign up for rental services such as VRBO.com or airbnb.com.
8. Write an enticing description of your home and upload pictures.
9. Type a contract template.
10. Book renters! Maybe your home's simplicity will inspire renters to change their lives, too.

Note: Some property managers can cover steps four through ten for a management fee.

5 RS CHECKLIST: 5 TIPS FOR OUTINGS

Refuse: Be proactive in rejecting the pizza stacker, the restaurant straw, and the airline earphones.
Reduce: Fly only when no other option is available.
Reuse: Bring your own shampoo and conditioner when staying in a hotel.
Recycle: Make your camping stove's butane can recyclable by puncturing it when completely empty.
Rot: Embrace trench composting when camping or traveling.

Getting Involved

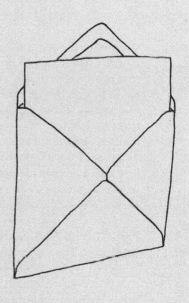

The tips covered in this book are intended to help you reduce waste throughout your home and move toward Zero Waste. Not there yet? Don't despair. Adopting Zero Waste alternatives does not happen overnight; as a matter of fact, the overall journey is likely to follow a progression:

1. **Obliviousness:** You started your journey unaware of environmental concerns. You lived as if the Earth offered unlimited resources, as if your body was invincible, as if your time did not matter. There was a time I stuffed plastic grocery bags into my kitchen trash can, lined with a plastic refuse bag, which I would then proceed to throw into the larger city can. Today it seems silly to me, but it all seemed normal back then. I put no thought into the consequences of my actions.

2. **Awareness:** Through the media or driven by your personal interest, you have gained a certain ecological knowledge. You have become aware of the effects of plastics on health and the environment; you have become familiar with such words as *parabens* and *BPA*; you realized that paper towels are made from trees; and maybe you have heard about the Great Pacific Garbage Patch. You think, "Oh my gosh! I can't believe what is happening!" This newfound knowledge resulted in three possible consequences: (a) denial followed by a disregard for future generations (you keep living your life as is); (b) eco-depression followed by action paralysis (you may talk the talk but do not walk the walk); or (c) motivation followed by action (you decide to make a difference). I hope that the fact that you are reading this book means you have chosen the latter path!

3. **Action:** You take action. You do something about those environmental issues, if not for yourself, at least for future generations. You try many of the alternatives presented in this book at a pace that fits your schedule, one room at time, one day, week, month at a time. You adopt reusables, find a bulk supplier, and cook from scratch. You find that food in glass is more appealing than food wrapped in plastic and that an uncluttered kitchen is easier to clean. Sometimes you run into road-

blocks (e.g., you can't find bulk or a store refuses to refill your jars), but then you remember that any change at all benefits the environment, your health, and your finances. Actively working on Zero Waste, at your own pace, is what really matters. It takes time out of your day today, but you know your efforts lead to future benefits. It is time well invested.

4. **Isolation:** Your awareness and motivation make you feel singled out. The carelessness of others sticks out like a sore thumb. You notice people carrying disposable coffee cups, friends microwaving food in plastic containers, family members wasting money on paper napkins. You do not understand why they won't change. You wish they, too, embraced the lifestyle. You are constantly torn between advising them and suppressing your concerns. As Bo Bennett wisely said, "Frustration, although quite painful at times, is a very positive and essential part of success." A friend or an online Zero Waste community, such as ZeroWasteHome.com forum page, provides support for the criticism that you endure. But over time you learn that there is a spectrum of choices and that what *you* do is what matters. There will always be naysayers. Some said that our household doesn't do enough because we are carnivores and travel to France, for example. Others said that we do too much, that our lifestyle is unrealistic or extreme. How is it unrealistic if I am living it? We coped with criticism by believing that what we were doing was just right *for us.*

5. **Confidence:** Perseverance prevails; you move beyond frustration as family and friends gradually accept your lifestyle change. Over time you adopt the methods that are sustainable for your lifestyle, drop those that are not; you implement an overall system that works for your household, a system that is simple and easy to stick to for the long term. You let the 5 Rs guide your decision making. Refusing, reducing, reusing, recycling, and rotting, in order, have become second nature to you. You have Zero Waste on autopilot.

6. **Involvement:** Now that you have Zero Waste all figured out and optimized for your household, you can fully enjoy the benefits of the lifestyle. Eat healthy, save money, and feel good about your environmental endeavors. You can use your time gains to organize get-togethers with friends, start a vegetable garden, or take a foraging class. But you yearn to do more and look for ways to give back to your community, to extend your efforts beyond your personal realm, to allow your exper-

tise to benefit the broader community. You can focus your efforts on:
(a) being an ambassador of the Zero Waste lifestyle, (b) letting your
voice be heard, and (c) taking the initiative.

BE AN AMBASSADOR OF THE LIFESTYLE

All that is necessary for evil to triumph is for good men to do nothing.
—Edmund Burke

Once we have adopted the Zero Waste lifestyle, by taking a positive outlook, we have the power to inspire others and to encourage them to adopt
waste-free alternatives. To become an ambassador of the Zero Waste lifestyle, simply adopt many of the suggestions mentioned throughout the
book. Also consider the following:

Add locations to my Bulk app.

Bring extra reusables for others to use at a picnic.

Contribute to collaborative consumption; make your assets available to
others.

Donate this book to friends or your local library.

Elect officials concerned about waste issues.

Fund charities that support Zero Waste initiatives.

Go to waste-related discussions, such as your city council's climate change
planning.

Hire services that support the lifestyle: a dry cleaner that reuses cloth
sleeves, a housecleaner who uses cloth and vinegar to clean, a pest
control company that uses natural treatments, etc.

Invest in mutual funds that support Zero Waste initiatives.

Join a sustainability organization in your community, and sit on the waste
committee.

Keep a positive attitude and a good sense of humor about the lifestyle;
brag about its benefits!

Leave a place cleaner than you found it: pick up as you go, whether camping, hiking, beachgoing, or walking the dog.

Make your extras available to others; contribute to the secondhand
market.

Network with like-minded people.

Open your home to green tours.

Praise good practices and good products.

Quote Gandhi: "Be the change you want to see in the world."

Reach out to help friends declutter their homes, and co-workers adopt paperless methods.

Sign petitions that support Zero Waste initiatives.

Talk to your kid's school about celebration alternatives.

Use the green programs already in place: public transportation, book library, tool library, garden exchange.

Volunteer in waste-related events such as trash pickups.*

Walk or bike everywhere!

XYZ, etc.: Every time you shop with reusables, refuse freebies, take your name off a junk mail list, or give a present wrapped in Furoshiki, your actions spread the word about Zero Waste and inspire others to follow your lead!

* Earth Day provides a great opportunity to participate in waste-related activities, but many environmental groups organize initiatives throughout the rest of the year. Refer to the "Resources" guide for links to volunteering websites. Street pickups or coastal cleanups, although not glamorous, are a great way to build awareness and contribute to your community.

LET YOUR VOICE BE HEARD

We cannot wait for the system to change. We individuals are the system.
—Colin Beavan, *No Impact Man*

The Zero Waste journey is not always a smooth ride. Considering the current practices in place, one is likely to face roadblocks along the way and be forced to adhere to unsustainable methods. Even though these obstacles create frustration, they provide an excellent opportunity to let government officials, manufacturers, suppliers, or organizations know how we feel and what we want! An email, call, or handwritten letter can effectively suggest the implementation of a sustainable practice or the modification of a wasteful one. Communicating our concerns is a powerful way to not only proactively support Zero Waste but also actively participate in and accelerate our society's ecological progress.

Don't have bulk in your town? Once you have adopted the many alternatives unrelated to bulk proposed in this book (refuse the unnecessary, reduce your belongings, adopt reusables, recycle, compost, etc.), you can focus your energy on convincing your grocery store to sell loose goods! Don't wait for change. Ask for it. Contact the owners of your local stores and make it happen. Don't use your lack of bulk as a reason to dismiss the Zero Waste lifestyle; use it as a reason to act.

Frustrated with flowers sold in plastic at the farmer's market? Talk to the florist or contact the stand's owner. Bring up the fact that many florists manage to sell theirs without it, that flowers look more attractive that way and that it could translate into increased sales and cost savings (by not having to buy the wrappers).

Love the local eatery but not its disposables? Urge the owner to swap its plastic utensils for the reusable kind, paper napkins for cloth ones. Emphasize that it would make their business look nicer and result in increased patronage.

Active Discards

Our patronage (or lack thereof) is our most important tool in supporting (or rejecting) current manufacturing practices. However, when we are forced to buy a wasteful product or packaging simply because we do not have an available or feasible alternative, communication is an effective fallback. While I have no hard statistics, I believe that when we act on a piece of trash and send it back to its originator, we offset its negative environmental impact. While inaction condones waste and perpetuates it, action, on the other hand, can initiate change. Shipping it back along with a suggestion letter shows dedication and provides a more powerful way to get your message across than words alone. The piece of trash then becomes what I call an "active discard."

In our previous life, we would have thrown the same piece of garbage "away" time after time, but today anything that goes into our quart-size jar or the recycling receptacle calls for further action. For example, I have sent plastic caps back to my milk producer to propose the adoption of flip tops on his bottles, plastic corks back to a good and affordable winery to suggest an alternative corking choice. And yes, I do think that using the extra fuel to send these active discards is worth it. I have seen my car insurance company switch from laminated to cardboard cards, the kids' school from a paper to digital directory, and an international cosmetic brand from clamshell packaging to cardboard!

How to Write a Suggestion Letter

No need to ramble on about your environmental concerns or the ideology behind your lifestyle. Keep your letter short and concise, your words tactful and courteous, and your content diplomatic and hopeful. In short, write a letter that you would like to receive.

1. Start with gratitude: state your appreciation for the company, such as the efficiency, affordability, or availability of their product or service.
2. Show understanding of the current practice employed.
3. Address the problem.
4. Propose up to three constructive solutions.
5. Support your solutions with working examples: how other companies have addressed the problem effectively.
6. Mention how the change would benefit your addressee, focusing on financial profit.
7. Gracefully conclude with a positive note.

Sample letters:

Dear Cosmetic Company:

I love your tinted moisturizer, as it embodies my lifestyle and ecological beliefs perfectly: it is time efficient, organic, and packaged in glass!

The two orders that I have placed online, however, came with samples. While I am sure samples increase your sales, I personally do not care to receive them, and I think they are a waste of resources (and your money!) if other customers and I do not have a use for them.

I propose that you offer them as an option at checkout. The online store [insert name], for example, uses that method. Those who wish to receive them can check a box! Those who do not, on the other hand, will save you money.

I think this method would endorse your environmental efforts beautifully, as well as sustain my patronage!
Thanks for listening.

> *A big fan,*
> *[your name]*

Or

Dear Movie Theater:
I am a simple moviegoer. I love the 3-D glasses that you provide; they are comfortable to wear and they look so much better than the flimsy cardboard/plastic ones we used to wear! More important, I appreciate the fact that the glasses are reused.
While I am sure that you are satisfied with the service that you use to refurbish the glasses, I find its sanitization, transport, and protective plastic sleeve to be a waste of resources.
I have been told that in New Zealand, the moviegoer buys a pair and reuses them over and over. I propose that you, too, charge for the glasses separately, a way for your clientele to understand that these are not a disposable freebie but a reusable purchase. It would save your theater time not having to pick them up after a movie and money not having to subscribe to a service.
I thank you for your time. I applaud your reuse efforts, and I look forward to seeing your environmental improvements.

> *Sincerely yours,*
> *[your name]*

TAKE THE INITIATIVE

There is much to do before our society comes to adopt Zero Waste. But in the meantime, your new awareness probably brought to your attention some organizational flaws, educational needs, or discrepancies in jurisdictional rules. Your expertise and personal strengths can benefit the greater good. Whether it is in the form of a nonprofit endeavor, or a profitable one, the future holds many opportunities. The possibilities are limited only to your imagination. If you put your mind to it, you can accomplish anything!

Here are a few ideas to get you thinking:

- Leverage your **organizational** skills. Coordinate a Zero Waste activity, such as a street cleanup, a Halloween costume swap, or an electronic-waste-collection event. Start your own buying club or a sustainability group if your town does not have one. Create a local branch of an organization that has already proved to be successful. Learn from these nonprofit organizations: Dump & Run, which collects valuable items from college campuses at the end of the year, resells them in the fall, and donates the profits to charitable causes; Cans for Kids, which collects recycling and funds scholarships with the redemption profits; Marin Open Garden Project, which organizes meetings for home gardeners to exchange excess fruit and vegetables, and harvests unwanted crops for people in need.
- Tap in to your **teaching** or **homemaking** skills. Teach a workshop on the Zero Waste alternatives mentioned in this book or on an activity such as foraging, composting, woodworking, darning, canning, sewing, cooking with leftovers, etc. If you are intimidated by the notion of teaching adults, start with kids in schools or after-school programs.
- Participate in the **democratic** process. Raise awareness about an issue; start a petition against a wasteful practice or law. To change a law, find a working example of the legislation you would like to change, seek the support of like-minded individuals or organizations, collect signatures through a website like Change.org, and approach the jurisdiction concerned: your town's councilman, county supervisor, congressman, senator, assemblyman, etc. If you must, run for office!
- Let loose your inner **entrepreneur.** Propose a Zero Waste business plan to your employer or change your career path and start a small business. Create a profitable program or product to promote or facilitate refusing, reducing, reusing, recycling, or composting.

While each of our individual journeys will differ in its practical applications, all of our abilities and strengths are required to make this a meaningful transition. Zero Waste holds surprises for each one of us. Who knows what you might discover about yourself through this lifestyle. For my part, I never expected to eat healthier, save money, have more time for my family and volunteering, find more meaning in holidays, increase my tolerance for others, make do with the available bulk at my local grocery store, rent our house when we travel, and discover a fantastic and supportive community through my blog. The lifestyle inspired both Scott and me to extend our efforts beyond the home and make career changes. While he focuses on changing the business world through his work, I aim at raising awareness about the lifestyle and implementing Zero Waste practices into homes, one house at a time, with my consulting practice ... and this book! While we still have much to learn and discover, I can surely attest that the biggest surprise is that Zero Waste can change your life ... for good and for the better.

The Future of Zero Waste

Never doubt that a small group of thoughtful committed citizens can change the world; indeed, it's the only thing that ever has.

—Margaret Mead

It will take time for people to understand that Zero Waste does not deprive one of life's pleasures but makes room for what truly matters. If it takes time for even one small household to implement Zero Waste methods, of course it's going to take a while for society to embrace it as a whole, to get past its preconceptions, and to realize its economic potential.

Today, Zero Waste is considered a waste-management strategy; tomorrow it will be regarded as an economic opportunity. Discards will not generate feelings of disgust, guilt, and uncertainty; instead they will be viewed, as they should be, as valuable resources. Today, waste is the result of deficient planning, design, and infrastructure; tomorrow it will adhere to a clear set of actions and reflect clever resource management.

I often hear: "If everyone lived like that you, our economy would collapse." But the fact is, we're headed for complete collapse if we hew to our present course. Seriously: What would the world really look like if we all adopted Zero Waste alternatives?

The way I see it . . .

Every household would go grocery shopping with cloth bags, jars, and totes; the supermarkets would sell only loose goods behind a counter, in bins, or with dispensers, including wine. Home pantries, refrigerators, and freezers would be filled with glass jars, the contents of which would be visible and rarely end up in the compost. Toilet seats would be outfitted with bidets, featuring Dyson technology dryers. Material excess would not be regarded as a sign of wealth but as a careless behavior. Refusing would be unnecessary, because material giveaways would be considered a waste of resources, and therefore regarded as ethically unacceptable. With a strong secondhand economy in place, people would share their belongings and learn to live with less.

Our health would improve: cancer, diabetes, and asthma rates would drop as we reduced our overall consumption of synthetics and junk food and owned fewer dust-collecting possessions. Living with less would help adults with chronic fatigue syndrome, as sufferers have testified on my blog, and kids with attention deficit disorders, sleep troubles, and an array of stress-related emotional symptoms. Kim John Payne covers these issues well in his book, *Simplicity Parenting*.

Zero Waste would be included in school curricula. In grade school, the focus would be on where materials come from and what happens to them when they are discarded. It would include a field trip to the local recycling and composting facilities. Home economics (now called family and consumer sciences) would be reinstated and taught to higher grades. The course would instill cooking abilities along with sustainability and survival skills, such as simple needle-and-thread repairs. Teachers would agree to a common set of supplies that students would be able to use from one grade level to the next. "Teachers would allow liquid homemade glue, and all school communication and work would be done on the computer," said Léo. Zero Waste would be incorporated into all college and university programs, and not just relegated to the environmental sciences and sustainability departments. And it would be applied to the site operations of school campuses at all levels, too. For example, all schools would provide bins to collect items that could be reused by subsequent generations of students.

Every community would organize a tool library and a free market where extra garden veggies, books, and clothing would be shared. We would contribute to urban foraging and allow others to profit from the harvests of our fruit trees. Reusable containers could be purchased at restaurants for people who forgot theirs. We would not need to own cars; we would subscribe to a fleet of electric ones, available in multiple models to meet our transportation needs. Solar-powered electric-vehicle charging stations would dot our landscape. We would not need to own bikes, either; a self-service would make them available at convenient locations.

Roads would be filled with cyclists riding in dedicated, well-marked bike lanes. Public spaces would be equipped with drinking fountains and bottle refilling stations and outfitted with recycling and composting receptacles, including the airport. Separate receptacles would collect dog poop for compost.

Every town would provide curbside pickup of organic materials for compost (including meat and fish bones), unusable items for recycling (including hard-to-recycle items such as worn-out textiles, shoes, or broken mirrors), and reusable ones for redistribution. Government agencies, such as sanitation, planning, and environmental bureaus, would work together and aim for a common Zero Waste goal. Landfilling would be highly taxed; its fees would be based on a pay-as-you-throw (PAYT) system across the country, but over time, as manufacturers worked on true cradle-to-cradle products, our need for it would become obsolete. An extended producer responsibility (EPR) legislation would hold manufacturers responsible for the safe disposal of their products. Recycling and composting would be mandatory for households and businesses; disposal regulations would be enforced. For example, hair salons would compost their clients' hair; the death care industry would adhere to green burial practices; contractors would take advantage of reuse outlets to properly dispose of construction debris. The reuse, recycling, and composting markets would provide business owners cheaper alternatives to landfill or incineration and would translate into reduced operating costs. Buy-back centers would be reinstated and offer high rewards for all materials. Litter would be nonexistent, as people would then rightly associate materials with resources value and monetary significance. Material recovery facilities (MRF) would offer hazardous waste and medication pickups, provide complimentary paper-shredding services, and make all reusable items, including the finished compost product, leftover paint, home improvement supplies, and household goods available to the community or donate them to independent salvage enterprises.

The future of Zero Waste includes extensive use of resale shops. Working closely with MRFs and relying on the community's goodwill, the available selection of these shops would surpass that of today's thrift stores. The same marketing tactics and aesthetic standards currently used to lure customers to new merchandise would be applied to secondhand goods. Attention to detail, attractive window and merchandise displays, compliance to cleanliness, organization, and quality standards would reclaim consumer confidence and boost the secondhand market. The reuse shops would be specialized, using the retail model. Office supplies, art and crafts materials, sporting equipment, electronics, clothes, shoes, furniture, and housewares would be sold in separate boutiques, thus facilitating space planning and maximizing selection, including the resale of trivial objects—no material would be disregarded for lack of space as current thrift stores do. Items that cannot be refurbished or repaired would be dismantled for parts. For example, a sewing store would provide buttons, ribbons, thread spools, fabric scraps, and knitting supplies, organized by color, size, and/or material. One could easily find and then purchase a single half-inch pearl button if needed, a convenience that retail stores cannot currently match since buttons are generally sold in a lot. These boutiques would be grouped into one location or located within a block of each other to encourage exchange of materials and provide convenience to the shopper. This "thrift mall" would also include a repair café: with the tools provided and the help of specialists, we could repair almost anything, from clothes and furniture to bicycles and appliances. Repair parts would be purchased loose from the secondhand hardware store. But products that are difficult to repair and require specialized care would be covered under the EPR program for manufacturers to take back.

Does this seem overzealous? Well, it isn't. Apart from the Dyson toilet seat, all the initiatives just mentioned already exist! (Check out "Resources.") They are unfortunately scattered all over the country and the world. Some have recently emerged, but others have been around for a very long time. For example, the transportation scenario that I have mentioned is being built in cities like Amsterdam—and my mall fantasy is an enhanced description of a reuse complex that I visit yearly in the South of France. Founded in 1949 by the French priest Abbé Pierre, Emmaus is a wonderful charitable organization that understands the profitability of resource recovery. Collecting, sorting, repairing, and reselling donated appliances, furniture, and household goods afford employment and shelter to otherwise socially excluded individuals all over the world. This nonprofit provides a snapshot of the work opportunities and economic growth that Zero Waste would offer on a grand scale. Reusing, recycling, and composting provide much more professional and economic opportunities than do landfilling or incinerating.

According to a 2009 report by the Cascadia Consulting Group, recycling creates ten times more jobs per ton of material in the collection, processing, brokering, and transporting practices than throwing "away," and it pays more, too! The future of Zero Waste holds even more employment opportunities in the reuse industry. Jobs in the arena of waste minimization would address the demand for the manufacture, implementation, and maintenance of reusables for the entirety of the supply chain (from suppliers to consumers): in grocery stores (bulk display and transportation containers), hotels (body product dispensers), and aircraft (catering), for example. Optimizing the marketability of secondhand items would create jobs in transporting, sorting, dismantling, repairing, cleaning, reconditioning, quality controlling, pricing, merchandising, inventory management, and sales, of course. Educational positions would aim to raise the population's awareness and to train people for the new job market. Although we would purchase less overall and reduce our demand for manufactured goods dramatically, we would spend less and therefore need to earn less. Additionally, the business of reusing would boost the local economy by not only creating employment but also keeping financial transactions within the community.

But the biggest jobs of all will be to set up the societal rules and regulations and establish the commercial cradle-to-cradle practices.

Just as we have developed preemptive household procedures to avoid waste from entering our home, laws need to be established to keep it from entering our society's waste stream in the first place. It is our responsibility to elect a government that can provide measures and that of manufacturers to collaborate in providing smart designs that are reusable, are long lasting, and close the waste loop. There is much to do in terms of establishing simple disposal standards and designing compliant products. Once we define a standard life cycle for products to follow, new products would need to pass recyclability or biodegradability codes and require manufacturers to prove that they have closed the loop. Within this system, materials without a recycling market could not prosper. Products and bulk containers would be labeled with a standardized disposal guideline for reuse, repair, and recycling or composting (according to the plan described earlier) and a carbon footprint index to help consumers make environmentally sound purchasing decisions. The current plethora of seals of approval (which confuse the end consumer) would not be necessary, because the collaboration of these organizations would have been included in the development of the manufacturing and disposal procedures.

How far are we from getting to a Zero Waste society? It all depends on *you* and the power of community: the joint efforts of elected officials, manufacturers, teachers, grocery store owners, etc. It's a change we can be excited about embracing. As you now understand that Zero Waste is not just about waste reduction—it's about enjoying simple pleasures, eating local and seasonal foods, living a healthier lifestyle, enjoying the outdoors more, getting involved in the community, and simplifying life to make room for things that matter—imagine a world where everyone could enjoy the benefits of this lifestyle! Imagine what a civilization could accomplish if its material wants would be disengaged and replaced with interior growth!

We could all consume less, work less, and live more.

OUR LEGACY

We cannot change the past, but we can focus on the future. The future of Zero Waste is what we teach our kids as much as it is what we plan on leaving behind. And we, the adults, have a choice to make: to either pass down heirlooms to our kids or to give them the knowledge and skills to help build a sustainable future.

From personal and professional experience, I have found that material heirlooms often carry with them the guilt of letting go. No matter our true feeling about the item, we hold on to it for fear of disappointing or forgetting our ancestors, of not conforming to the traditions or erasing a family story. In a way, our predecessors keep partial control over those items. Barry Lubetkin, a psychologist and the director of the Institute for Behavior Therapy in Manhattan, who has observed this *heirloom guilt* in a number of patients, stated in a *New York Times* article: "It's an unhealthy setup, in which people become slaves to inanimate objects [. . .] Once you're defining it as something you can't get rid of, you're not in control of your life or your home." I sure do not wish to impose such a slavishness to objects onto my kids.

I plan on leaving behind a different type of heirloom, one that can be passed down indefinitely and resist damages or loss, one that is worthy of sustaining my descendants, one that my children can enjoy today: knowledge and skills. They are worth so much more than housewares and tchotchkes! My dedication to the simplifying, cooking, and canning savoir faire and to the environment will benefit my kids and generations to come.

To have or to be? What will your legacy be?

Acknowledgments

I wish to thank those without whom I could not have completed this book.

My husband, Scott: For believing in me, for reading all my drafts, and for taking on household chores!

My mom, Maman: For being a homemaking risk taker and passing on her knowledge (may it live on through future generations).

My editor, Shannon Welch: For her responsiveness, patience, and reassurance.

My agent, Amy Williams: For finding a book idea in me!

My friends Robin and Kress: Robin, for holding my hand when I embarked on the lifestyle and Kress, for being there when I needed a break from writing.

The Wednesday Walkers: For lending an ear to my blabber every week and offering advice when I needed it.

And of course, my blog readers: For being open to change and for spreading the word about Zero Waste.

Resources

Please visit ZeroWasteHome.com:
>   To view how-to tutorials and find seasonal recipes.
>   To locate products mentioned in this book, including reusables and books.
>   To find support in the community's forum.
>   To download my free bulk locator app, Bulk.
>   And if you're interested: To see pictures and videos of my home.

The 5 *Rs*

>   To view a wonderful animated video on production and consumption patterns: storyofstuff.org/movies-all/story-of-stuff
>   To understand plastic recycling: ecologycenter.org/recycling/recycledcontent _fall2000/plastics_qa.html#faq3
>   To learn about plastic pollution: plasticpollutioncoalition.org
>   To find out more about collaborative consumption: collaborativeconsump tion.com/the-movement/snapshot-of-examples.php
>   To donate or sell your extras (worldwide): amazon.com, craigslist.org (large items and free items), ebay.com (small items of value), freecycle.org, habitat.org (building materials, furniture, and/or appliances), nikereusea shoe.com/get-involved/drop-off-locations (athletic shoes), lionsclubs.org /EN/our-work/sight-programs/eyeglass-recycling (eyeglasses)
>   In the US only: salvationarmyusa.org, crossroadstrading.com/used-clothes-store, diggerslist.com (home improvement), dressforsuccess.org/locations.aspx, homelessshelterdirectory.org, womensshelters.org/, aspca.org/findashelter
>   In the US and Canada: locator.goodwill.org
>   In the UK only: bhf.org.uk, preloved.co.uk

To locate recycling locations near you: earth911.com (Canada and US),
www.recyclenow.com/ (UK)

To learn basics on composting: composting101.com

Kitchen and Grocery Shopping

Bulk food stores in my area (from closest to farthest): wholefoodsmarket.
com, rainbow.coop, goodearthnaturalfoods.net, newleaf.com

To learn how to store veggies without plastic: myplasticfreelife.com/2010/05
/how-to-store-produce-without-plastic

To find a farmer's market, a co-op, a farm, or a CSA near you: localharvest.org
(US), localfoods.org.uk/ (UK)

To start your own co-op: coopdirectory.org

To find a local egg producer: eggzy.net

To locate dairies that use glass bottles for milk: mindfully.org/Plastic/Dairies-
Glass-Bottles-Milk.htm#1 (US), findmeamilkman.net (UK)

To learn how to prepare bulk foods: wholefoodsmarket.com/department
/bulk

To store recipes online and access them from anywhere: drive.google.com/start
or dropbox.com

To try seasonal recipes: harvesteating.com or bbc.co.uk/food/seasons

To find recipes for your leftovers: lovefoodhatewaste.com/recipes/list

To learn a few napkin folding tricks: kitchen.robbiehaf.com/NapkinFolds

Bathroom, Toiletries, and Wellness

To find out more about Return to Origins Recycling Program: origins.com
/customer_service/aboutus.tmpl#/Commitment

To locate an Origins store: origins.com/locator/index.tmpl (US and Canada)

To dispose of old prescriptions: www.deadiversion.usdoj.gov/drug_disposal
/takeback (US), returnmed.com.au (Australia), medicationsreturn.ca
(Canada)

To look up the toxicity levels of your cosmetics: ewg.org/skindeep

To know more about the Dirty Dozen: davidsuzuki.org/issues/health/science
/toxics/dirty-dozen-cosmetic-chemicals

To locate a shelter to donate hygiene disposables: homelessshelterdirectory.org
(US), uk.local.yahoo.com/search.html?fr=sfp&fr2=&p=Homeless+shelter&
poi=UK&s=Search+Local (UK)

To learn how to shave using a straight edge razor: youtube.com/watch?v=qDR
_1hg-xNs&feature=related

To learn how to sew a reusable menstrual pad: youtube.com/watch?v=zaRtF0
Aafds&feature=related

To locate a kohl powder container and integrated applicator: enter the keywords
'kohl container' on ebay.com

To prepare henna sold in bulk: hennapage.com/henna/how/index.html

To see how to take a navy shower: wikihow.com/Take-a-Navy-Shower

Bedroom and Wardrobe

To locate your nearest thrift store (for purchases and donations): salvation
armyusa.org or locator.goodwill.org (US), charityretail.org.uk/locator.
php (UK)

To swap clothes: clothesswap.meetup.com

To view a short video on how to turn a man's shirt into other garments without
sewing: youtube.com/watch?v=2JwdZC31nQU

To learn more about Patagonia's sustainable efforts: patagonia.com/us/common-
threads

To find a Reuse-A-Shoe program near you: nikereuseashoe.com/get-involved
/drop-off-locations

Housekeeping and Maintenance

To find crocheted cotton mop pads: etsy.com

To donate cleaning products and gardening supplies (including plants) or
locate used repair materials: freecycle.org or craigslist.org

To know more about EWG's cleaning product warnings: static.ewg.org
/reports/2012/cleaners_hallofshame/cleaners_hallofshame.pdf

To get information on how to fix something: ifixit.com

To borrow a tool from a neighbor: sharesomesugar.com (US), uk.zilok.
com (UK)

To buy dog treats in bulk: petco.com (US)

Workspace and Junk Mail

To locate shared office space: desksnear.me or worksnug.com (US) officeshare.
co.uk or sharemyoffice.co.uk/ (UK), openoffices.com.au/ (Australia)

To sell your books: amazon.com

To find out more about ACMI nontoxic seals: acminet.org/SealText.htm

To purchase paper clips in bulk: stores.staples-locator.com/staples (US)

To refill ink cartridges: cartridgeworld.com or walgreens.com/topic/inkrefill
/printer-cartridge-refills.jsp (US)

To subscribe to a free cloud storage and sharing service: drive.google.com
/start or dropbox.com

To recycle Tyvek envelopes and electronic wrap: plasticbagrecycling.org
/plasticbag/s01_consumers.html.

To send Tyvek envelopes for recycling: www2.dupont.com/Tyvek_Envelopes
/en_US/tech_info/tech_environ.html

To donate bubble wrap, packing peanuts or Styrofoam for reuse: call the
Plastic Loose Fill Council's Peanut Hotline 1-800-828-2214 (US)
or ups.com/dropoff

To find out more about Best Buy's recycling program: bestbuy.com/site
/Global-Promotions/Recycling-Electronics/pcmcat149900050025
.c?id=pcmcat149900050025 (US)

To receive voice mail transcripts in your email inbox: google.com/voice

To stop receiving direct mail: dmachoice.org (US), www.mpsonline.org.uk
/mpsr/ (UK)

To stop receiving credit and insurance offers (US): optoutprescreen.com

To stop receiving catalogs (US): catalogchoice.org

To opt out of the yellow pages: yellowpagesoptout.com (US), www.yell.com
/contactus/contactform.html (UK), delivery.ypg.com/en/US/Home/Index
/form.php (Canada)

To hire a service to stop junk mail for you (US): 41pounds.org, catalogchoice.
org, slotguard.com

To download the USPS PS 1500 form (US): about.usps.com/forms
/ps1500.pdf

To stop receiving unaddressed mail in the UK: email optout@royalmail.com
to request an opt-out form.

To download CutePDF Writer: cutepdf.com/Products/CutePDF/Writer.asp

To see how to reduce page margins in your Word document: youtube.com
/watch?v=1DFK_fOUbJo

To fax electronically: hellofax.com (send your document to an email address or phone number).

To sign, notarize and share a legal document without printing it: signnow.com

To recycle your credit card (PVC, Plastic #3 only): earthworkssystem.com

To advertise your business using Zero Waste strategies: elementsixmedia.com

To help your business reduce waste: zerowastescotland.org.uk

Kids and School

To go geocaching with your kids: geocaching.com

To locate a local library: nces.ed.gov/surveys/libraries/librarysearch (US), gov.uk/join-library (UK)

To read a great article on the toxicity of art supplies and labels: greenamerica. org/livinggreen/toxicart.cfm

To donate used toys to a shelter: homelessshelterdirectory.org or http://www. womenshelters.org/ (US)

To donate new toys to Operation Christmas Child: samaritanspurse.org /index.php/OCC (US), operationchristmaschild.org.uk/ (UK)

To locate specific school supplies: ebay.com

To create healthy lunches for your child: www.choosemyplate.gov, laptop lunches.com/healthy-lunches-bored.php

To find a Furoshiki-style cloth to wrap your child's lunch: furoshiki/techniques

To choose age-appropriate media for your kids: commonsensemedia.org

To hire a composting diaper service within the San Francisco Bay Area: earth-baby.com or tinytots.com

Holidays and Gifts

To find a volunteering activity during the holiday season: volunteermatch.org (US), do-it.org.uk (UK)

To participate in Operation Christmas Child: samaritanspurse.org/index. php/OCC (US), operationchristmaschild.org.uk (UK)

To drop off or trade your incandescent Christmas lights in the US (Lowes recycles them in their stores): lowes.com/StoreLocatorDisplayView?store Id=10151&langId=-1&catalogId=10051

To recycle your greeting, birthday and thank-you cards: send them to St. Jude's Ranch for Children, Recycled Card Program, 100 St. Jude's Street, Boulder

City, NV 89005 or visit stjudesranch.org/shop/recycled-card-program
for more info.

To learn how to sew a fillable fabric Easter egg: oneinchworld.com/blog
/index.php/2009/04/fillable-soft-egg-tutorial

To get inspired for a homemade costume: thedailygreen.com/green-homes
/latest/recycled-halloween-costume-470708

To host or participate in a costume swap: greenhalloween.org/CostumeSwap
/index.html (US)

To recycle candy wrappers through TerraCycle Inc.: terracycle.com

To locate a local food bank: feedingamerica.org/foodbank-results.aspx (US),
trusselltrust.org/foodbank-projects (UK)

To locate a candy buy-back location: halloweencandybuyback.com (US)

To give a movie ticket: fandango.com (US), movietickets.com (UK)

To give digital gifts: netflix.com, hulu.com, itunes.com, skype.com

To give the gift of photo scanning: scancafe.com (US), photoscanning.ca
(Canada), iphotoscanning.co.uk (UK), remba.com.au (Australia)

To learn origami bill-folding tricks: origami-instructions.com/dollar-bill
-origami.html

To give a charitable gift card: justgive.org (US), globalgiving.co.uk (UK),
http://www.canadahelps.org/GiftCards/CharityGiftCard.aspx (Canada)

To purchase used gifts: craigslist.org, freecycle.org, ebay.com

To purchase used sporting equipment: playitagainsports.com/locations (US),
adpost.com/uk/sports_equipment (UK)

To purchase a handmade gift: etsy.com

To learn how to wrap different-shaped items using Furoshiki techniques:
furoshiki.com/techniques

Out and About

To find out more about the Slow Food movement: slowfood.com

To find out more about the effects of Styrofoam on our health and the environment: earthresource.org/campaigns/capp/capp-styrofoam.html

To send your tent poles for repair: tentpoletechnologies.com

To plan a trip to the San Francisco Bay Area using transit: 511.org

To purchase carbon offsets: terrapass.com/individuals-families/carbon-footprint-
calculator/#air or carbonfund.org/individuals (US), climatecare.org (UK)

To locate a farmer's market when traveling: localharvest.org (US), localfoods.
org.uk (UK)

To rent your home: VRBO.com or airbnb.com (you can also rent only a room).

To rent your car: relayrides.com or getaround.com (US), whipcar.com or easycar.com/car-club/join-car-club.aspx (UK)

Getting Involved

To start your own buying club: coopdirectory.org

To host or participate in a costume swap: greenhalloween.org/CostumeSwap /index.html (US)

To locate volunteer opportunities: volunteermatch.org (US), do-it.org.uk (UK), idealist.org or allforgood.org (worldwide)

To start or sign petitions: change.org

To get inspired to start your own project: dumpandrun.org, cans4kids.com, opengardenproject.org

To participate in activism, such as signing a petition or writing/calling an elected official with credoaction.com (US), or raising awareness through social media, oneworldgroup.org

The Future of Zero Waste

Check out the Zero Waste initiatives already in place:

Household

Supermarkets that only sell loose goods: beunpackaged.com, in.gredients.com

Specialty stores selling loose goods: la-cure-gourmande.fr (cookies), fionas sweetshoppe.com/about.htm (candy)

Store that sells exclusively behind counters: www.avignon-leshalles.com

Supermarket wine dispenser: geekosystem.com/diy-wine-pump-france

Schools

Grade schools curriculum that include Zero Waste: zerowasteeducation.co.nz, calepa.ca.gov/education/eei/curriculum/Grade12/1231/1231SE.pdf

School field trip to local recycling and composting facilities: dsgardencenter. com/irecycle.asp

Home economics program: doe.k12.ga.us/Curriculum-Instruction-and-
    Assessment/CTAE/Pages/Family-and-Consumer-Sciences.aspx
Zero Waste college program: ivc.edu/careered/certificates/Pages/zerowaste.aspx
Zero Waste university class: sustainable.colorado.edu/index.php?option=com
    _content&view=article&id=107
Zero Waste campuses: museschool.org, grrn.org/page/zero-waste-campuses
Reuse collection bins in schools:
    montgomeryschoolsmd.org/departments/studentaffairs/sao/supplies

Community

Tool library: oaklandlibrary.org/locations/tool-lending-library
Free market: reallyreallyfree.org
Harvest share: opengardenproject.org
Book exchange: bayareafreebookexchange.com
Clothes swap: clothesswap.meetup.com
Urban foraging maps: urbanedibles.org, fallenfruit.org/index.php/media/maps
Reusable containers available for purchase at a restaurant:
    nmsu.edu/atnmsu /cur/taostogoprogram.html
Electric car fleet: bmwusa.com/activee, car2go.com
Electric-vehicle charging stations: plugshare.com, ev-network.org.uk/
Bike fleet: velib.paris.fr
Roads filled with cyclists: amsterdam.info/transport/bikes, thisbigcity.net
    /amsterdam-urban-form-created-ideal-cycling-city

Public Spaces

Drinking fountains and bottle refilling stations: sfwater.org/index.aspx?
    page=447, tapitwater.com, aquafil.com.au
Airport recycling and composting receptacles: flysfo.com/web/page/index.jsp
Dog poop compost receptacles: envirowagg.com/englewood.html

Town

Curbside pickup of organic materials for compost (including meat and fish
    bones): sunsetscavenger.com/residentialCompost.htm

Curbside recycling for hard-to-recycle items:
eurekarecycling.com/page.cfm?ContentID=4#Clothes (worn-out textiles), www.
crrwasteservices.com/recycling/pdf/CRR_Winter_11.pdf (worn-out shoes)
Recycling of broken mirrors: buildingresources.org/tumbled_glass.html
Landfilling based on a pay-as-you-throw (PAYT) system: epa.gov/epawaste/
conserve/tools/payt/index.htm
Extended producer responsibility (EPR): electronicstakeback.com/how-to-
recycle-electronics/manufacturer-takeback-programs
Mandatory recycling and composting: sfenvironment.org/zero-waste
/overview/zero-waste-faq, environment.westchestergov.com/recycling
/recycling-enforcement
Hair salon that composts their clients' hair: keenanrecycling.co.uk/news
/news-0022.asp
Green burial: nativewoodland.co.uk
Mandatory reuse of construction debris: www.sjrecycles.org/construction
-demolition/cddd.asp
Buy-back centers: marinsanitary.com/customer-service/recycling-information-
directory/marin-sanitary-service/marin-recycling-center, calrecycle.
ca.gov/BevContainer
Hazardous waste pickups: wmatyourdoor.com/public-access/household-
materials-pickup-.aspx
Medication pickups: highlandvillage.org/index.aspx?NID=598
Paper-shredding services: marinsanitary.com/document-shredding (this one
requires a fee, though)

Reusable items offered back to residents:

ci.berkeley.ca.us/ContentDisplay.aspx?id=5606 (finished compost)
recologysf.com/hazardousWastePaintRecycling.htm (leftover paint)
toronto.ca/reuseit/centres.htm (home improvement supplies)
middlebury.edu/offices/business/recycle/mrf/reuse (household goods)
Specialty reuse store examples: scrap-sf.org (art materials), playitagainsports.
com (sporting equipment), renewcomputers.com (electronics), buildin-
gresources.org/donations_inventory.html (building supply), tripsforkids.
org/marin/recyclery.htm (bikes).
Thrift mall: emmaus-france.org (the organization of the sewing department
of the store in Joncquières particularly caught my attention).
Repair café: thegoodlifecentre.co.uk/repair-cafe

Index

accessories, 118, 121, 122, 123, 124, 131
advertising, 16, 34, 82, 118, 140, 174–75, 192, 238, 271
air travel. *See* travel
allergies, 34, 97, 107, 108, 115, 116, 118, 122, 189, 238
aluminum, 26, 42, 46, 50, 90, 109, 238, 247
alum stone, 90
anchovies, salt-packed, 73
antibacterial products, 140, 141, 155
antiques shops and markets, 21, 23
antiperspirants, 90
appliances, 21, 44, 76, 264, 268
art supplies, 21, 164, 272, 276
ASPCA, 268
athletic shoes, donating, 268
auction houses, 21

bakeries, 7, 51, 55–56, 58, 61, 239, 248
baking soda, 6, 65, 67, 81, 89, 91, 94, 105, 108, 138, 139, 148, 155
balm, 63, 102, 130, 132, 139, 205, 230
Band-Aids, 84, 110, 193
bartering, 23
bathrooms
    cleaning supplies for, 83, 137
    collection in, 87–88
    composting and, 87–88
    decluttering, 82, 85–86
    energy tips for, 111
    5 Rs checklist for, 111
    landfill use and, 88
    recycling in, 87
    reusability in, 86
    setup of, 82–88

simplicity in, 82–86
time tips for, 112
water tips for, 111–12
batteries, 24, 27, 156, 169, 190, 232
bedrooms, 115–16
    decluttering, 115
    resources for, 270
    simplicity and, 115–16
beer bottles, recycling, 244
beer kegs (growlers), 58, 69
beauty products. *See* cosmetics
bee house, 206
bill-folding tricks, 231, 273
bike fleets, 275
biking, 20, 118, 129, 185, 228, 255, 275, 276
biodegradable diapers, 195–96
birthday cards, 217, 272
birthday parties, 189, 193, 234
blush, 98
board games, 186, 188, 191, 228, 232
body bronzer, 132–33
bones, composting, 29, 30, 49, 66, 263, 275
bone soup, 227
book exchanges, 275
borrowing, 23, 125, 152, 155, 234, 270
bottle refilling stations, 263, 275
bottles
    glass. *See* glass bottles
    insulated stainless-steel, 47, 232, 247
bread, 7, 49, 55–56, 58, 61, 64, 66, 76
bread-and-butter pickles, 241
bread bags, 55–56
bread pudding, 63, 66, 75
bronzers, 133

play, and kids, 186, 201
play dough, 204, 207
pollution, 16, 32, 116, 268
potlucks, 236, 241
power strips, 180
preschools, donating to, 21
prescriptions, 82, 115, 158
   expired, discarding, 83, 84, 269, 276
   5 Rs approach to, 107, 111–12
presents. *See* gifts
prevention, and wellness, 107
printers, 164, 169
printer ink cartridges, 167–68, 169, 271
printing, used paper for, 175, 176
produce, shopping for, 5, 54, 55, 60–61,
   185, 214, 248
prostate problems, home remedy for, 108
pumice stones, 86, 134
pumpkin-seed topping, 225
pumpkin serving dish, 225
pumpkin soup, 225–26
purses, 125, 130, 131, 187
putty, from dryer-lint, 205

Q-tips, 84, 86

razors, 84, 92, 134, 269
receipts
   digitizing for safekeeping, 175
   refusing, 17, 18, 61
rechargeable batteries, 24, 156, 169, 190,
   232
recipes
   decluttering, 62–63
   dinner planning and, 64
   organizing, 63
   storing online, 63–64, 269
recycle step in Zero Waste, 24–27
   buying new decision and, 32
   camping and, 244
   cosmetics and, 83
   craft projects and, 203, 204
   curbing consumption and, 24
   electronics and, 169
   green economy and, 25–26
   holidays and, 234
   home checklist for, 27
   home collection containers for, 27
   housekeeping and, 155
   kids and schools and, 207

kitchens and, 46, 50
labeling in, 25
landfill use versus, 26
mandatory, 276
outings and, 250
reduce step and, 20
reuse differentiated from, 22
wardrobe and, 118, 127–28, 133
workspace and, 179
recycling facilities, 27, 262, 268, 274, 275
recycling programs
   collection sites in, 25, 26, 27, 35, 152,
     168
   curbside, 25, 27, 30–31, 50, 168, 263,
     275
   lack of regulations covering, 24–25
   variables affecting, 24–25, 27
reduce step in Zero Waste, 19–22
   advantages from, 20–22
   bedrooms and, 115
   comfort level and, 20
   holidays and, 234
   housekeeping and maintenance, 155
   kids and schools and, 207
   options for usable items in, 21
   outings and, 250
   practices implemented in, 19–20
   recycle step and, 26
   reuse step and, 22–23
   simplicity and, 35
   workspace and, 179
refrigerators, 55, 56, 61–62, 76, 146, 199,
   240, 261, 156
refuse step in Zero Waste, 15–19
   curbing consumption in, 15–16
   holidays and, 234
   housekeeping and maintenance, 155
   kids and schools and, 207
   opportunities in, 16–17
   outings and, 250
   recycle step and, 26
   reuse step and, 22–23
   simplicity and, 35
   toys and, 191–93
   ways to approach, 17–18
   workspace and, 179
regifting, 21
renting
   cars, 23, 249, 273
   financial advantage of, 33, 249

renting (*cont.*)
  Halloween costumes, 222, 234
  houses, 22, 23, 116, 129, 151, 249–50, 273
  short-term, while traveling, 249
repair cafés, 264, 276
repairs, 23
  camping equipment and, 244
  materials for, 151–52, 264, 269
  proactive approach to, 150–51
repurposing
  junk mail envelopes and, 176
  reusing and, 22
  wardrobe and, 118, 125–27, 133
  workspaces and, 163, 176, 179
resale shops, 121, 122, 128, 263–64. *See also* secondhand stores; thrift stores
restaurants and takeout, 237–40
  disposables to refuse in, 239–40
  leftovers and takeouts from, 238–40
  reusable containers in, 237, 238, 275
  sustainable practices and, 237, 238
  Zero Waste approach to, 237
returning items for reuse, 23
reusability, 35
  bathroom setup and, 86
  kids and school and, 198
  kitchen setup and, 43, 46–47, 54
  shopping and, 54, 69
  wardrobe and, 119, 120–22
  workspace and, 165
reusables
  basic checklist for, 24
  cleaning supplies and, 145–46
  locating, 268
  offering back to residents, 276
  reduce step and choosing, 20
  restaurant containers as, 275
  shopping with, 23
  swapping disposables for, 23
  toys as, 190
  wardrobe with, 119, 120–27
  wrapping as, 233
reuse step in Zero Waste, 22–24
  basic checklist for reusables in, 24
  collection bins in, 275
  healthy lifestyle and, 34
  holidays and, 234
  housekeeping and maintenance, 155
  kids and schools and, 207

  outings and, 250
  recycle step and, 26
  recycling differentiated from, 22
  reduce step and, 22–23
  resource depletion alleviated by, 23
  shipping materials, 166
  shoes and, 128, 270
  useful life of necessities in, 23–24
  wasteful consumption eliminated in, 23
  workspace and, 179
  wrapping and, 233–34
  See also buying used; collaborative consumption; sharing
rolling pins, 43, 45
rot step in Zero Waste, 27–32
  bathrooms and, 111
  bedrooms and, 133
  camping or traveling and, 250
  collection and, 35
  crafts with kids and, 207
  holidays and, 214
  kitchens and, 75
  housekeeping and, 155
  outings and, 250
  workspace and, 179
  See also compost
rummage sales, 21
runny nose, home remedy for, 108
rust remover, 139

salad bars, 55, 61
salads, 59, 64, 66, 69, 77, 199
salad spinners, 19, 43, 45
salt-packed anchovies, 73
salvage yards, 21, 152, 154, 203, 263
sandwich bags, 41, 46, 47
scanning photos, 273
scarves, 117, 125, 126, 130, 131
schools, 197–201
  donating usable items to, 21
  extracurricular activities and, 201
  field trips by, 262, 274
  5 Rs checklist for, 207
  lunches in, 183, 198–201, 272
  resources for, 272
  reuse collection bins in, 275
  Zero Waste initiatives in, 274–75
school supplies, 197–98, 272
scrubbers and scrub brushes, 146, 155
scrubbing powder, 148–49